T0290811

Managing Your Environmental Responsibilities:

A Planning Guide for Construction and Development

Use this document to fulfill your environmental obligations in every stage of your construction project:

◆ **Pre-Bid** – Learn what is required of you and factor in the cost.

◆ **Pre-Construction** – Assign environmental responsibility to all parties before breaking ground.

◆ **During Construction** – Find answers to ongoing environmental questions and conduct comprehensive self audits.

This Page Is Intentionally Left Blank

EPA/305-B-04-003

EPA Office of Compliance

Managing Your Environmental Responsibilities:
A Planning Guide for Construction and Development

April 2005

Office of Compliance
Office of Enforcement and Compliance Assurance
U.S. Environmental Protection Agency
1200 Pennsylvania Avenue, NW (MC 2224-A)
Washington, D.C. 20460

DISCLAIMER

This document has been developed to provide a general overview of the federal environmental requirements for the construction industry. This document contains a general discussion on the common requirements pertaining to the construction industry. Detailed aspects of each requirement are not included. This document also contains a checklist to facilitate discussion and assignment of environmental responsibilities among the parties involved in a construction project. Additionally, self-audit checklists are provided in Part II of the document. These checklists can be used once the construction project has commenced. This document is intended solely as guidance on the federal requirements, and readers should consult with their states for state-specific requirements. Any variation between applicable regulations and the information provided in this document is unintentional, and, in the case of such variations, the requirements of the regulations govern.

This guidance does not constitute rulemaking by EPA and may not be relied on to create a substantive or procedural right or benefit enforceable by any person. EPA may take action at variance with this guidance and its internal procedures.

This document also identifies governmental and non-governmental resources that may be helpful to the construction industry. EPA does not make any guarantee or assume any liability with respect to either the use of any information or recommendation made by these resources. The use of non-governmental resources provided in this document is not to be viewed as an endorsement of these resources by EPA.

Foreword

A s a participant in the construction and development process, your success may depend on how well you identify, analyze, and manage your environmental risks. Simply being unaware of your environmental obligations does not relieve you of your liability.

This planning guide was developed in a collaborative effort between U.S. EPA and its partners. Its purpose is to help you to:

- Recognize the federal environmental requirements and factor in the associated expenses for the project;

- Designate the responsible party to fulfill these requirements;

- Complete the requirements by filing the necessary paperwork, performing the required activities, and obtaining the essential permits; and

- Identify additional sources of information to help implement these requirements throughout your project.

The guide contains two parts. Part I presents background information on environmental requirements for the construction and development industries. It also contains a checklist to help assign environmental responsibilities. Part II contains seven self-audit checklists that help construction companies evaluate their compliance status in these seven areas once the project has commenced.

This guide can be used at the following stages of your project:

Pre-Bid

A clear understanding of the federal environmental requirements is necessary even at the pre-bid phase. Not including the cost of complying with environmental requirements up front can lead to cost over-runs or profit loss in the future. By using this document, owners/developers will be able to determine the level of effort needed to comply with the requirements, and the contractors/subcontractors can more accurately include environmental compliance costs in their bids.

Pre-Construction

If you do not assign responsibility for environmental compliance before you start the project, some important steps may be omitted during construction. Prior to breaking ground, you should sit down with the other members of the construction team, and use this document to assign responsibility for meeting your environmental obligations. Section II in Part I of this guide contains a checklist of required tasks for each federal environmental regulation associated with the construction process. By completing these checklists prior to breaking ground, you will help ensure that your environmental requirements are not overlooked during construction.

During Construction

No matter how thoroughly you prepare for a construction project, you may still encounter unexpected situations requiring environmental knowledge and understanding. You can use this guide as a reference tool to find answers to questions that you encounter during the construction process. It identifies many resources you will find useful. Additionally, the seven self-audit checklists contained in Part II of this guide will help you apply the knowledge gained in Part I to your actual construction site.

With the help of this document, you can properly manage your environmental responsibilities, and therefore reduce the risk of future enforcement actions and penalties.

Document Contents

Part I - A Planning Guide for Construction and Development

Part II - Self-Audit Checklists

Part I

Managing Your Environmental Responsibilities:

A Planning Guide for Construction and Development

This Page Is Intentionally Left Blank

TABLE OF CONTENTS FOR PART I

This Page Is Intentionally Left Blank

I. Introduction

Are you involved in construction projects? Are you an owner, developer, contractor, subcontractor, architect, construction manager, or design engineer? If so, you may be responsible for meeting requirements of federal, state, and local environmental regulations. This guide presents information on your federal environmental responsibilities. While the guide can be used during all stages of construction projects, the best time to begin using this guide is before a project is bid.

Part I of this guide is intended to facilitate discussions among the various parties involved in construction projects to ensure that federal environmental requirements are addressed. If you are an owner, developer, general contractor, subcontractor, architect, or another party involved in a construction project, you should review this guide before the project begins to know the federal environmental requirements. During your discussions, you also should determine who is responsible for each requirement, so you can better assess project costs and reduce the potential risks and liability for all parties.

Section XIV of Part I of this guide contains a map of the EPA Regions and a glossary of the terms and acronyms used throughout this guide. Part II of this guide provides self-audit checklists for you to determine if your operations are in compliance with EPA's requirements. This guide complements the Federal Environmental Requirements for Construction guide located at http://www.cicacenter.org/links.

A. How Can This Guide Help You?

At the onset of a construction project, it is important to clearly identify who will address the environmental requirements. Because many parties are involved in construction projects, different parties may be responsible for addressing different environmental requirements. For example, some requirements may be more appropriately addressed by the owner or developer, while others may be more appropriately addressed by contractors or subcontractors. This guide is intended to help you determine "who is doing what" and to help you avoid potential liabilities and penalties associated with not addressing these requirements.

Section II of Part I of this guide contains a list of questions that you should answer prior to starting a construction project. Next to each question is a space to indicate who will address the requirement. You can use this section to help determine and keep a record of who is responsible for each item.

Sections III through XIII of Part I of this guide contain additional details on the specific environmental requirements. These sections will help you to:

- Learn about the environmental requirements for construction projects including the types of environmental permits you may need;

- Learn about possible penalties associated with not following the environmental requirements; and

- Find additional resources and information.

The seven self-audit checklists in Part II of this guide can help you monitor your operations and ensure compliance in these areas to avoid violations and fines.

B. Some Key Points To Keep In Mind

When reading this guide, keep in mind the following:

1. This guide presents information on federal environmental requirements. However, in many cases, **state and local requirements may apply to your construction site** and may be more stringent than the federal requirements. You should always check with your state and local agencies before starting a construction project to make sure that you are addressing all relevant requirements. You can find information on state-specific requirements and contact information for state environmental departments at the *Construction Industry Compliance Assistance Center* (http://www.cicacenter.org).

2. Many of the environmental regulations do not specifically define the responsible party (e.g., owner, developer, contractor). Therefore, it is possible that **all involved parties may be liable** (i.e., be subject to penalties) if requirements are not met. Use this guide to start a dialogue with all parties involved to ensure that the requirements are met. Where available, the guide presents examples of entities that have been held liable in past cases.

3. This guide presents information on potential penalties if environmental requirements are not met. However, **citizen lawsuits and delayed projects are also potential consequences**. These impacts can be far more damaging than the monetary penalties presented in this guide.

This guide presents specific information on a number of federal environmental requirements for general construction projects. In addition to these requirements, you should also be aware that when a federal agency makes a decision to entirely or partly finance, assist, conduct, regulate or approve a construction project, the project may also be subject to requirements in cross-cutting environmental laws. There are three different federal requirements that are pertinent to the construction industry that were not developed and promulgated by EPA. They are the Endangered Species Act (ESA), the National Environmental Policy Act (NEPA), and the National Historic Preservation Act (NHPA), discussed in Sections XI through XIII of Part I of this guide, respectively. Although EPA does not have jurisdiction over these requirements, they are discussed briefly to raise awareness. EPA recommends that you reference the specific agencies and listed resources for more information.

C. Key References to Supplement the Guide

The following table contains a list of web sites that you can use to quickly access additional information on each of the topics discussed in this guide. Other supplemental resources are provided at the end of each section in Part I of this guide.

Key References

Key References for Information on Environmental Responsibilities:

The Construction Industry Compliance Assistance Center: **http://www.cicacenter.org/index.cfm**

The National Environmental Compliance Assistance Clearinghouse: **http://www.epa.gov/clearinghouse/**

EPA's "Where you live" page contains links to state environmental agencies: **http://www.epa.gov/epahome/whereyoulive.htm**

EPA's Office of Wastewater Management, NPDES Stormwater Program: **http://www.epa.gov/npdes/stormwater**

EPA's Office of Wetlands, Oceans, and Watersheds (OWOW): **http://www.epa.gov/owow/**

EPA's Office of Solid Waste and Emergency Response: **http://www.epa.gov/epaoswer/osw/laws-reg.htm**

EPA's Oil Program Web Site: **http://www.epa.gov/oilspill/**

EPA's Superfund Web Site: **http://www.epa.gov/superfund/index.htm**

EPA's Polychlorinated Biphenyl (PCB) Homepage: **http://www.epa.gov/pcb/**

EPA's Air Program Mobile Sources Page: **http://www.epa.gov/ebtpages/airmobilesources.html**

EPA's Asbestos Management and Regulatory Requirements Web Site: **http://www.epa.gov/fedsite/cd/asbestos.html**

EPA's Cleanup Enforcement (CERCLA or Superfund) Web Site: **http://www.epa.gov/compliance/cleanup/**

The U.S. Fish and Wildlife Service Endangered Species Program Web Site: **http://endangered.fws.gov/**

National Oceanic and Atmospheric Administration (NOAA) Fisheries, National Marine Fisheries Service Web Site: **http://www.nmfs.noaa.gov/endangered.htm**

This Page Is Intentionally Left Blank

II. List of Questions for Owners and Contractors

his section contains a list of questions to help owners and contractors assign who is responsible for ensuring compliance with the applicable environmental regulations discussed in this guide. You should make these assignments prior to beginning any construction activity. If you are unfamiliar with these environmental regulations, you should reference the corresponding detailed section (Sections III through XI of Part I) of the guide for more information. These sections contain detailed information and helpful resource links related to each regulation. Please note that this section does not include checklists for NEPA and NHPA. For more information on these regulations, go to http://ceq.eh.doe.gov/nepa/nepanet.htm and http://www.achp.gov.

A. Stormwater Permits (detailed discussion starting on page 17 of this guide)

Assigned To

Getting a Permit

A.1.   Who will determine if you need a stormwater permit?
        (A permit is generally required when at least one acre of land is disturbed.)   _____

A.2.   Who will find out what agency issues the stormwater permit
        for your location (i.e., U.S. EPA, state, or local government) and
        get the permit? To determine your permitting authority, go to the
        following web site: http://cfpub.epa.gov/npdes/stormwater/
        authorizationstatus.cfm. If your construction activity occurs in an area
        where the state issues permits, contact your state for further information
        about applicable requirements.   _____

A. Stormwater Permits (continued)

Assigned To

Getting a Permit

The following questions specifically apply to the Federal Construction General Permit.

A.3.   Who will submit the Notice of Intent (NOI) before the start of the
        construction project and submit the Notice of Termination (NOT)
        to EPA when the construction project is complete?   _____

A.4.   Who will comply with the Endangered Species Act requirements?   _____

A.5.   Who will determine if the receiving waters are covered under a
        Total Maximum Daily Load (TMDL) requirement?   _____

A.6.   Who will develop the stormwater pollution prevention plan (SWPPP)
        includes selection of appropriate BMPs?   _____

Meeting Permit Requirements

A.7.   Who will perform and document the inspections?   _____

A.8.   How often will inspections be performed?   _____

A.9.   Who will install and maintain Best Management Practices (BMPs) and
        stormwater controls?   _____

A.10.   Who will notify site personnel of the permit requirements (e.g.,
        ensuring controls are in place and telling the recordkeeper of any
        site changes)?   _____

A.11.   Who will modify the SWPPP during the construction project (including
        updating records and documenting inspection results)?   _____

A.12.   Who will update the site map?   _____

A.13.   Who will be the recordkeeper?   _____

B. Dredge and Fill Wetlands (Section 404) Permit Requirements (detailed discussion starting on page 25 of this guide)

Assigned To

Getting a Permit

B.1.   Who will determine if wetlands are present at the construction site?   _____

B.2.   Who will determine whether the construction project will impact waters of the United States (i.e., will fill materials or pollutants be discharged into wetland areas)?   _____

B.3.   Who will determine if the Section 404 permit requirements apply to your construction project (including a review of exempt activities)? Contact your state environmental department and the Army Corps of Engineers (COE) District Office for requirements.   _____

B.4.   Who will determine if Section 401 state certification is required, or if the state has already granted certification for any general permits in the area?   _____

B.5.   Who will perform (or hire someone to perform) the wetland delineation, if required?   _____

B.6.   Who will determine if a Nationwide Permit (or regional or state general permit) is applicable to your construction project?   _____

B.7.   Nationwide Permits: Who will submit a preconstruction notification, if required?   _____

B.8.   Individual Permits: Who will submit the application for an individual permit and check that the permit is received?   _____

Meeting Permit Requirements

B.9.   Who will perform mitigation activities under your permit?   _____

B.10.   Who will ensure that any general or special conditions in the permit are met (applies to general and individual permits)?   _____

B.11.   Who will maintain the necessary documentation?   _____

B.12.   Who will submit a compliance certification once the construction is complete, if required?   _____

C. Oil Spill Prevention Requirements (detailed discussion starting on page 33 of this guide)

Assigned To

Spill Prevention Control and Countermeasures (SPCC) Requirements

C.1. Who will determine if SPCC requirements apply (i.e., determining oil storage capacity at the site and whether the site location poses a hazard)?   _____

C.2. Who will develop the SPCC Plan?   _____

C.3. Who will keep the SPCC Plan?   _____

C.4. Who will update the SPCC Plan with changes to the construction site and maintain documentation/records?   _____

C.5. Who will be responsible for implementing the plan? See Section III.D in Part I of this guide for more information.   _____

C.6. Who will maintain any secondary containment or diversionary structures?   _____

C.7. Who will perform the necessary inspections?   _____

C.8. Who will inspect the integrity of the storage tanks?   _____

C.9. Who will train site personnel?   _____

C.10. Who will ensure fuel transfer requirements are met?   _____

C.11. Who will report any oil spills to the National Response Center and state and local authorities?   _____

C.12. Who will perform any necessary response actions following an oil spill?   _____

D. Hazardous and Non-Hazardous Solid Waste Requirements (detailed discussion starting on page 39 of this guide)

Assigned To

Determining Applicability

D.1.   Who will determine if hazardous wastes are present at the construction site (e.g., fluorescent bulbs containing mercury removed during demolition, contaminated soil)?   _____

D.2.   Who will identify whether additional hazardous wastes will be generated during construction activities (e.g., ignitable paint wastes, degreasing solvents, remediation waste that is also considered a hazardous waste)?   _____

D.3.   Who will submit the preliminary notification to EPA or the state once hazardous waste is generated?   _____

D.4.   Who will get the EPA ID number?   _____

D.5.   Who will determine whether the site is a large, small, or conditionally exempt small quantity generator?   _____

Following are Hazardous Waste Requirements for Generators

D.6.   Who will be responsible for proper management and disposal of any hazardous wastes present at the construction site?   _____

D.7.   Who will establish and maintain hazardous waste storage requirements?   _____

D.8.   Who will develop the contingency plan and emergency procedures, as required?   _____

D.9.   Who will maintain the necessary documentation?   _____

D.10.   Who will ensure that site personnel are trained to handle hazardous waste? _____

D.11.   Who will determine whether a RCRA permit or Remedial Action Plan (RAP) is required (i.e., who will keep track of how long hazardous waste is stored at the site)?   _____

D.12.   Who will get the hazardous waste permit, if required?   _____

D.13.   Who will hire a licensed hazardous waste hauler?   _____

D.14.   Who will properly package the hazardous waste for transport?   _____

D.15.   Who will mark and label the package?   _____

D. Hazardous and Non-Hazardous Solid Waste Requirements (continued)

Assigned To

Determining Applicability

D.16. Who will complete and sign the Uniform Hazardous Waste Manifest?   _____

Solid Waste/Construction and Demolition Debris Requirements

D.17. Who will contact the state environmental department for any applicable solid waste or construction and demolition debris requirements?   _____

D.18. Who will review the state requirements and designate responsibility?   _____

D.19. Who will meet state recycling standards, if applicable?   _____

E. Hazardous Substances (Superfund Liability) Requirements (detailed discussion starting on Page 49 of this guide)

Assigned To

Pre-Planning Issues

E.1.   Who will conduct the historical review (to determine the possible presence of hazardous substances) of the construction site?   _____

E.2.   If this is a Superfund or brownfield property, who will identify and analyze if there are specific issues associated with the site (e.g., are there ongoing or remaining cleanup or long-term maintenance obligations associated with the site)?   _____

E.3.   Who will ensure that soil, air, and water samples are collected and analyzed, if necessary?   _____

E.4.   If a hazardous substance is found, who will contact the National Response Center?   _____

E.5.   Who will coordinate with EPA regarding any necessary site cleanup activities?   _____

E.6.   Who will follow the steps of the Brownfields Program if the construction site is a brownfield site?   _____

E.7.   Who will maintain documents/records containing hazardous substance information?   _____

Project-Related Wastes

E.8.   Who accepts responsibility for generated wastes? The waste "generator" is the person whose activity first "produces" the waste.   _____

E.9.   Who will ensure proper handling, storage, transport, and disposal of wastes?   _____

E.10.   Who will ensure that reporting obligations are met?   _____

E.11.   Who will work with EPA to conduct site cleanup, if necessary?   _____

F. Polychlorinated Biphenyl (PCB) Waste Requirements (detailed discussion starting on Page 55 of this guide)

Assigned To

Identifying PCB Materials

F.1.   Who will determine if PCB materials or equipment are at your site?   _____

F.2.   Who will label all PCB-containing materials?   _____

F.3.   Who will determine the actual PCB concentrations?   _____

F.4.   Who will determine what items will be stored for reuse or removed for disposal?   _____

F.5.   Who will look for old spills or leaks?   _____

Handling PCB Materials

F.6.   Who will be responsible for handling any PCB remediation issues?   _____

F.7.   Who will be responsible for cleaning up new spills?   _____

F.8.   Who will contact the National Response Center in case of a spill emergency?_____

F.9.   Who will complete and file the PCB Activity Form?   _____

F.10.   Who will prepare the materials for storage or disposal?   _____

F.11.   Who will determine if the site has an allowable permanent PCB waste storage area?   _____

F.12.   Who will inspect PCB waste storage areas?   _____

F.13.   Who will complete and sign the waste manifest?   _____

F.14.   Who will keep all of the records including the activity form, the manifest, the certification of disposal, and any on-site inspection reports?   _____

F.15.   Who will identify and hire the companies that will be used to transport and dispose of PCBs?   _____

G. Air Quality Requirements (detailed discussion starting on Page 63 of this guide)

Assigned To

Getting a State Implementation Plan (SIP) Permit

G.1.   Who will determine if you need an air permit? A permit may be required for the uncontrolled open burning of debris, dust generation, vehicle emissions, and combustion gases from oil-fired equipment.   _____

G.2.   Who will be responsible for getting the air permit?   _____

G.3.   Who will be responsible for implementing the requirements of the SIP permit?   _____

Getting a New Source Performance Standard (NSPS) Permit

G.4.   Who will determine if an NSPS permit is required (i.e., if a rock crusher, cement plant, or hot mix asphalt plant is operated on site)?   _____

G.5.   Who will notify site personnel of the permit requirements if a large source of emissions such as a rock crusher, cement plant, or a hot mix asphalt plant is located at the construction site (e.g., ensuring that proper recordkeeping and monitoring are completed)?   _____

Ozone Depleting Substances (CFCs)

G.6.   Who will determine if equipment containing ozone depleting substances is located at the site?   _____

G.7.   Who will be responsible for disposing of any equipment containing ozone depleting substances located at the site?   _____

G.8.   Who will determine if the equipment containing ozone depleting substances will be removed for treatment off site or treated on site before demolition activities are begun?   _____

G.9.   Who will maintain copies of records from the disposal contractor verifying that the ozone depleting substances have been removed from the appliances?   _____

G.10.   Who will determine if the Transportation Conformity Rule applies?   _____

G.11.   Who will determine if the project meets the requirements of the Transportation Conformity Rule?   _____

H. Asbestos Requirements (detailed discussion starting on Page 69 of this guide)

Assigned To

Asbestos NESHAP

H.1.   Who will schedule the site inspection with a certified asbestos inspector?   _____

H.2.   If asbestos is present, who will determine if it will be disturbed in amounts greater than the "threshold" quantities?   _____

H.3.   Who will ensure that an approved laboratory is used for testing the asbestos?   _____

H.4.   Who will complete and submit the notification form?   _____

H.5.   Who will hire the asbestos removal/remediation company and ensure that they have the proper licenses and certifications?   _____

H.6.   Who will notify the state Health Department (if required)?   _____

H.7.   Who will receive the notification form?   _____

H.8.   Who will be responsible for proper handling of asbestos materials (e.g., wetting the material)?   _____

H.9.   Who will maintain the records of asbestos inspections and notifications?   _____

I.   Endangered Species Act (ESA) Requirements (detailed discussion starting on Page 75 of this guide)

Assigned To

Asbestos NESHAP

I.1.   Who will determine whether your construction activity involves a
       federal action?   _____

Responsible Party

I.2.   Who will check during the planning process whether the federal agency
       or another party will be fulfilling the ESA requirements?   _____

Environmental Assessment

I.3.   Who will contact state or federal fish and/or wildlife agencies to determine
       whether state or ESA-listed species or habitat may be affected?   _____

I.4.   Who will maintain the necessary documentation (e.g., communication for
       federal fish and/or wildlife agencies, biological assessments)?   _____

       **If listed threatened or endangered species or critical habitat for listed species are found in
       your construction area:**

I.5.   Who will evaluate whether your construction project will adversely impact
       the listed species/habitat (i.e., perform/coordinate biological evaluation
       or assessment)?   _____

I.6.   Federal Action Projects: Who will submit the biological evaluation/assessment
       to the National Oceanic and Atmospheric Administration (NOAA)-Fisheries
       for marine species or the U.S. Fish & Wildlife Service (USFWS)
       for all other species?   _____

       **If assessment determines that your activities will impact listed threatened or endangered
       species or critical habitat:**

I.7.   Who will ask the USFWS/National Marine Fisheries Service (NMFS) or
       appropriate state environmental protection agency for advice on how to
       reduce potential impacts?   _____

I.8.   Who will develop alternate project scopes to avoid adverse impacts? _____

I.   Endangered Species Act (continued)

Assigned To

If assessment determines that impacts cannot be avoided:

I.9.   Federal Action Projects: Who will request a formal consultation
(Section 7 consultation) in writing with the USFWS/NMFS or appropriate
state environmental protection agency? The request must include:
1) description of the activity, affected area, listed species/habitat potentially
impacted, how the activity will impact the species/habitat, and analysis of
cumulative effects; 2) relevant reports; and 3) other relevant documentation
including all previous communication with NOAA-Fisheries/USFWS.   _____

I.10.   Non-Federal Action Projects: Who will apply for an ESA permit and coordinate
with USFWS/NMFS (process is referred to as a Section 10 consultation)?
Your application needs to include a habitat conservation plan and
additional measures.   _____

I.11.   Who will be responsible for ensuring a permit is received from
USFWS/NMFS?   _____

Meeting ESA Requirements

I.12.   Who will ensure that habitat enhancement requirements are met,
if required?

I.13.   Who will ensure that any restrictions on construction activities are met?   _____

III. Stormwater Permit Requirements for Construction Projects

Before beginning any construction project, you must consider the stormwater discharges from your site. These discharges are generated by runoff from or across disturbed land, vegetative areas, and impervious areas (e.g., paved streets, parking lots, and building rooftops) during rainfall and snow events. Stormwater discharges often contain pollutants in quantities that could adversely affect water quality. If your project disturbs one or more acres, or disturbs less than one acre but is part of a larger common plan of development or sale that will disturb one or more acres, you may need a stormwater permit. To get a permit, you must meet either the requirements of the EPA Construction General Permit (CGP), state-specific general stormwater permits, or site-specific stormwater permits.

Definitions

Construction Activities—Can include but is not limited to: grading; excavation; road building; construction of residential houses, office buildings, and industrial sites; demolition and other construction-related activities.

Land Disturbance—Exposed soil due to clearing, grading, or excavation activities.

Operator—The party (ies) that has: (1) operational control of construction project plans and specifications, including the ability to make modifications to those plans, or (2) day-to-day operational control of stormwater compliance activities.

Stormwater—Stormwater runoff, snow melt runoff, and surface runoff and drainage.

Waters of the United States—All waters currently used, or used in the past, or may be susceptible to use in interstate or foreign commerce, including all waters that are subject to ebb and flow of the tide. Waters of the United States include, but are not limited to, all interstate waters and intrastate lakes, rivers, streams (including intermittent streams), mudflats, sandflats, wetlands, sloughs, prairie potholes, wet meadows, play lakes, or natural ponds. See 40 Code of Federal Regulations (CFR) Part 122.2 for the complete definition.

The EPA CGP is developed under the National Pollutant Discharge Elimination System (NPDES) program, which stems from the Clean Water Act (CWA). The regulatory text discussing this program (40 CFR Part 122) can be found at http://ecfr.gpoaccess.gov under "Title 40 - Protection of the Environment." Your state may have authority to issue permits for the NPDES program, rather than EPA. Section III-E of Part I of this guide identifies states that do not issue their own permits (i.e., where EPA is the permitting authority). Note that states' requirements may differ. If you are located in a state that stormwater permits, contact your state environmental department for further information. You can also search for your state requirements at the Construction Industry Compliance Assistance Center (http://www.cicacenter.org/).

Acronyms

BMP—Best Management Practice

CFR—Code of Federal Regulations

CGP—Construction General Permit

CWA—Clean Water Act

NOI—Notice of Intent

NOT—Notice of Termination

NPDES—National Pollutant Discharge Elimination System

SWPPP—Stormwater Pollution Prevention Plan

A. Is a Stormwater Permit Required for Your Construction Project?

To determine if your project requires a stormwater permit for construction activities, consider the following questions:

- Will your construction project disturb one or more acres of land?

- Will your construction project disturb less than one acre of land but is part of a larger common plan of development or sale that will disturb a total of one or more acres of land?

- Will your construction project disturb less than one acre of land but is designated by the NPDES permitting authority (state agency or EPA) as a regulated construction activity?

- Will stormwater from the construction site flow to a municipal separate storm sewer system (MS4) or a water of the United States?

> **For more information on the NPDES Stormwater Program go to:**
> **http://www.epa.gov/npdes/stormwater**

If you have answered "Yes" to any of the first three questions AND "Yes" to the fourth question, then you need a stormwater permit for your construction activities. **Please note that some municipalities also are required to implement stormwater control programs; therefore, check with your municipality for their own requirements.**

B. Are You Responsible for the Permit?

For EPA's CGP, you are responsible for getting a stormwater permit if you are considered to be an "operator" of the construction site. (If your site is in a location where the stormwater program is run by the state rather than EPA, keep in mind that the state authority may have different requirements regarding who is required to obtain permit coverage). Depending on your site and the relationship between all of the parties (e.g., owner, developer, general contractor, subcontractors), there can either be a single site operator or multiple operators.

For most construction projects, multiple parties are involved; several parties may meet the definition of operator and therefore be required to obtain coverage under EPA's CGP.

Are You Responsible for Getting a Permit?

EPA requires each party who is considered an "operator" to get permit coverage by submitting your application to EPA or the state authority. The owner, developer, general contractor, and architect could all be considered "operators" and may be required to obtain permit coverage. (Again, some states may have requirements different from EPA regarding permit coverage. To determine those requirements, you will need to consult the specific permit in the state you are operating. EPA's "Where you live" page contains links to state environmental agencies: http://www.epa.gov/epahome/whereyoulive.htm.) Prior to obtaining permit coverage, you will need to develop a stormwater pollution prevention plan (SWPPP).

Are You Responsible for Meeting Permit Requirements?

For EPA's CGP, you must obtain permit coverage if you meet either of the following criteria:

- *Do you have control of construction project plans and specifications, including the ability to make modifications to those plans and specifications?*

- *Do you have day-to-day control of those activities that are necessary to ensure compliance with a SWPPP for the site or other permit conditions (e.g., are you authorized to direct workers at a site to carry out activities required by the SWPPP or other permit conditions)?*

If you answer "Yes" to one or both of these questions, you are likely responsible for meeting the permit requirements.

After you obtain permit coverage, you must follow the requirements of the permit (e.g., maintaining soil and erosion controls, updating your SWPPP, conducting inspections, keeping records) as discussed in Section III-D of this guide. Typically, the contractor or subcontractor carries out activities to meet the permit requirements and notes any changes to the SWPPP.

C. What Are the Penalties?

The goal of the CWA is to "restore and maintain the chemical, physical, and biological integrity of the Nation's waters." The CWA prohibits the discharge of pollu-

---

Case Studies

In May 12, 2004, the Department of Justice and EPA, along with the U.S. Attorney's office for the District of Delaware and the States of Tennessee, and Utah reached a CWA settlement for stormwater violations at Wal-Mart store construction sites across the country. Under this settlement, Wal-Mart agreed to pay a $3.1 million civil penalty and conduct an environmental project costing $250,000 that will protect sensitive wetlands or waterways in one of the affected states. This settlement also requires Wal-Mart to comply with stormwater permitting requirements and ensures rigorous oversight of its 150 contractors. Wal-Mart will be required to use qualified personnel to oversee construction, conduct training and frequent inspections, report to EPA and take quick corrective action.

If all parties involved (Wal-Mart store personnel and contractors) had discussed the stormwater requirements and followed through with meeting those requirements before starting construction at these sites, penalties for all parties could have been avoided.

---

tants by any person from a point source into waters of the United States, except in compliance with various sections of the Act. As defined by the CWA, "person" means any individual, corporation, partnership, association, state, municipality, commission, subdivision of a state, or interstate body.

EPA may impose administrative, civil, and criminal sanctions on a property owner and/or a contractor for failure to comply with the CWA. Administrative penalties can reach $157,500 and civil penalties – imposed in a judicial proceeding – can reach $32,500 per violation per day. Under certain circumstances, the CWA also authorizes criminal penalties. The CWA allows private citizens to bring civil actions against any person for any alleged violation of "an effluent standard or limitation." In a citizen suit, a court may issue an injunction and/or impose civil penalties, litigation costs, and attorney's fees. In addition to fines, you may need to pay legal fees and face project delays. If legal action is taken against your construction site, you also may be subject to increased scrutiny at all of your other construction sites by regulatory agencies and the public.

EPA has pursued enforcement actions against different parties involved in construction projects: owners, developers, general contractors, subcontractors, etc. For this reason, it is critical to define, before the start of the project, who will be responsible for complying with the stormwater requirements; assuming another party is "taking care of it" does not absolve you from any liability, and more than one party may be responsible.

While owners, contractors, and consulting engineers all may be found liable for discharging pollutants without a permit, the remedy imposed on each may vary, depending on their respective degrees of control, responsibility, or involvement in the illegal activity.

D. In General, What Are the Permit Requirements?

If you are located in an area requiring a federal permit, you must meet the EPA CGP requirements. If your location requires a state permit, you must meet the state's general permit requirements. In either case, you can apply for an individual permit in lieu of general permit coverage; however, the individual permit process can take significantly longer than the general permit process. One of the requirements of the EPA CGP is to assess the potential effects of your activities on federally listed endangered and threatened species and any designated critical habitat that exists on or near your site. More information on the Endangered Species Act (ESA) and its requirements is included in Section XI of Part I of this guide.

Requirements

The federal CGP, as well as most state general permits, has three major requirements. Because your site may have multiple responsible parties, before construction activities begin, the parties should decide, in writing, who will be held responsible for meeting each requirement. The requirements are:

1. <u>Develop and implement a Stormwater Pollution Prevention Plan (SWPPP)</u> — You must prepare this plan prior to submitting a Notice of Intent to EPA; it should include:

   • A site description identifying sources of pollution, including a site map;

   • A description of how you will prevent erosion, sediment, and other pollutants from contaminating stormwater;

- A description of how you will control stormwater flow from your site;

- Documentation supporting permit eligibility with regard to the Endangered Species Act;

- Documentation supporting permit eligibility with regard to local Total Maximum Daily Load (TMDL) requirements;

- Clearly outlined roles and responsibilities of different operators; and

- The protocol you will use to inspect your site.

> To complete an NOI online or to check the status of your NOI in the electronic database go to: http://cfpub.epa.gov/npdes/stormwater/enoi.cfm. If you do not have Internet access call the NOI Processing Center toll free at: 1-866-352-7755
>
> For a fact sheet on the CGP including detailed information on SWPPP requirements go to: http://www.epa.gov/npdes/pubs/cgp2003_fs.pdf

You also must maintain records of the self-inspections performed and the times and locations of major land disturbance and stabilization activities. Make sure these records are legible and be prepared to show the SWPPP and records to government inspectors who may visit your site. Do not submit the SWPPP to EPA, but if you are in a state that administers this program, you may be required to submit the SWPPP to the state. Keep the SWPPP on site and revise it as needed. For more detail on SWPPP contents, read the CGP.

2. <u>Submit a Notice of Intent (NOI)</u> — This notice triggers coverage under the general permit and includes general information and a certification that the activity will not impact endangered or threatened species or any historic places. You may begin work once your NOI is shown in "Active" status on the EPA eNOI web site. Note that your NOI will appear on the eNOI web site even if you submit the NOI in paper form. EPA holds your NOI for seven days before moving it to "Active" status; therefore, you must submit your NOI at least seven days (or longer if submitting it by postal mail) prior to beginning land disturbance (e.g., clearing, grading). Note that states may have different notice requirements (e.g., submission of a NOI 30 days prior to construction, approval prior to construction).

3. <u>Submit a *Notice of Termination* (NOT)</u> — You need to submit this to EPA within 30 days after one or more of the following:

- Final stabilization has been achieved on all portions of the site for which the permittee is responsible,

- Another operator/permittee assumes control over all areas of the site that have not achieved final stabilization,

- Coverage has been obtained under an individual or alternative NPDES permit, or

- For residential construction only, temporary stabilization has been achieved and the residence has been transferred to the homeowner.

Waivers

EPA may grant permit waivers for certain construction projects where it is highly unlikely that the activity will have negative impacts on water quality. These waivers can apply when operators certify to either one of two conditions:

1. Low predicted rainfall potential (i.e., project occurs during a negligible rainfall period); or

2. Controls are not necessary based on an EPA-established or -approved Total Maximum Daily Load (TMDL) that indicates stormwater will not impact water quality.

You can get more details on the waivers at EPA's NPDES web site (http://cfpub.epa.gov/npdes/ stormwater/waiver.cfm).

Other Permits

Note that many states have a variety of construction permits that may apply to your project. Some of them, like erosion or sediment control permits, have components that are similar to those in the EPA-based stormwater permit. Keep in mind that complying with these other parallel or unrelated state programs does not release you from the need to get a stormwater permit from EPA or your state. Go to http://www.cica-center.org/swp2.html for a link to state permit programs.

E. Where Do You Get a Permit?

If your construction project is located in one of the following states or territories, you must get a federal stormwater permit from EPA:

- Alaska
- American Samoa
- Guam
- Idaho
- Massachusetts
- New Hampshire

- New Mexico
- Northern Mariana Islands
- Puerto Rico
- Trust Territories
- Tribal Lands (most but not all)
- Washington, D.C.

Additionally, there are several other instances where the CGP applies, including construction related to oil and gas activities in Texas; oil and gas and certain agricultural and silvicultural activities in Oklahoma; and construction of federal facilities in Colorado, Delaware, Vermont, and Washington. Refer to Attachment A of the stormwater checklist in Part II of this guide for more details.

For coverage under the federal CGP, you can submit your NOI and NOT to http://cfpub.epa.gov/npdes/stormwater/enoi.cfm or to the following addresses:

Regular U.S. Mail Delivery
Stormwater Notice of Intent
U.S. EPA - Ariel Rios Building
Mail Code 4203M
U.S. EPA
1200 Pennsylvania Ave., NW
Washington, DC 20460

Overnight/Express Mail Delivery
Stormwater Notice of Intent
U.S. EPA - East Building, Room 7420
U.S. EPA
1201 Constitution Ave., NW
Washington, DC 20004

If your construction project is in one of the other 45 states or the U.S. Virgin Islands, you generally must get a stormwater permit from the state or territory (note that for certain activities in specific states, such as oil and gas construction activities in Texas, your project may require a federal permit). Construction projects in states authorized to administer the stormwater program may be subject to requirements that are different from the CGP requirements. **In all cases, check with your EPA region or state to determine the stormwater requirements that apply. You can find information on state-specific stormwater permit requirements and contact information for state environmental departments at the Construction Industry Compliance Assistance Center (http://www.cicacenter.org).**

F. What Questions Do You Need to Answer Before Starting Your Construction Project?

You can use the questions in Section II of Part I of this guide to start a discussion among all parties involved in the construction project and to assign tasks to ensure all environmental requirements are met. Each question has a space next to it to designate who will take the lead on each task. Note that designating a responsible party does not absolve you of your own obligation to meet environmental requirements or liability for failing to meet these requirements.

G. Where Can You Get Additional Information?

Many tools are available to assist you with the stormwater permit requirements, including the following:

- The Stormwater Self-Audit Checklist in Part II of this guide;

- The Construction Industry Compliance Assistance Center provides plain language explanations of environmental rules for the construction industry, including tools to identify state-specific requirements, permits, and contacts: http://www.cicacenter.org/stormwater.html;

- The National Environmental Compliance Assistance Clearinghouse contains a search engine to help you find compliance assistance tools, contacts, and EPA-sponsored programs: http://www.epa.gov/clearinghouse/;

- The Office of Wastewater Management, NPDES Stormwater Program provides information about the NPDES stormwater program: http://www.epa.gov/npdes/stormwater;

- The NPDES Construction Site Stormwater Runoff Control web page provides factsheets on a variety of stormwater best management practices (BMPs): http://cfpub.epa.gov/npdes/stormwater/menuof-bmps/con_site.cfm;

- Does Your Construction Site Need a Stormwater Permit? A Construction Site Operator's Guide to EPA's Stormwater Permit Program is a brochure that provides construction companies with a brief overview of EPA's CGP and its requirements: http://www.epa.gov/npdes/pubs/sw_cgp_brochure.pdf;

- Resource List for Stormwater Management Programs lists resources to help stormwater program managers start developing or improve their stormwater programs: http://www.epa.gov/npdes/pubs/sw_resource_list.pdf;

- The Stormwater Manager's Resource Center contains a series of factsheets for stormwater BMPs that include information on soil type, slope, and cost: http://www.stormwatercenter.net/; and

- EPA's "Where you live" page contains links to state environmental agencies: http://www.epa.gov/epahome/whereyoulive.htm.

IV. Dredge and Fill/ Wetlands (Section 404) Permit Requirements for Construction Projects

I f your construction project requires you to perform work in waters of the United States or wetlands, most likely you will need to obtain a Clean Water Act (CWA) Section 404 permit. The regulatory text discussing this program (40 CFR Parts 230-233) can be found at http://ecfr.gpoaccess.gov under "Title 40 - Protection of the Environment." The U.S. Army Corps of Engineers (COE) and EPA regulate the discharge of dredged or fill material into waters of the United States under Section 404 of the CWA. You need a Section 404 permit if your construction project will result in the discharge of dredged material (i.e., material excavated from waters) or fill material (i.e., material placed in waters such that dry land replaces water—or a portion thereof—or the water's bottom elevation changes) into a water of the United States. You must obtain a permit (or permit coverage) prior to starting construction. Approval of individual permits might take approximately three months, although general permit authorizations typically take far less time.

Definitions and Acronyms

Dredged Material—Material that is excavated or dredged from waters in the United States.

Fill Material—Material placed in waters of the United States where the material has the effect of either replacing any portion of water of the United States with dry land or changing the bottom elevation of any portion of a water of the United States. Examples include rock, sand, soil, clay, plastics, construction debris, wood chips, overburden from mining or other excavation activities, and materials used to create any structure or infrastructure in waters of the United States.

Definitions and Acronyms

Waters of the United States—All waters that are currently used, or were used in the past, or may be susceptible to use in interstate or foreign commerce, including all waters which are subject to ebb and flow of the tide. Waters of the United States generally include all interstate waters as well as lakes, rivers, streams (including intermittent streams), mudflats, sandflats, wetlands, sloughs, prairie potholes, wet meadows, playa lakes, or natural ponds. See 40 CFR Part 232.3 for the complete definition.

Wetlands—Areas inundated or saturated by surface or ground water at a frequency and duration sufficient to support, and that under normal circumstances do support, a prevalence of vegetation typically adapted for life in saturated soil conditions. Wetlands generally include swamps, marshes, bogs, and similar areas.

CFR—Code of Federal Regulations

COE—Army Corps of Engineers

CWA—Clean Water Act

Waters of the United States include wetlands. You must determine whether any wetlands or other waters are present in your construction area. COE and EPA define wetlands as "areas inundated or saturated by surface or ground water at a frequency and duration sufficient to support, and that under normal circumstances do support, a prevalence of vegetation typically adapted for life in saturated soil conditions. Wetlands generally include swamps, marshes, bogs, and similar areas." Wetlands are covered by water or have waterlogged soils for parts of the growing season. Some wetlands are easy to recognize (e.g., swamps and marshes); however, others may be dry during part of the year and difficult to recognize (e.g., bottomland forests, pocosins, pine savannahs, wet meadows, and wet tundra). Contact your COE district office or state environmental department for further information.

> **Use the following web site to locate your COE district office:**
> **http://www.usace.army.mil/where.html**

A. Is a Section 404 Permit Required for Your Construction Project?

Answering the following questions will help you determine whether a Section 404 permit is required for your construction project.

Does your construction project (or any part thereof) occur in or impact a water of the United States?

The COE Wetlands Delineation Manual contains information that you can use to help identify a wetland. However, you should consult trained personnel to help you identify jurisdictional waters of the United

States, and to identify and delineate (i.e., identify and mark its boundaries) wetlands. Some basic questions you can ask when determining if your site contains a wetland include the following:

- Is your area in a flood plain or otherwise has low spots in which water stands at or above the soil surface during the growing season?

- Does your area have plant communities that commonly occur in areas having standing water for part of the growing season (e.g., cypress-gum swamps, cordgrass marshes, cattail marshes, bulrush and tule marshes, and sphagnum bogs)?

- Does your area have peat or muck soils?

- Is your area periodically flooded by tides, even if only by strong, wind-driven, or spring tides?

> **Find the COE Wetlands Delineation Manual online at http://www.saj.usace.army.mil/ permit/documents/87manual.pdf**

- Are one or more of the wetland indicators (vegetation, soil, and hydrology) present in your area? See the Wetlands Delineation Manual for specific details.

Will your project involve the discharge of dredged or fill material?

COE defines discharges of dredged material at 33 CFR Part 323. These discharges, which require permits under Section 404 of the CWA, include:

- The addition of dredged material to a specified discharge site located in waters of the United States;

- The runoff or overflow from a contained land or water disposal area; and

- Any addition, including redeposit other than incidental fallback, of dredged material, including excavated material, into waters of the United States that is incidental to any activity, including mechanized land clearing, ditching, channelization, or other excavation.

COE also defines discharges of fill material at 33 CFR Part 323. These discharges, which require permits under Section 404 of the CWA, include:

- Placement of fill necessary for the construction of any structure or infrastructure in a water of the United States;

- Building of any structure, infrastructure, or impoundment in waters of the United States requiring rock, sand, dirt, or other material for its construction;

- Site-development fills in waters of the United States for recreational, industrial, commercial, residential, or other uses;

- Causeways or road fills, dams and dikes, artificial islands, beach nourishment, levees, and artificial reefs;

- Property protection and/or reclamation devices such as rip rap, groins, seawalls, breakwaters, and revetments;

- Fill for structures such as sewage treatment facilities;

- Intake and outfall pipes associated with power plants and subaqueous utility lines;

- Placement of fill material in waters of the United States for construction or maintenance of any liner, berm, or other infrastructure associated with solid waste landfills; and

- Placement of overburden, slurry, or tailings or similar mining-related materials in waters of the United States.

Are your activities exempt from a Section 404 permit?

Certain activities are exempt from the requirement to get a Section 404 permit. These include discharging dredged or fill material from normal and ongoing farming, forestry (silviculture), and ranching activities; maintaining currently serviceable structures such as dikes and dams, including emergency reconstruction of recently damaged parts; constructing/maintaining farm or stock ponds or irrigation ditches; maintaining drainage ditches; constructing temporary sedimentation basins on a construction site (does not include placing fill material into navigable waters); certain construction/maintenance activities for farm roads, forest roads, and temporary roads for moving mining equipment; and other activities meeting certain Section 404 requirements. The exemption applies as long as the activity purpose is NOT to bring an area of the navigable waters into a use to which it was not previously subject (i.e., the flow or circulation of navigable waters may not be impaired or the reach

> **Contact your state's environmental department and the COE District Office to determine whether your construction project requires a 404 permit.**

of such waters may not be reduced). If the activity performed results in bringing an area of the navigable waters into a new use, then a Section 404 permit is required for your construction project. See Section 404 at http://www.epa.gov/OWOW/wetlands/regs/sec404.html for further details on the exemptions.

If you answered "yes" to the first two questions and "no" to the third, then you will need a Section 404 permit.

B. Are You Responsible for the Permit?

All parties associated with construction projects that impact waters of the United States could be held liable. Therefore, the owner, developer, contractor, and other parties involved should ensure that any necessary permits are obtained prior to starting construction.

Are You Responsible for Getting a Permit?

Typically, either the owner, developer, contractor, or architect will get the necessary permit. Owners or developers usually determine whether any wetlands are at the site and if they will be impacted. Before receiving a permit, you also must get approval for your project from your state (Section 401 certification).

There are two types of Section 404 permits: general permits and individual permits.

General Permits. COE issues general permits on a nationwide, regional, or state basis for particular categories of activities resulting in minimal individual and cumulative impacts to aquatic resources. To determine if your construction project is covered by a Nationwide Permit, or by a regional or state general permit, contact the COE District Office or the state environmental department. You can review the existing Nationwide Permits on the Corps web site.

Individual Permits. For projects with greater anticipated impacts, individual permits may be issued for a specific construction project. You must submit an application to the COE District Office and receive permit approval prior to beginning any construction.

Are You Responsible for Meeting Permit Requirements?

If your project is covered by a general permit, you must follow the conditions listed in that permit. The COE District Engineer also may add specific conditions

> **For detailed information on Nationwide Permits go to http://www.usace.army.mil/inet/ functions/cw/cecwo/reg/nwpfinal.pdf**

to your general permit. If your project is covered by an individual permit, you must meet the requirements listed in that permit. Typically, contractors and subcontractors who perform the work on site need to follow these requirements.

While owners, contractors, and consulting engineers all may be found liable for discharging dredge or fill material without a permit, the remedy imposed on each may vary, depending on their respective degrees of control, responsibility, or involvement. For this reason, it is critical to define, before beginning a project, who will be responsible for complying with the Section 404 requirements; assuming another party is "taking care of it" does not absolve you from any liability, and more than one party may be responsible.

C. What Are the Penalties for Working Without the Proper Permit?

The goal of the CWA is to "restore and maintain the chemical, physical, and biological integrity of the nation's waters."

> ## Case Studies
>
> Landowners, contractors, and consultants have been found liable for discharging into U.S. waters without a permit.[1] In one case, the court found both the owner and the contractor to be liable, ruling that the contractor was responsible for the discharge activity, despite his reliance on the owner to get the necessary permits. Even where the contractor or consultant did not directly cause the violation, he or she still may be held responsible.
>
> ---
>
> [1] U.S. v. Florida Keys Comm. Coll., 531 F. Supp. 267 (S.D. Fla 1981); U.S. v. Weisman, 489 F. Supp. 1331 (M.S. Fla 1980)

The CWA prohibits the discharge of pollutants by any person from a point source into waters of the United States, except in compliance with various sections of the CWA. As defined by the CWA, "person" means any individual, corporation, partnership, association, state, municipality, commission, subdivision of a state, or interstate body.

EPA may impose administrative, civil, and criminal sanctions on a property owner and/or a contractor for failure to comply with the CWA. Administrative penalties can reach $157,500 and civil penalties – imposed in a judicial proceeding – can reach $32,500 per violation per day. Under certain circumstances, the CWA also authorizes criminal penalties. In addition, the CWA allows private citizens to bring civil actions against any person for any alleged violation of "an effluent standard or limitation." In a citizen suit, a court may issue an injunction and/or impose civil penalties, litigation costs, and attorney's fees.

In addition to fines, you may need to pay legal fees and face project delays. If legal action is taken against your construction site, you may also be subject to increased scrutiny at all of your other construction sites by regulatory agencies and the public.

C. In General, What Are the Permit Requirements?

Section 404 specifies that you may not discharge dredged or fill material if a practicable alternative exists that is less damaging to the aquatic environment or if the nation's waters would be significantly degraded. As mentioned in Section IV-B of Part I of this guide, there are two types of Section 404 permits: general permits and individual permits. For discharges that have only minimal adverse effects, COE issues general permits. General permits may be issued on a nationwide, regional, or state basis for particular categories of activities. Individual permits are usually required for activities with potentially significant impacts.

When applying for an individual permit (and certain general permits), you must demonstrate compliance with mitigation provisions by showing that you will:

- Avoid wetland and water impacts where practicable;

- Minimize potential impacts to wetlands and waters; and

- Compensate for any remaining, unavoidable impacts to wetlands or waters through activities to enhance or create wetlands and/or waters.

Demonstration of the above is referred as wetland/water mitigation.

Prior to COE issuing a Section 404 permit, your state also must approve the project by granting certification under Section 401 of the CWA. Your state may have already granted certification for any general permits in your area, which will reduce your burden.

If your construction project requires an individual permit, you must submit an Application for Department of Army Permit to COE and/or the state where the construction project is being done. After public notice and comments, COE, EPA, the state, and any other interested federal agencies will evaluate your application. You will be either granted or denied a permit.

A Nationwide Permit (or regional or state permit) may require you to notify the COE District Engineer of the construction project in a preconstruction notification. If a preconstruction notification is required, you may not begin construction until one of the following occurs:

1. The District Engineer notifies you that the activity may proceed. This notification may include special conditions for your construction project.

2. The District Engineer notifies you that an individual permit is required (and you must apply for and be issued an individual permit).

The COE District Engineer should contact you within 45 days regarding your preconstruction notification. If you have not heard from the District Engineer within 45 days, you should follow up with the District Engineer regarding the status of the notification. Prior to issuing the Section 404 permit, the COE or EPA may require an Endangered Species Act Section 7 consultation if threatened or endangered species may be adversely impacted by your construction activity. However, the permit-issuing agency (e.g., COE) is responsible for completing the consultation. See Section XI of Part I of this guide for more information on requirements for endangered species.

E. Where Do You Get a Permit?

In most states, you must obtain a Section 404 permit or verify coverage under a general permit from your COE District Office. A list of COE district offices is available at:
http://www.usace.army.mil/inet/functions/cw/cecwo/reg/district.htm.

Currently, two states (Michigan and New Jersey) have assumed the role of the COE to issue Section 404 permits; however, several other states have enacted laws and regulations to protect wetlands. In many cases, these rules define the state's role in the Section 404/Section 401 permitting process. Some state laws may also have other impacts. For example, a state may define wetlands or regulated activities differently from federal regulations. This could qualify an area as a wetland on the state level even if it does not meet the federal definition. Therefore, always check with your state to determine if there are any additional requirements that you must follow.

F. What Questions Do You Need to Answer Before Starting Your Construction Project?

You can use the questions in Section II of Part I of this guide to start a discussion among all parties involved in the construction project and to assign tasks to ensure all environmental requirements are met. Each question has a space next to it to designate who will take the lead on each task. Note that designating a responsible party does not absolve you of meeting environmental requirements or liability for failing to meet these requirements.

G. Where Can You Get Additional Information?

For further information on Section 404 permits, you can check the following resources:

- The Dredge and Fill/Wetlands (Section 404) Self-Audit Checklist in Part II of this guide;

- The Construction Industry Compliance Assistance Center (http://www.cicacenter.org/wetlands.html) provides resources specific to Section 404 permits and wetlands including state requirements and contacts;

- The National Environmental Compliance Assistance Clearinghouse contains a search engine to help you find compliance assistance tools, contacts, and EPA-sponsored programs: http://www.epa.gov/clearinghouse/;

- U.S. Army Corps of Engineers (COE) web site (http://www.usace.army.mil/) provides a list of District Offices, including phone numbers that you can call concerning permits for construction activities impacting waters of the United States, information on Nationwide Permits, and the application for individual permits;

- U.S. EPA Office of Wetlands, Oceans, and Watersheds (OWOW): http://www.epa.gov/owow/;

- Wetlands Helpline: 1-800-832-7828; and

- EPA's "Where you live" page contains links to state environmental agencies: http://www.epa.gov/epahome/whereyoulive.htm.

V. Oil Spill Prevention Requirements for Construction Activities

If you are using, consuming, storing, transferring, or otherwise handling oils at your construction site, you will need to take the appropriate actions to prevent spills, and be prepared to take action in case of a spill. You will need to follow EPA's Spill Prevention Control and Countermeasures Plan (SPCC Plan) requirements, which were developed under authority of Section 311 of the Clean Water Act (CWA). The regulatory text discussing this program (40 CFR Part 112) can be found at http://ecfr.gpoaccess.gov under "Title 40 - Protection of the Environment." On July 16, 2002, EPA promulgated a revised final SPCC Regulation that became effective August 17, 2002. EPA subsequently extended the regulatory compliance schedule included in the new SPCC rule.

Definitions and Acronyms

Bulk Storage Container—Any container used to store oil. These containers are used for purposes including, but not limited to, the storage of oil prior to use, while being used, or prior to further distribution in commerce. Oil-filled electrical, operating, or manufacturing equipment is not a bulk storage container. Bulk storage containers include items such as tanks, containers, drums, and mobile or portable totes.

Oil—Oil of any kind or in any form, including, but not limited to: petroleum; fuel oil; sludge; oil refuse; oil mixed with wastes other than dredged spoil; fats, oils or greases of animal, fish, or marine mammal origin; vegetable oils, including

oil from seeds, nuts, fruits, or kernels; and other oils and greases, including synthetic oils and mineral oils.

Storage Capacity - The shell capacity of the container (i.e., the maximum volume of the storage container used to store oil, not the actual amount of product stored in the container).

CFR—Code of Federal Regulations

CWA—Clean Water Act

SPCC—Spill Prevention Control and Countermeasures

The current compliance dates for the new rule are as follows:

- February 17, 2006: Facilities must prepare and certify (using a Professional Engineer, or P.E.) an SPCC Plan in accordance with the new SPCC rule.

- August 18, 2006: The revised SPCC Plan must be implemented.

Affected facilities that start operations between August 16, 2002 and August 18, 2006 must prepare and implement an SPCC Plan by August 18, 2006. Affected facilities that become operational after August 18, 2006 must prepare and implement an SPCC Plan before starting operations.

The SPCC rule includes spill prevention and countermeasure plans for spills from aboveground and certain underground storage tanks. Completely buried storage tanks that are subject to all the technical requirements of the underground storage tank regulation (40 CFR Part 280/281) and any permanently closed underground storage tanks are not required to comply with SPCC provisions. For more information on underground storage tanks, go to http://www.epa.gov/swerust1/.

A. Do Oil Spill Requirements Apply to Your Construction Project?

Your construction project must meet SPCC regulatory requirements if it meets the following three criteria:

- It stores, uses, transfers, or otherwise handles oil;

- It has a maximum aboveground storage capacity greater than 1,320 gallons of oil (which includes both bulk and operational storage volumes) OR total underground storage capacity greater than 42,000 gallons of oil; AND

- There is a reasonable expectation (based on the location of your site) that an oil spill would reach navigable waters or adjoining shorelines of the United States.

> Calculate your total aboveground storage capacity by adding together the storage capacity of all of your storage tanks as well as the fuel and fluid (e.g., hydraulic fluid) tanks on your mobile and operational equipment. In this calculation, include only those tanks that have more than 55 gallons of storage capacity.

The following items at your construction site are exempt from SPCC requirements and are not included in the storage capacity calculations:

- Completely buried tanks that are subject to all the technical requirements of the underground storage regulations;

- Storage containers with less than 55-gallon storage capacity (both aboveground and belowground tanks); and

- Permanently closed tanks.

When calculating your storage capacity, you must include the capacity of the fuel and fluid tanks on your mobile and operational equipment (e.g., fuel tanks on bulldozers, cranes, backhoes of greater than 55 gallons). Also, note that individual aboveground storage tanks with storage capacities of greater than 660 gallons, which had been regulated under the 1974 rule, are no longer regulated unless the total site capacity is greater than 1,320 gallons.

In addition to SPCC requirements, the CWA also includes requirements for Facility Response Plans for "substantial harm" sites (see 40 CFR 112.20 and 112.21.) Construction sites are not expected to meet the definition of "substantial harm;" therefore, these requirements are not discussed in this guide. If you transfer oil over water and use vessels that have a total oil storage capacity of 42,000 gallons or more OR your site has a total oil storage capacity greater than one million gallons, you should review the Facility Response Plan requirements (see http://www.epa.gov/oilspill/frps/index.htm).

B. Are You Responsible for Meeting Oil Spill Prevention Requirements?

All parties associated with construction projects that store (or spill) oil can be held liable if the SPCC requirements are not met. Therefore, the owner, developer, contractor, and other parties as applicable should determine up front who will:

- Decide if SPCC requirements apply by calculating the total oil storage capacity on the site and then determining whether an oil spill could reach navigable waters or adjoining shorelines of the United States (It is recommended that you use a Professional Engineer to decide if the requirements apply.);

- Develop the SPCC plan, which should include the following: procedures the site will use to prevent oil spills; control measures the site will install to prevent oil from entering navigable waters or adjoining shorelines; and countermeasures the site will use to contain, clean up, and mitigate the effects of an oil spill; and

- Meet the SPCC plan requirements.

If no party complies with the SPCC regulations, all parties can be found liable for violating federal law. If oil is brought on site for construction, the contractor or subcontractor is also responsible for meeting any SPCC requirements. If a spill occurs (regardless of the source), all parties need to make sure that the spill is properly reported and handled.

C. What Are the Penalties?

If you are the responsible party to an oil spill, you may be required to pay for any damages and cleanup costs resulting from that oil spill. Third parties also may be held responsible for damages and removal costs if the responsible party shows that the spill resulted from an incident caused solely by an act or omission by a third party. Administrative penalties can reach $157,500 and civil penalties imposed in a judicial proceeding can reach $32,500 per violation per day, or $1,100 per barrel of oil spilled if the oil reaches waters of the United States or adjoining shorelines.

The fine for failing to notify the appropriate federal agency of an oil spill can reach a maximum of $250,000 for an individual or $500,000 for an organization. The maximum prison term is five years. The criminal penalties for violations have a maximum fine of $250,000 and 15 years in prison.

The SPCC regulation is implemented at the federal level; however, states and localities may also have oil programs through which they may impose additional penalties (including unlimited liability), funding mechanisms, requirements for removal actions, and fines and penalties for responsible parties.

D. In General, What Are the Oil Spill Requirements?

The SPCC regulations require the owners and operators of facilities to prepare and implement spill prevention plans to avoid oil spills into navigable waters or adjoining shorelines of the United States. Your plan must identify operating procedures in place and control measures installed to prevent oil spills, and countermeasures to contain, clean up, or mitigate the effects of any oil spills

> **For more specific details on SPCC requirements, you can refer to the regulations or to EPA's "Required Elements of SPCC Plans" web page, http://www.epa.gov/oilspill/spccmust.htm.**

that occur. The plan must be updated as conditions change at your construction site. Specific items in the SPCC Plan include, but are not limited to, the following:

- Professional Engineer certification;
- For plans not following the format listed in the rule (e.g., plans developed for a combined SWPPP and SPCC Plan), a cross-reference to the requirements in 40 CFR Part 112.7;
- Site diagram, identifying the location and contents of each container (including completely buried tanks that are otherwise exempted from the SPCC requirements);
- For each container, the type of oil stored and the storage capacity;
- Discharge prevention measures, including procedures for oil handling;
- Predictions of direction, rate of flow, and total quantity of oil that could be discharged from the site as a result of a major equipment failure;
- Site drainage;
- Site inspections;
- Site security;
- Five-year plan review (if construction lasts five years);
- Management approval;
- Requirements for mobile portable containers (e.g., totes, drums, or fueling vehicles that remain on facility grounds);
- Appropriate secondary containment or diversionary structures;
- Secondary containment for fuel transfer;
- Personnel training and oil spill prevention briefings;
- Tank integrity testing;
- Bulk storage container compliance; and
- Transfer procedures and equipment (including piping).

For information on the SPCC requirements, go to EPA's Oil Spill Program web site, http://www.epa.gov/oilspill/. Regional SPCC contacts are listed at http://www.epa.gov/oilspill/spcccont.htm.

Spill Response Requirements

If a spill occurs, you must follow the spill response procedures outlined in your SPCC plan. These procedures should include identifying the spilled material, restricting the flow of any remaining material within the original container, confining the spill area with absorbent materials or dikes, beginning remediation and decontamination of the affected areas, and notifying all of the appropriate parties.

The following groups should be notified in the event of a spill:

- The site Emergency Coordinator and any client representatives;

- The National Response Center at 1-800-424-8802 for spills that trigger the "sheen rule";

- The State Emergency Response Commission for spills with the potential to harm people off site; and

- Local Emergency Planning Committees or the local fire department for spills with the potential to harm people off site.

> EPA does not define an oil spill based on the volume of the spill. Rather, an oil spill is defined as a discharge in quantities that:
>
> - Violate applicable water quality standards;
>
> - Cause a film or "sheen" upon, or discoloration of, the surface of the water or adjoining shorelines; or
>
> - Cause a sludge or emulsion to be deposited beneath the surface of the water or upon adjoining shorelines.
>
> This definition is known as the "sheen rule" (see 40 CFR Part 110 for more information).

If an oil spill adversely impacts an Endangered Species Act listed species, an emergency Section 7 consultation may be needed (see Section XI-A of Part I of this document for more information).

EPA must be notified of any spills over 1,000 gallons or of any two spills over 42 gallons within a 12-month period. Additionally, the site should add a copy of the report with oil spill details to the SPCC Plan documentation for any reportable oil spills. The oil spill details should include correction actions taken, cause of discharge, and additional preventive measures taken.

E. What Questions Do You Need to Answer Before Starting Your Construction Project?

You can use the questions in Section II of Part I of this guide to start a discussion among all parties involved in the construction project and to assign tasks to ensure all environmental requirements are met. Each question has a space next to it to designate who will take the lead on each task. Note that designating a responsible party does not absolve you of meeting environmental requirements or liability for failing to meet these requirements.

F. Where Can You Get Additional Information?

For more information on oil spill requirements, review the following:

- The Oil Spill Prevention Self-Audit Checklist in Part II of this guide;

- EPA Oil Program web site: http://www.epa.gov/oilspill/;

- Spill Prevention Plan and Countermeasure Control Fact Sheet Guidance from EPA: http://www.epa.gov/oilspill/pdfs/spccbluebroch2002.pdf;

- EPA's "Where you live" page contains links to state environmental agencies: http://www.epa.gov/epahome/whereyoulive.htm;

- The Construction Industry Compliance Assistance Center provides information on requirements that apply to the construction industry: http://www.cicacenter.org/index.cfm; and

- The National Environmental Compliance Assistance Clearinghouse contains a search engine to help you find compliance assistance tools, contacts, and EPA- sponsored programs: http://www.epa.gov/clearinghouse/.

VI. Hazardous and Non-Hazardous Solid Waste Requirements for Construction Projects

D uring your construction project, you will likely generate solid wastes. EPA classifies solid wastes as being either non-hazardous or hazardous, as discussed later in this section. These wastes are regulated under the Resource Conservation and Recovery Act (RCRA). The regulatory text discussing this program (40 CFR Parts 260-299) can be found at http://ecfr.gpoaccess.gov under "Title 40 - Protection of the Environment." Construction projects typically generate much more non-hazardous waste than hazardous waste; however, you should understand the requirements for both types of wastes to assure proper handling and disposal of these wastes.

Definitions and Acronyms

Disposal—The discharge, deposit, injection, dumping, leaking, or placing of any solid or hazardous waste into or on any land or water so that the solid or hazardous waste or any constituent may enter the environment.

Generator—Any person, by site, whose act or process produces hazardous waste identified or listed in RCRA Subtitle C or whose act first causes a hazardous waste to become subject to regulation. For example, an action such as unearthing soil contaminated with a hazardous substance causes the contaminated soil to be subject to RCRA regulations.

Hazardous Waste—A solid waste, or combination of solid wastes, which because of its quanti-

ty, concentration, or physical, chemical, or infectious characteristics may either cause, or significantly contribute to, an increase in mortality or an increase in serious irreversible or incapacitating reversible illness; or pose a substantial present or potential hazard to human health or the environment when improperly treated, stored, transported, or disposed of, or otherwise managed.

Storage—When used in connection with hazardous waste, means the containment of hazardous waste, either on a temporary basis or for a period of years, in such a manner as not to constitute disposal of such hazardous waste.

Definitions and Acronyms

Universal Waste—Federal Universal Wastes are batteries such as nickel-cadmium (Ni-Cd) and small sealed lead-acid batteries, agricultural pesticides that are recalled under certain conditions and unused pesticides that are collected and managed as part of a waste pesticide collection program, thermostats that can contain as much as 3 grams of liquid mercury, and lamps that are the bulb or tube portion of electric lighting devices that have a hazardous component.

CESQG—Conditionally Exempt Small Quantity Generators

CFR—Code of Federal Regulations

DOT—Department of Transportation

LQG—Large Quantity Generators

RCRA—Resource Conservation and Recovery Act

SQG—Small Quantity Generators

TSDF—Treatment, Storage, and Disposal Facility

EPA regulates hazardous wastes at the federal level; however, always check with your state agencies for additional hazardous waste requirements. EPA does not regulate non-hazardous wastes at the federal level; these are regulated at the state and local level. Since this guide focuses on EPA regulations, most of this section discusses EPA's hazardous waste requirements as they apply to construction projects. However, since most of the solid wastes generated at construction sites are non-hazardous, Section VI-A of Part I of this guide briefly discusses non-hazardous wastes.

A. What are Your Non-Hazardous Waste Requirements?

Non-hazardous solid waste requirements vary from state to state. Common non-hazardous solid wastes generated at construction sites include:

- Scrap wood (used or unused);
- Dry wall;
- Bricks;
- Concrete;
- Plaster;
- Asphalt;

- Plumbing fixtures and piping;
- Insulation (non-asbestos);
- Roof coverings (e.g., shingles);
- Metal scraps; and
- Electrical wiring and components.

States have differing requirements for handling and disposing of these wastes. For example, some states allow you to grind drywall for use as on-site fill material while others do not. In addition, some states may classify certain wastes as hazardous while others do not. In many cases, if you dispose of non-hazardous construction waste, you are required to do so in a construction waste-specific landfill. Before construction begins, you

> **Always check with your state environmental agency for the applicable non-hazardous waste requirements. For a list of state agency contacts, go to http://www.epa.gov/epaoswer/ hotline/rcntcts.htm.**

should discuss who will be responsible for identifying any state requirements (e.g., recycling standards and proper disposal of solid wastes) and who will be responsible for complying with these requirements. For more information on state non-hazardous waste regulations that apply to the construction industry, go to the Construction Industry Compliance Assistance Center: http://www.cicacenter.org/hazwaste.html.

You may also choose to recycle or reuse your non-hazardous construction and demolition waste. For more information on local construction and demolition waste recyclers, go to the Construction Waste Management Database located at http://www.wdbg.org/ccbref/cwm.php. This database enables you to find waste recyclers based on your waste type and location.

B. What are Hazardous Wastes?

Your solid wastes may also meet the federal definition of hazardous waste. If that is the case, you are responsible for proper handling, storing, transporting, and/or disposing of them according to the federal requirements of RCRA and/or state requirements, from the point of generation to ultimate disposal. While states have the sole responsibility for regulating non-hazardous construction and demolition debris, they may also have authorization to implement EPA's RCRA Subtitle C - Hazardous Waste Program. State hazardous waste programs are at least as stringent as the federal hazardous waste program. Always contact your state authority to determine which state requirements apply to your site.

To determine if you must follow hazardous waste management requirements, you must first determine if your construction project will generate (i.e, produce or have present on site) hazardous wastes. RCRA Subtitle C defines solid waste as hazardous in one of two ways. Either the waste is one of the over 500 RCRA-listed wastes or it has one of the four following characteristics:

- Ignitable (flashpoint of less than 140 degrees), such as paint thinners, paints, paint and varnish strippers, epoxy resins, adhesives, degreasers, and spent cleaning solvents.

Examples of hazardous wastes:

- Used oil, hydraulic fluid, diesel fuel, or jet fuel;

- Soil contaminated with toxic or hazardous pollutants (e.g., soil contaminated with used oil, hydraulic fluid, diesel fuel, or jet fuel);

- Waste paints, varnish, solvents, sealers, thinners, resins, roofing cement, adhesives, machinery lubricants, and caulk;

- Cleanup materials (such as rags) contaminated with the items listed above;

- Drums and containers that once contained the items listed above;

- Waste carpeting (due to formaldehyde contents);

- Lead-based paint, lead flashing, or lead solder;

- Computer monitors and televisions with cathode ray tubes;

- Gypsum drywall (due to sulfate);

- Mercury-containing demolition wastes (e.g., fluorescent bulbs, broken mercury switches, batteries, or thermostats); and

- Other items that may have inseparable hazardous constituents.

- Corrosive (acids with a pH less than 2 or bases with a pH greater than 12.5), such as rust removers, cleaning fluids, and battery acids.

- Reactive (explosive or violently reactive), such as cyanide, plating waste, bleaches, and waste oxidizers.

- Toxic (meeting certain concentrations), such as materials containing metals (e.g., mercury, cadmium, or lead) or solvents (e.g., carbon tetrachloride or methyl ethyl ketone). Materials may include adhesives, paints, coatings, polishes, varnishes, thinners, or treated woods.

Listed wastes are divided into the four following waste codes:

- The "F" List contains nonspecific source wastes from specific industrial or manufacturing processes (e.g., spent solvents used to strip paint).

- The "K" List contains specific source waste (this list does not typically include waste from construction and demolition sites).

- The "P" and "U" Lists contain pure or commercial grade unused chemicals (e.g., left-over chemicals or container residues such as toluene or acetone). Note that unused pesticides and their containers are covered by the Federal Insecticide, Fungicide, and Rodenticide Act (FIFRA).

Additionally, some commonly recycled materials are considered to be "universal wastes." These are hazardous wastes that are subject to less stringent requirements. Universal wastes include the following hazardous wastes:

- Batteries;
- Pesticides (as defined by the Universal Waste definition);
- Thermostats; and
- Lamps.

In 2002, EPA proposed to add mercury-containing materials to the list of universal wastes. A final ruling on this proposal is expected in 2005.

For more information on hazardous wastes, refer to the resources listed in Section VI-G of Part I of this guide. You can also reference the Notification of Regulated Waste Activity, Instructions and Forms booklet. A list of commonly found hazardous wastes can be found at http://www.epa.gov/epaoswer/hazwaste/data/form8700/8700-12.pdf. The complete list of RCRA-listed chemicals is included in the text of the 40 CFR Part 261, Subpart D and can be found at http://ecfr.gpoaccess.gov under "Title 40 - Protection of the Environment."

C. Are You Responsible for Meeting Hazardous Waste Requirements?

If you generate (or discover) hazardous waste during construction activities, you may be responsible for the proper handling, storing, transporting, and disposal of the waste. In a typical construction activity, hazardous wastes are generated in one of two ways:

> **If you discover hazardous waste on your construction site, you should notify your state and local authorities or the National Response Center Hotline at 1-800-424-8802.**

- Hazardous wastes are discovered during construction activities (e.g., grading or digging) or removed during demolition (e.g., mercury-containing fluorescent bulbs); or
- Hazardous wastes are produced by construction activities (e.g., spent materials such as paints and degreasers, used oil).

When hazardous wastes are already present at the site, the contractor or subcontractor who first discovers the material is responsible for notifying the general contractor, developer, and/or owner. You should also notify local, state, and federal authorities. Because the hazardous waste was present at the site prior to construction activities, the developer or owner typically is responsible for ensuring that the hazardous wastes are handled and disposed of properly.

> ## Case Studies
>
> In one court case, two construction companies pleaded guilty to criminal charges for failing to handle discovered hazardous waste properly. The construction contractors discovered canisters containing hazardous waste left by a previous owner; however, they failed to notify the owner and did not remove the canisters. The canisters were improperly removed from the site, ultimately resulting in the death of one person. If the contractors had notified the owner and had the canisters removed and disposed of properly, criminal charges may not have been filed against them.

When hazardous wastes are produced at the site, the contractor or subcontractor who produces the hazardous waste typically is responsible for ensuring its proper handling and disposal. NOTE: Hazardous materials stored at your site that are being used for their intended purpose are not considered "wastes" and may be stored on site indefinitely. However, once the material is no longer usable, the material is considered a waste and RCRA storage requirements (e.g., time limit before a permit is needed) apply.

D. What Are the Penalties for Not Meeting the Hazardous Waste Requirements?

Federal environmental laws give a range of enforcement options to EPA, state agencies, and individual citizens. Most laws authorize EPA to: (1) issue an administrative order or impose an administrative penalty, (2) file a civil action in a federal court for injunctive relief or a civil penalty, or (3) file a criminal action in a federal court to impose criminal sanctions.

In addition to fines, you may need to pay legal fees and face project delays. If legal action is taken against your construction site, you may also be subject to increased scrutiny at all of your other construction sites by regulatory agencies and the public.

If you do not follow the hazardous waste management and permitting standards listed in RCRA Subtitle C, you may be fined in civil penalties up to $32,500 per day per violation. You can lose any existing permits for your site and/or need to stop work until you meet EPA requirements. You also may face criminal penalties under RCRA if you knowingly endanger another person while managing hazardous waste.

In addition, you could face penalties or actions for past or present handling, storage, treatment, transportation, or disposal of any waste that may be a hazard to human health or the environment. Not only are there civil and criminal penalties for violating hazardous waste laws, but a construction company can be required to pay the cost of cleaning up any contamination resulting from a violation. These ""cleanup"" costs can be significant.

E. In General, What Are the Hazardous Waste Requirements?

If you generate hazardous waste, you must identify the waste and determine your generator status based on monthly data because waste storage and management requirements vary based on how much hazardous waste you generate. If you generate 220 pounds or less of hazardous waste per month, or 2.2 pounds or less of acute hazardous waste per month, you are a conditionally exempt small quantity generator (CESQG). Most

> **Conditionally Exempt Small Quantity Generators generate ≤220 lbs/month**
>
> **Small Quantity Generators generate >220 lbs/month and <2,200 lbs/month**
>
> **Large Quantity Generators generate ≥2,200 lbs/month**

construction sites are classified as conditionally exempt small quantity generators. If you generate between 220 and 2,200 pounds of hazardous waste per month, you are a small quantity generator (SQG). Some construction sites may be classified as small quantity generators. If you generate 2,200 pounds of hazardous waste per month or greater, or greater than 2.2 pounds of acute hazardous waste per month, you are a large quantity generator (LQG). Conditionally exempt small quantity generators have significantly fewer requirements than other generators, as discussed below. Acute hazardous wastes are denoted with the hazardous waste code "H" or are P-listed RCRA

> **Hazardous waste must be treated and disposed of at a facility permitted or licensed for that purpose by the state or Federal Government.**

wastes. Keep in mind that requirements vary between states; therefore, contact your state environmental department for hazardous waste requirements regardless of the amount of waste you generate.

You are not allowed to transport hazardous wastes off your construction site unless you follow EPA's standards for transporting hazardous waste to a designated treatment, storage, and disposal facility (TSDF). This guide does not address transportation requirements; contact your local Department of Transportation for information on these requirements.

Conditionally Exempt Small Quantity Generators

Most construction sites are conditionally exempt small quantity generators (generate less than 220 pounds of hazardous waste per month). Under RCRA, these generators must meet RCRA storage limit requirements (2,200 pounds of hazardous waste/month) and ensure proper transportation, waste treatment, and disposal (i.e., meet all DOT requirements and use permitted or licensed facilities for hazardous waste treatment and/or disposal). Although you are not required to meet the further stipulations listed below for small and large quantity generators, some states may have additional requirements (e.g., obtaining an EPA ID number) that do apply. If your site exceeds the storage limit (2,200 pounds of hazardous waste/month), you become a small quantity generator and must meet additional requirements.

Small and Large Quantity Generators

If you generate hazardous waste as a small or large quantity generator, you must get an EPA ID number and notify EPA (or your state) within 90 days after initial waste generation. In addition, you need to provide subsequent notifications if one of the following occurs:

- Your business moves to another location;
- Your site contact changes;
- The ownership of your site changes;
- An additional owner is added or replaced; or
- The type of regulated waste activity changes.

To get an EPA ID number and notify EPA of hazardous waste generation, you need to file a Form 8700-12, Notification of Regulated Waste Activities. The form and instructions are available on line at http://www.epa.gov/epaoswer/hazwaste/data/form8700/8700-12.pdf. The instructions include a list of state contacts for submitting forms and asking for assistance.

If you store hazardous waste for longer than 180 days (for small quantity generators) or 90 days (for large quantity generators), you must get a RCRA permit. You should plan ahead to avoid storing hazardous wastes longer than allowed without a permit. If you exceed the storage limits and need a RCRA permit, additional regulations apply. If you need a RCRA permit, you may be eligible to meet only those requirements for Remedial Action Plans (RAPs). As with permits, you must submit an application for a RAP to the permitting authority (e.g., EPA or designated states). For more information on RAP requirements go to http://www.epa.gov/epaoswer/hazwaste/id/hwirmdia/hwrmedfr.pdf.

In addition, small and large quantity generators must meet the following requirements for handling hazardous waste:

- Document the amount of hazardous waste stored on site.
- Keep waste in proper containers.
- Properly mark containers.
- Put emergency procedures in place.
- Train on-site personnel to handle hazardous waste.
- Get a licensed hazardous waste hauler to transport the waste.
- Properly package and label hazardous waste for transport.
- Complete a Uniform Hazardous Waste Manifest for transporting hazardous waste. The manifest allows all parties involved in hazardous waste management (e.g., generators, transporters, TSDFs, EPA, state agencies) to track the movement of hazardous waste from the point of generation to the point of ultimate treatment, storage, or disposal.

If your construction project is located in Iowa or Alaska, contact your EPA Region for hazardous waste information. If your construction project is located in one of the other 48 states, contact your state environmental agency for hazardous waste information. Note that states may control some RCRA provisions, but not others.

For more detailed information on the hazardous waste requirements, use the resources listed in Section VI-G of Part I of this guide.

Universal Wastes

You can store universal wastes at your site for up to one year. Small quantity handlers of universal waste store less than 11,000 pounds and large quantity handlers of universal waste store 11,000 pounds or more.

Universal waste handlers must meet the following requirements:

- Prevent environmental releases of the wastes;

- Respond immediately to any releases; and

- Educate employees on basic waste handling and emergency procedures (including information distribution).

Large quantity handlers of universal waste must meet additional requirements, including maintaining shipment documentation, getting an EPA ID number, and meeting stricter employee training requirements.

When transporting universal wastes, you do not need to meet the RCRA hazardous waste manifest requirements; however, DOT or state requirements may apply.

> **A good guide for safe lead work practices can be found at http://www.epa.gov/lead/leadsafetybk.pdf**

Lead-Based Paint Debris

During construction projects, you may discover lead-based paint debris. In most cases, lead-based paint debris is considered to be a hazardous waste under RCRA; however, certain activities involving this type of debris are exempt. If you generate lead-based paint debris from construction in homes and other residences (e.g., during abatement, renovation, and remodeling), you can treat the debris as "household waste." You can dispose of the debris as household garbage in municipal waste landfills, construction and demolition debris landfills, or in municipal solid waste combustion units, unless other state requirements apply. You cannot dump (dispose on or off site) or open-burn lead-based paint debris.

While not a regulatory requirement, using safe work practices when disturbing lead paint can greatly reduce the risk of household occupants, workers, and even workers' families from being exposed to hazardous quantities of lead. Also, check with your state for any additional requirements.

If your project involves construction in homes or other residences, several rules and policies may apply, all developed under the Residential Lead-Based Paint Hazard Reduction Act of 1992 (Title X). The authority for these regulations falls under the Toxic Substances Control Act (TSCA), Title IV (Lead Exposure Reduction).

National Lead Laboratory Accreditation Program (TSCA Section 405(b)): Establishes protocols, criteria, and minimum performance standards for laboratory analysis of lead in paint, dust, and soil;

- Hazard Standards for Lead in Paint, Dust, and Soil (TSCA Section 403): Establishes standards for lead-based paint hazards and lead dust cleanup levels in most pre-1978 housing and child-occupied facilities;

- Training & Certification Program for Lead-Based Paint Activities (TSCA Section 402/404): Ensures that individuals conducting lead-based paint abatement, risk assessment, or inspection are properly trained and certified, that training programs are accredited, and that these activities are conducted according to reliable, effective and safe work practice standards;

- Pre-Renovation Education Rule (TSCA Section 406(b)): Ensures that owners and occupants of most pre-1978 housing are provided information concerning potential hazards of lead-based paint exposure before beginning certain renovations on that housing;

- Disclosure Rule (Section 1018 of Title X): Requires disclosure of known lead-based paint and/or lead-based paint hazards by persons selling or leasing housing constructed before the phase-out of residential lead-based paint use in 1978; and

- Lead-Based Paint Debris Disposal: Regulatory status of waste generated by contractors and residents from lead-based paint activities conducted in households.

For more information on these programs, go to http://www.epa.gov/lead/regulation.htm.

F. What Questions Do You Need to Answer Before Starting Your Construction Project?

You can use the questions in Section II of Part I of this guide to start a discussion among all parties involved in the construction project and to assign tasks to ensure all environmental requirements are met. Each question has a space next to it to designate who will take the lead on each task. Note that designating a responsible party does not absolve you of meeting environmental requirements or liability for failing to meet these requirements.

G. Where Can You Get Additional Information?

For more information on hazardous and non-hazardous solid waste requirements, you can check the following resources:

- The Hazardous Solid Waste Self-Audit Checklist in Part II of this guide;
- The Construction Industry Compliance Assistance Center provides information on hazardous and toxic waste regulations that apply to the construction industry: http://www.cicacenter.org/hazwaste.html;
- The National Environmental Compliance Assistance Clearinghouse contains a search engine to help you find compliance assistance tools, contacts, and EPA- sponsored programs: http://www.epa.gov/clearinghouse/;

- EPA's Office of Solid Waste and Emergency Response provides information on RCRA regulations, including permitting, state authorization, and other requirements: http://www.epa.gov/epaoswer/osw/laws-reg.htm;

- EPA's Office of Solid Waste provides information on remediation waste, recycling construction wastes, and other resources: http://www.epa.gov/osw/;

- List of commonly reported hazardous wastes in EPA's Notification of Regulated Waste Activities: Instructions and Forms (available on-line at http://www.epa.gov/epaoswer/hazwaste/data/form8700/8700-12.pdf);

- Your state or EPA Region (for a list of state agency contacts, go to www.epa.gov/epaoswer/hotline/rcntcts.htm);

- Federal Facility Hazardous Waste Identification Flow Chart helps you to decide if your waste is hazardous as defined by RCRA (some states have different definitions): http://www.epa.gov/fedsite/hazwaste/flowchart.html;

- EPA's "Where you live" page contains links to state environmental agencies: http://www.epa.gov/epahome/whereyoulive.htm; and

- EPA's Office of Site Remediation Enforcement provides information on RCRA cleanup regulations and enforcement at: http://www.epa.gov/compliance/cleanup/.

VII. Hazardous Substances (Superfund Liability) Requirements for Construction Activities

Before beginning any construction or demolition activities at your construction site, you should evaluate the site for existing hazardous substances as defined by the Comprehensive Environmental Response, Compensation, and Liability Act (CERCLA, also known as "Superfund"). CERCLA was originally enacted to address hazardous substances at inactive or abandoned sites. The Superfund program is administered by EPA in cooperation with individual states and tribal governments. The program includes a revolving Trust Fund used by EPA and other agencies to clean up hazardous waste sites where no responsible party can be identified. CERCLA also requires you to immediately report to the National Response Center any releases of hazardous substances at your construction site if the amount released meets or exceeds the reportable quantity.

Definitions and Acronyms

Brownfield—Property where any expansion, redevelopment, or reuse may be complicated by the presence or potential presence of a hazardous substance, pollutant, or contaminant, not including sites that are part of a planned or ongoing removal action or are on the National Priorities List.

Extremely Hazardous Substances (EHSs)—Chemicals that most likely induce serious acute reactions following short-term airborne exposure

(defined at 40 CFR Part 355). The list of extremely hazardous substances subject to EPCRA reporting requirements can be found in EPA's Consolidated List of Chemicals Subject to the Emergency Planning and Community Right-To-Know Act (EPCRA) and Section 112(r) of the Clean Air Act (EPA 550-B-01-003). Note that an extremely hazardous substance may also be included on the CERCLA list of hazardous substances.

Definitions and Acronyms

Hazardous Substances—Defined in CERCLA Section 101(14) and includes hazardous air pollutants (designated in Section 112(b) of the Clean Air Act), radionuclides, toxic pollutants (designated in Section 307(a) of the Clean Water Act), elements and compounds that present an imminent danger to public health when discharged into waters of the United States (designated in Section 311(b)(2)(A) of the Clean Water Act), TSCA substance that EPA has taken action against (currently none), RCRA-listed hazardous wastes, and RCRA characteristic wastes. The list of hazardous substances subject to CERCLA and EPCRA reporting requirements can be found in EPA's Consolidated List of Chemicals Subject to the Emergency Planning and Community Right-To-Know Act (EPCRA) and Section 112(r) of the Clean Air Act (EPA 550-B-01-003). Certain substances are excluded from CERCLA and/or EPCRA reporting requirements (see Section VII-F of this document for web sites and hotlines where you can obtain additional information).

National Priorities List—The list of national priorities among the known releases or threatened releases of hazardous substances, pollutants, or contaminants throughout the United States and its territories. The NPL is intended primarily to guide the EPA in determining which sites warrant further investigation.

Release—Any spilling, leaking, pumping, pouring, emitting, emptying, discharging, injecting, escaping, leaching, dumping, or disposing into the environment, including abandonment or discarding of barrels, containers, and other closed receptacles containing any hazardous substance.

Reportable Quantity—Amount of hazardous substance (or extremely hazardous substance) released into the environment within a 24-hour period that must be met or exceeded before emergency release notification requirements are triggered. Reportable quantities are listed in EPA's Consolidated List of Chemicals Subject to the Emergency Planning and Community Right-To-Know Act (EPCRA) and Section 112(r) of the Clean Air Act (EPA 550-B-01-003).

CERCLA—Comprehensive Environmental Response, Compensation, and Liability Act

CFR—Code of Federal Regulations

EPCRA—Emergency Planning and Community Right-to-Know Act

LEPC—Local Emergency Planning Committee

NPL—National Priorities List

SERC—State Emergency Response Commission

SARA Title III, better known as the Emergency Planning and Community Right-to-Know Act (EPCRA), originated from CERCLA. EPCRA requires the use of emergency planning and provides citizens, local governments, and local response authorities with information regarding the potential hazards in their community. The regulatory text discussing these programs (40 CFR Part 302 and Parts 350-372) can be found at http://ecfr.gpoaccess.gov under "Title 40 - Protection of the Environment."

Prior to beginning the bidding process, the owner or developer should research the construction site to identify any history of hazardous substance use or disposal at the site. If you conduct this research prior to construction, it will help to avoid significant project delays and possible project cancellation if hazardous substances are discovered during construction. Contractors should also make sure that this review has been completed prior to starting any construction activities to better understand potential risks and liabilities prior to bidding a job.

EPCRA establishes State Emergency Response Commissions (SERC) and Local Emergency Planning Committees (LEPC). If EPCRA applies to your construction project, you may need to provide information to your SERC/LEPC on the presence of hazardous chemicals and their releases (accidental or routine). In addition, your SERC/LEPC may have additional requirements. EPA has found that most construction sites are not subject to EPCRA planning requirements.

> **To make sure that your construction site is not a Superfund site or on the National Priorities List (NPL), go to: http://cfpub.epa.gov/supercpad/ cursites/srchsites.cfm.**

In addition to planning requirements, EPCRA also has reporting requirements for hazardous substances and extremely hazardous substances. You must report to your SERC/LEPC any releases of these substances at your construction site if the amount released meets or exceeds the reportable quantity.

A. Does Your Construction Project Site Contain Hazardous Substances?

Your facility can be affected by Superfund or EPCRA if hazardous substances are discovered during construction activities (e.g., grading or digging) or removed during demolition (e.g., drums of spent chemicals). Prior to any construction activity, you should make sure that a thorough historical evaluation of your site has been completed. This should include, but not be limited to, a review of historical records to determine previous uses of the site, a review of historical aerial photographs to identify potential areas of contamination, and a review of state and local files to identify past

> **To determine if test results indicate the presence of hazardous substances at your site contact the National Response Center Hotline, 1-800-424-8802.**

environmental concerns at the site. If your site was previously used for industrial or commercial activities that may have generated hazardous substances, or there is some indication of waste disposal at the site, you should consider testing the soil, surface water, and groundwater prior to beginning any construction activities.

There may still be instances where, during construction, you discover hazardous substances at a site that was never used for industrial or commercial activities or waste disposal (i.e., illegal dumping grounds). If this happens, stop your construction activities and immediately notify the owner/developer and the National Response Center Hotline at 1-800-424-8802. See Section VII-B of Part I of this guide for more information.

If your construction site is considered a brownfield site, you should already be aware of any potential hazardous contamination. A brownfield site is a piece of property that is undesirable for development due either to contamination by a hazardous substance or the perception of contamination. Brownfields do not include sites that are part of the Superfund process. EPA implements a Brownfields Program to encourage states, communities, and other stakeholders to work together to prevent, assess, safely clean up, and reuse brownfields. The Brownfields Program provides grant money to communities to help fund the evaluation and cleanup of these sites. For more information on this program, go to EPA's Brownfields Cleanup and Redevelopment web site at http://www.epa.gov/swerosps/bf/index.html.

EPCRA Planning Requirements

Your construction site is subject to EPCRA emergency planning requirements (Section 302) if it meets both of the following:

- It stores an extremely hazardous substance, as defined at http://yosemite.epa.gov/oswer/cep-poweb.nsf/
content/chemicalinfo.htm; or stores any substance regulated by your state or local authority; and

- It stores the substance above the designated Threshold Planning Quantity, which varies by substance. A definition of Threshold Planning Quantities can be found at
http://yosemite.epa.gov/oswer/ceppoweb.nsf/vwResourcesByFilename/title3.pdf/$File/title3.pdf.

However, EPA has found that most construction sites do not work with the listed extremely hazardous substances and are not subject to the requirements of EPCRA. Therefore, this guide does not discuss EPCRA planning requirements further. If you discover hazardous substances at your site, you should consult the references listed above to determine if EPCRA applies.

> **More information on brownfields cleanup enforcement is available on line at: http://www.epa.gov/ enforcement/cleanup/brownfields.**

B. Are You Responsible for Meeting CERCLA/EPCRA Requirements?

If hazardous substances are discovered during construction activities, the contractor or subcontractor who first discovers the material is responsible for notifying the general contractor, developer, and/or owner. Because the hazardous substance was present at the site prior to construction activities, the developer or owner typically is responsible for ensuring that the hazardous substances are handled and disposed of properly.

However, if you excavate or spread soils containing a hazardous substance (e.g., waste pesticides), you may be responsible under CERCLA as an operator, arranger, or transporter. For example:

- You may be an operator if you spread soil that contains a hazardous substance on the land.

- You may be an arranger if you dispose of a hazardous substance or arrange to have it removed from the construction site. For example, if you excavate soil that contains pollutants buried by a previous owner, you may be liable for disposal of a hazardous substance.

- You may be a transporter if you move hazardous substance from one location to another. For example, you may be liable if you transport dioxin-contaminated soil even if you did not know the soil contained dioxin.

If there is a hazardous substance release exceeding the reportable quantity for CERCLA, you must immediately notify the National Response Center at 1-800-424-8802 and your SERC/LEPC. If there is an extremely hazardous substance release exceeding the reportable quantity for EPCRA, you

> **If you discover a hazardous substance on your construction site, you should notify your state and local authorities or the National Response Center Hotline, 1-800-424-8802.**

must immediately notify your SERC/LEPC. If no notification occurs, both the owner and operator (e.g., contractor, subcontractor) may be held responsible.

C. What Are the Penalties?

Federal environmental laws give a range of enforcement options to EPA, state agencies, and individual citizens. Most laws authorize EPA to: (1) issue an administrative order or impose an administrative penalty, (2) file a civil action in a federal court for injunctive relief or a civil penalty, or (3) file a criminal action in a federal court to impose criminal sanctions.

EPA may impose administrative, civil, and criminal sanctions on a property owner and/or a contractor for failure to comply with Superfund requirements. Administrative penalties and civil penalties – imposed in a judicial proceeding – can reach $32,500 per violation per day. In addition to fines, you may need to pay legal fees and face project delays. If legal action is taken against your construction site, you may also be subject to increased scrutiny at all of your other construction sites by regulatory agencies and the public.

CERCLA authorizes EPA to negotiate with parties that helped create hazardous waste sites (responsible parties, also known as PRPs) to get them to clean up the sites. If those parties refuse to cooperate, EPA can order them to conduct the cleanup, or EPA can conduct the cleanup using money from the Superfund Trust Fund. Regardless of how the cleanup is conducted, CERCLA gives EPA the authority to recover any costs it incurs as part of the response. Therefore, any responsible party may be required to pay for the entire cleanup cost. For more information on the types of costs EPA can recover, go to http://www.epa.gov/compliance/cleanup/superfund/recovercosts/index.html.

D. In General, What are the Steps for Cleanup?

If you discover hazardous materials, contaminated soil, or contaminated groundwater, your construction site may be entered into the Comprehensive Environmental Response, Compensation, and Liability Information System (CERCLIS), EPA's computerized inventory of potential hazardous substance release sites. When this happens, the responsible parties are required to work with EPA to evaluate the severity of the problem and develop remedies. EPA and the responsible party will evaluate the potential for a release of hazardous substances from the site through these steps in the Superfund cleanup process:

- Preliminary Assessment/Site Inspection (PA/SI) - Investigate the site conditions;
- Hazard Ranking System (HRS) Scoring - Based on the results of the PA/SI, rate the site and determine if it should be placed on the National Priorities List; and
- National Priorities List (NPL) Site Listing Process - Based on the HRS score, EPA lists the most serious of the sites for further investigation and possible long-term cleanup.

If a site is placed on the NPL, the responsible parties are required to work with EPA to conduct several steps to clean up the site, including:

- Remedial Investigation/Feasibility Study (RI/FS) - Investigate the NPL sites to determine the nature and extent of contamination as well as the potential treatment options;
- Records of Decision (ROD) - Use the results of the RI/FS to explain which cleanup alternatives will be used at the NPL site;

- Remedial Design/Remedial Action (RD/RA) - Design the cleanup technology and begin the site cleanup process;

- Cleanup Completion - Complete any required cleanup activities or, remove the site from the NPL; and

- Post Cleanup Completion - Once cleanup is complete, implement maintenance programs that will provide for the long-term protection of human health and the environment.

Releases that require immediate or short-term response actions are addressed under the Emergency Response program of Superfund.

E. What Questions Do You Need to Answer Before Starting Your Construction Project?

You can use the questions in Section II of Part I of this guide to start a discussion among all parties involved in the construction project and to assign tasks to ensure all environmental requirements are met. Each question has a space next to it to designate who will take the lead on each task. Note that designating a responsible party does not absolve you of responsibility for meeting environmental requirements or liability for failing to meet these requirements.

F. Where Can You Get Additional Information?

Many tools are available to assist you with your CERCLA and EPCRA requirements, including the following:

- The Hazardous Substances (Superfund Liability) Self-Audit Checklist in Part II of this guide;

- EPA's Superfund web site: http://www.epa.gov/superfund/index.htm;

- EPA's Brownfields homepage: http://www.epa.gov/swerosps/bf/;

- EPCRA web site: http://yosemite.epa.gov/oswer/ceppoweb.nsf/content/epcraoverview.htm;

- EPCRA Hotline: 1-800-424-9346;

- EPA's "Where you live" page contains links to state environmental agencies: http://www.epa.gov/epahome/whereyoulive.htm;

- EPA's Office of Site Remediation and Enforcement (OSRE) staff assist with issues such as lender liability, prospective purchasers, comfort letters, and municipal solid waste. OSRE web sites include: http://www.epa.gov/compliance/cleanup/ and specifically for brownfields, http://www.epa.gov/enforcement/cleanup/brownfields;

- The Construction Industry Compliance Assistance Center provides information on hazardous and toxic substances regulations that apply to the construction industry: http://www.cicacenter.org/hazwaste.html; and

- The National Environmental Compliance Assistance Clearinghouse contains a search engine to help you find compliance assistance tools, contacts, and EPA- sponsored programs: http://www.epa.gov/clearinghouse/.

VIII. Polychlorinated Biphenyl (PCB) Waste Requirements for Construction Activities

B efore beginning any construction activities on existing buildings, you should evaluate the potential for generating PCB-laden waste. The PCB regulations and requirements apply to both PCB waste materials and PCBs still in use. Because of potential harmful effects on human health and the environment, federal law banned U.S. production of PCBs as of July 2, 1979. However, PCB-containing materials may be present at construction and demolition sites.

Definitions and Acronyms

Polychlorinated Biphenyls (PCBs)—Any chemical substance that is limited to the biphenyl molecule that has been chlorinated to varying degrees or any combination of substances that contain such a substance. Due to their non-flammability, chemical stability, high boiling point, and electrical insulating properties, PCBs were used in hundreds of industrial and commercial applications including electrical, heat transfer, and hydraulic equipment; as plasticizers in paints, plastics, and rubber products; in pigments, dyes, and carbonless copy paper; and many other applications.

PCB—Polychlorinated Biphenyl

RCRA—Resource Conservation and Recovery Act

TSCA—Toxic Substances Control Act

A. Could Your Construction Project Site Contain PCBs?

PCBs were used in hundreds of industrial and commercial applications including electrical (e.g., capacitors and transformers), heat transfer, hydraulic, and lighting equipment. Items with a PCB concentration of 50 parts per million (ppm) or greater are regulated for disposal under 40 CFR Part 761. The regulatory text discussing this program (40 CFR Part 302 and Part 761) can be found at http://ecfr.gpoaccess.gov under "Title 40 - Protection of the Environment." The most likely sources of PCBs at construction sites are:

- Mineral-oil filled electrical equipment such as motors or pumps manufactured prior to July 2, 1979;

- Capacitors or transformers manufactured prior to July 2, 1979;

- Plastics, molded rubber parts, applied dried paints, coatings or sealants, caulking, adhesives, paper, Galbestos, sound-deadening materials, insulation, or felt or fabric products such as gaskets manufactured prior to July 2, 1979;

- Fluorescent light ballasts manufactured prior to July 2, 1979;

- Waste or debris from the demolition of buildings and equipment manufactured, serviced, or coated with PCBs; and

- Waste containing PCBs from spills, such as floors or walls contaminated by a leaking transformer.

For demolition activities, the building owner should have an inventory of all items containing PCBs. However, if the equipment is not marked and if no records exist, you will need to identify any PCB-containing materials. PCBs are difficult to locate and identify. PCB concentrations may vary from item to item and

PCB Trade Names and Other Synonyms To Help You Identify PCB-Containing Equipment

Aceclor	Chorinol	Hyrol	Polychlorinated diphenyl
Adkarel	Clophen	Hyvol	Polychlorinated diphenyls
ALC	Clophenharz	Inclor	Polychlorobiphenyl
Apirolio	Cloresil	Inerteen	Polychlorodiphenyl
Apirorlio	Clorinal	Inertenn	Prodelec
Arochlor	Clorphen	Kanechlor	Pydraul
Arochlors	Decachlorodiphenyl	Kaneclor	Pyraclor
Aroclor	Delor	Kennechlor	Pyralene
Aroclors	Delorene Diaclor	Kenneclor	Pyranol
Arubren	Dicolor	Leromoll	Pyroclor
Asbestol	Diconal	Magvar	Pyronol
ASK	Diphenyl, chlorinated	MCS 1489	Saf-T-Kuhl
Askael	DK	Montar	Saf-T-Kohl
Askarel	Duconal	Nepolin	Santosol
Auxol	Dykanol	No-Flamol	Santotherm
Bakola	Educarel	NoFlamol	Santothern
Biphenyl, chlorinated	EEC-18	Non-Flamol	Santovac
Chlophen	Elaol	Olex-sf-d	Solvol
Chloretol	Electrophenyl	Orophene PCB	Sorol
Chlorextol	Elemex	PCB's	Soval
Chlorinated biphenyl	Elinol	PCBs	Sovol
Chlorinated diphenyl	Eucarel	Pheaoclor	Sovtol
Chlorinol	Fenchlor	Phenochlor	Terphenychlore
Chlorobiphenyl	Fenclor	Phenoclor	Therminal
Chlorodiphenyl	Fenocloro	Plastivar	Therminol
Chlorphen	Gilotherm	Polychlorinated biphenyl	Turbinol
Chorextol	Hydol	Polychlorinated biphenyls	

within classes of items. If you cannot locate and identify PCB-containing materials yourself, you will need to contact a company that specializes in environmental engineering, remediation, or sampling and analytical services. Your state environmental agency may be able to assist in locating or recommending such companies. EPA's Home Page contains a "Where you live" link that contains links to state environmental agencies: http://www.epa.gov/epahome/whereyoulive.htm.

B. Are You Responsible for Addressing PCB Wastes?

The PCB regulations at 40 CFR Part 761 define the "generator" as being responsible for handling, storing, transporting, and disposing of PCB wastes. The "generator" is considered the party that owns the material. **For most construction projects, multiple parties will be involved; all may be liable if the PCB handling and disposal requirements are not followed.**

In a typical construction project, PCB wastes are generated in one of two ways:

> **The PCB regulations can be found at http://www.epa.gov/pcb/laws.html.**

- PCB-contaminated soils and materials are discovered during grading or digging (i.e., remediation wastes); or

- PCB-contaminated buildings or equipment are discovered during demolition.

In these situations, the contractor or subcontractor who first discovers the PCB-containing material typically is responsible for notifying the general contractor, developer, and/or owner. Because the PCB-containing material was present on the site prior to construction activities, the developer or owner typically is responsible for ensuring that all PCB wastes are handled and disposed of properly.

Because PCBs were banned as of 1979, it is unlikely that a contractor or subcontractor will bring PCB-bearing materials on site during a construction project. However, if this happens, that contractor or subcontractor typically would be responsible for complying with the PCB requirements.

C. What Are the Penalties?

Federal environmental laws give a range of enforcement options to EPA, state agencies, and individual citizens. Most laws authorize EPA (1) to issue an administrative order or impose an administrative penalty, (2) to file a civil action in a federal court for injunctive relief or a civil penalty, or (3) to file a criminal action in a federal court to impose criminal sanctions.

In addition to fines, you may need to pay legal fees and face project delays. If legal action is taken against your construction site, you also may be subject to increased scrutiny at all of your other construction sites by regulatory agencies and the public.

If you do not follow the PCB waste management and permitting standards listed in 40 CFR Part 761, you may be fined in civil penalties of up to $32,500 per day per violation. You also may be fined if you release PCB waste into the environment. You can lose any existing permits for your construction site and/or need to stop work until you meet EPA requirements.

You also may face penalties or actions for past or present handling, storage, treatment, transportation, or disposal of PCB waste that may be a hazard to human health or the environment.

D. In General, What are the Storage and Disposal Requirements?

The general requirements for handling PCB materials and equipment identified on site prior to demolition or remodeling projects consist of: identifying and labeling the material, notifying EPA, properly storing the material, and properly disposing of the material. If you discover PCB wastes during grading or digging (e.g., buried transformers), the storage and handling requirements can be very complex and depend on the amounts and concentrations of the waste. Contact your EPA Regional office for guidance on how to properly handle PCB materials, equipment, and wastes.

Identification and Labeling

Before you begin any demolition or remodeling activities, identify and label all PCB-containing equipment or material that will be disturbed. You can find an example of the two approved PCB labels in 40 CFR Part 761.45. Large mark (ML) is the larger, preferred label and is square from 6 inch by 6 inch to 2 inch by 2 inch. Small mark (MS) is the smaller label that should be used only on items that will not accommodate the ML and is rectangular from 1 inch by 2 inch to 0.4 inch by 0.8 inch. The following items must be labeled:

> **You may find a list of EPA Regional PCB coordinators at http://www.epa.gov/pcb/coordin.html and a list of EPA Headquarters PCB contacts at http://www.epa.gov/pcb/contactus.html.**

- PCB containers;
- Large PCB transformers, PCB low- and high-voltage capacitors, and equipment containing these transformers or capacitors at the time of removal from use if not already marked;
- Large PCB high-voltage capacitors at the time of manufacture, at the time of distribution in commerce if not already marked, and at the time of removal from use if not already marked;
- Electric motors using PCB coolants;
- Hydraulic systems using PCB hydraulic fluid;
- Heat transfer systems (other than PCB transformers) using PCBs;
- PCB article containers containing articles or equipment that must be marked; and
- Each storage area used to store PCBs and PCB items for disposal.

(Note - Items containing PCBs cannot be reused or recycled; there is no provision in the Toxic Substances Control Act for using, reusing, or recycling items or materials containing PCBs. However, items or materials containing less than 2 ppm PCBs may be used, reused, or recycled without restriction.)

For PCB waste disposal, there are two ways to determine regulatory status of items or materials suspected of containing PCBs: assume "worst case" (greater than or equal to 50 ppm) and remove and dispose the suspect item(s); or, analyze samples of the items for PCB concentration. The PCB rules do not require you to test, although EPA recommends it. Note that sampling and analysis may be expensive. It may be more cost-effective to assume a "worst case" scenario. EPA developed the following guidelines to assist you with your assumptions.

PCB Concentration Assumptions
(for Equipment Manufactured Prior to July 2, 1979)

Item	Concentration Assumption
Transformers with <3 lbs of fluid Circuit breakers Reclosers Oil-filled cable Rectifiers with unestablished PCB concentrations	<50 ppm PCB (not regulated by TSCA)
Mineral-oil filled electrical equipment without any established PCB concentration (pole-top and pad-mounted distribution transformers are considered mineral-oil filled)	>50 ppm and <500 ppm
Transformers with >3 lbs of fluid Capacitors	>500 ppm

Notification

If you are storing or disposing of PCB waste, complete a Notification of PCB Activity Form (see http://www.epa.gov/pcb/data.html) and mail it to the Fibers and Organics Branch of the National Program Chemicals Division in EPA's Office of Pollution Prevention and Toxics (OPPT). EPA will assign an identification number (ID number) to the construction site for handling PCBs. This ID number is for activities involving PCBs and may not be used for any other waste activities. If the construction site has already received an ID number for other regulated wastes (e.g., RCRA), EPA will verify the number and assign the same ID number for the site's PCB activities. It is not necessary to have a RCRA ID number to receive a PCB ID number.

Storage and Disposal

Storage requirements for PCB-containing materials depend on the end use of those materials. You can store approved materials for reuse for up to five years in an approved, permanent, PCB storage area. (Note - The storage-for-reuse provisions at 40 CFR Part 761.35 are meant to capture equipment such as transformers. The equipment must be manufactured for a particular use. It is not meant for any item or material containing PCBs. See the definition of "PCB Article" at 40 CFR Part 761.3.) You can store materials for disposal for up to 30 days in a temporary storage area or for up to one year in a permanent PCB storage location. In all cases, you must mark the items with the date they were removed from service and inspect the area every 30 days for any spills or leaks. A temporary storage for disposal area must meet the following requirements:

- Be marked with a PCB ML label;
- Have a roof and walls to protect the materials from rain or snow;

- Have impermeable floor with 6-inch curbing and no drains;

- Have containment volume equal to at least two times the volume of the largest PCB article or 25 percent of the total volume of all PCB articles, whichever is greater;

- Not be located in a 100-year flood plain; and

- Have all leaking equipment stored in a nonleaking PCB container with absorbents and have non-leaking equipment on pallets.

You can also store PCB material in an area permitted by RCRA to store hazardous wastes. If you operate an on-site storage area, you need to complete the Notification of PCB Activity Form as discussed above.

If at any time during site inspection or material handling you discover a spill or leak, you must clean it up within 72 hours of discovery. EPA has provided a detailed spill cleanup policy in 40 CFR Part 761, Subpart G. The requirements of this plan vary depending on the size and concentration of the spill but can include the following:

> **For information specific to fluorescent light ballast disposal, see http://www.epa.gov/pcb/ Ballastchart.pdf.**
>
> **Note that fluorescent light ballasts containing mercury are considered universal wastes; see Section V-E of Part I of this guide for more information.**

For high concentration spills (defined as 500 ppm or greater PCBs, or low concentration spills involving more than one pound PCBs by weight, or more than 270 gallons of untested material) within 24 hours of the spill or within 48 hours for spills involving PCB transformers:

- Notify the National Response Center at 1-800-424-8802 if the spill involved 10 pounds or more by weight of PCBs;

- Notify local environmental agencies;

- Notify local authorities immediately if there was a fire;

- Restrict and label the visible spill area;

- Record and document the extent of PCB contamination of the estimated spill area;

- Immediately begin cleanup of the visible spill area; once the concentration level of the PCB spill is determined, begin the appropriate cleanup depending upon the release location, exposure risk, PCB concentration, and future use of the site; and

- Test the area to confirm that the PCB concentration met EPA-specified levels.

For low concentration spills (defined as less than 500 ppm PCB, or less than one pound of PCBs by weight, or less than 270 gallons of untested material):

- Double wash/rinse all contaminated surfaces within 48 hours of the spill, properly dispose of the wash water; and

- Collect a standard wipe test sample from smooth surfaces, using hexane wipe samples to detect PCB contamination and confirm that the concentration is not more than 10 micrograms per 100 square centimeters.

At the completion of cleanup, records and certification forms must be maintained for a period of 5 years. Your records should contain the following:

- Identification of the source of the spill (e.g., type of equipment);

- Estimated or actual date and time of the spill;

- The date and time cleanup was completed or terminated (if cleanup was delayed by emergency or adverse weather, include the nature and duration of the delay);

- A brief description of the spill location;

- Pre-cleanup sampling data used to establish the spill boundaries if required;

- A brief description of the sampling methodology used to establish the spill boundaries;

- A brief description of the solid surfaces cleaned and of the double wash/rinse method used;

- Approximate depth of soil excavation and the amount of soil removed; and

- A certification statement signed by the responsible party stating that the cleanup requirements have been met and that the information contained in the record is true to the best of his/her knowledge.

Any spills that are deemed greater than 72 hours old must be cleaned up (remediated) by the methods listed in 40 CFR Part 761.61. These methods are not allowed to clean up the following:

- Surface or ground waters;

- Sediments in marine and freshwater ecosystems;

- Sewers or sewage treatment systems;

- Any private or public drinking water sources or distribution systems;

- Grazing lands; or

- Vegetable gardens.

Remediation cleanup requirements include characterizing the cleanup site and notifying, in writing, the EPA Regional Administrator, the Director of the state or tribal environmental protection agency, and the Director of the county or local environmental protection agency where the cleanup will be conducted at least 30 days prior to the date that the cleanup of a site begins.

For PCB waste disposal, you must find an approved PCB waste disposer. (Note - transporters do not need to be approved, but the generator or whoever is offering the waste for shipment must ensure that the transporter has submitted a Notification of PCB Activity Form and received an ID number for their PCB activities. In addition to the waste going to an approved disposer, that disposer must also have notified and received an ID number for their PCB activities.) To transport the waste for either commercial storage or disposal, you must complete a hazardous waste manifest. You can get a hazardous waste manifest from either your hazardous waste transporter or from your state hazardous waste coordinator. When you complete the manifest, sign it and keep a copy for your records. Once the waste has reached its final destination, the hazardous waste storer/disposer will sign the manifest and return a copy to you.

You also must keep an annual documentation log for certain storage and disposal activities. For details on the specific requirements of the annual documentation log, see 40 CFR Part 761.180.

E. What Questions Do You Need to Answer Before Starting Your Construction Project?

You can use the questions in Section II of Part I of this guide to start a discussion among all parties involved in the construction project and to assign tasks to ensure all environmental requirements are met. Each question has a space next to it to designate who will take the lead on each task. Note that designating a responsible party does not absolve you of meeting environmental requirements or liability for failing to meet these requirements.

F. Where Can You Get Additional Information?

Many tools are available to assist you with the PCB permit requirements, including the following:

*   The Polychlorinated Biphenyl (PCB) Self-Audit Checklist in Part II of this guide;

*   The Construction Industry Compliance Assistance Center provides information on hazardous and toxic waste regulations that apply to the construction industry: http://www.cicacenter.org/hazwaste.html;

*   The National Environmental Compliance Assistance Clearinghouse contains a search engine to help in finding compliance assistance tools, contacts, and EPA-sponsored programs: http://www.epa.gov/clearinghouse/;

*   EPA's PCB Homepage includes links to the regulatory text (40 CFR Part 761) as well as lists of approved PCB waste handlers: http://www.epa.gov/pcb/;

*   The Office of Pollution Prevention and Toxics (OPPT) has compiled a summary of PCB wastehandlers in the United States: http://www.epa.gov/pcb/waste.html;

*   The Minnesota Pollution Control Agency has prepared a series of fact sheets summarizing the federal regulations:

    —   Use and Servicing of Equipment Containing PCBs
        http://www.pca.state.mn.us/waste/pubs/4_48a.pdf,

    —   Labeling and Marking Requirements for Equipment Containing PCBs
        http://www.pca.state.mn.us/waste/pubs/4_48b.pdf,

    —   Storage and Disposal of PCB-Contaminated Equipment and Wastes
        http://www.pca.state.mn.us/waste/pubs/4_48c.pdf,

    —   Required Recordkeeping for PCB-Contaminated Equipment and Wastes
        http://www.pca.state.mn.us/waste/pubs/4_48d.pdf,

    —   Manifest Requirements for Shipping PCB Wastes
        http://www.pca.state.mn.us/waste/pubs/4_48e.pdf,

    —   Managing PCBs in Fluorescent Light Ballasts
        http://www.pca.state.mn.us/waste/pubs/4_48f.pdf, and

    —   PCB Spill Cleanup Policy http://www.pca.state.mn.us/waste/pubs/4_48g.pdf; and

*   EPA's "Where you live" page contains links to state environmental agencies: http://www.epa.gov/epahome/whereyoulive.htm.

IX. Air Quality Requirements for Construction Activities

A ir regulations for construction activities are designed to limit the generation of particulate and ozone precursor emissions. The air quality issues of concern to the construction industry include:

- Uncontrolled open burning of debris;
- Dust generation;
- Vehicle emissions;
- Combustion gases from oil-fired equipment; and
- Releases of chlorofluorocarbons (CFCs).

Definitions and Acronyms

Hot Mix Asphalt Plant—Facility or equipment used to prepare hot aggregate and mineral filler for mixing to make hot mix asphalt.

Portland Cement Plant—Any manufacturing facility producing Portland cement by either the wet or dry process.

Rock Crushing Plant—All activities to crush or grind nonmetallic minerals that include the crusher, grinding mill, screening, bucket elevator, conveyer, bagging, storage bin, and loading.

Sick Building Syndrome—Condition in which building occupants experience acute health and comfort effects that appear to be linked to indoor air quality and time spent in buildings.

CFC—Chlorofluorocarbons

DOT—Department of Transportation

SIP—State Implementation Plan

TIP—Transportation Improvement Plan

VOC—Volatile Organic Compound

For large construction sites, especially road construction activities, you may require a portable rock crusher, cement plant, or a hot mix asphalt plant for your operations. These sources are generally large emitters of particulate matter, combustion gases, and hazardous air pollutants. These sources are regulated under 40 CFR Part 60 - Standards of Performance for New Stationary Sources. Subpart F applies to Portland Cement Plants, Subpart I applies to Hot Mix Asphalt Facilities, and Subpart OOO applies to Nonmetallic Mineral Processing Plants. These facilities and regulations are not discussed in detail in this document because they are not common to most construction sites. If you own, operate, or maintain one of these facilities, you will need to follow all of the proper recordkeeping and monitoring requirements. For more information on each of these subparts, go to http://www.epa.gov/docs/epacfr40/chapt-I.info/60tc.html. The permitting requirements and the permit exemptions for these sources vary from state to state. Even if a New Source Performance Standard does not apply to your source, you should still consult with the proper state and local agencies to determine your permitting requirements.

A. What Clean Air Act (CAA) Programs Apply to Your Construction Project?

Ozone Depleting Substances

Before beginning any demolition or renovation activities on existing buildings, you should evaluate the potential for releasing ozone depleting substances such as chlorofluorocarbons (CFCs) that are in refrigerators, air conditioners, and other chiller units. EPA 40 CFR Part 82 (Protection of Stratospheric Ozone; Refrigerant Recycling) states that no person disposing of appliances may knowingly vent or otherwise release into the environment any CFC used as a refrigerant. You must ensure that all equipment containing ozone-depleting substances such as CFCs is properly disposed of. This will require following EPA recycling and recovery practices and using certified recycling and recovery equipment. Typically, this involves having items such as small air conditioners or chilling units sent to a recovery facility to have the CFCs removed by a certified specialist. If large industrial chillers are located at the site, then a certified CFC recovery specialist will have to remove the CFCs on site before demolition of the unit can begin. You will be required to maintain signed statements from the disposal contractor indicating that they have removed the refrigerant from the appliance.

State Implementation Plans

Currently, there are no federal CAA requirements for mobile and stationary sources that apply to construction activities. CAA requirements are implemented primarily by states through their State Implementation Plans (SIP). The following construction-related emissions may require a state permit under a SIP:

* Nitrogen oxides (NOx) and fine particulates from diesel engines;
* Dust from vehicle traffic;
* Dust from loading and unloading of construction materials at transfer points;
* Dust from conveyor systems transporting building materials;
* Visible stack emissions from off-road equipment;
* Emissions from open burning of debris (illegal in many areas);

- Volatile organic compounds (VOCs) from paint and cleaning solvents; and

- Combustion gases from oil-fired heaters.

States have differing requirements for air emissions. Check with your local permitting authority to determine if you need a permit for your activities.

Transportation Conformity Rule

Projects requiring funding or approval from the Department of Transportation (DOT), the Federal Highway Administration, the Federal Transit Administration, or the Metropolitan Planning

> **Transportation conformity requirements can be found at:**
> **http://www.epa.gov/otaq/transp/ traqconf.htm**

Organization must comply with the Transportation Conformity Rule issued by DOT on November 24, 1993. These projects include federal road construction activities. These requirements may affect projects in an area that does not meet one or more of EPA's air quality standards.

The Transportation Conformity Rule was established to control the impacts of transportation-related emissions on air quality. The rule requires that Metropolitan Planning Organizations develop a transportation improvement plan (TIP) that is consistent with a SIP. Before a construction project begins, you should determine if the Transportation Conformity Rule applies. If it does, you should verify that your project meets the requirements of the Transportation Conformity Rule. You should also confirm consistency between the TIP and SIP for the area where the road project is located. In most cases, this analysis occurs during the planning phases of a project, but the contractor should confirm that this analysis has occurred to avoid project delays or shut-down.

Voluntary Diesel Retrofit Program

To address air pollution from existing diesel construction equipment and heavy-duty vehicles, EPA has developed a Voluntary Diesel Retrofit Program

> **Information concerning the Voluntary Diesel Retrofit Program can be found at:**
> **http://www.epa.gov/otaq/retrofit/.**

through which it is developing incentives to encourage construction equipment manufacturers and operators to implement control technology to reduce emissions. The most common types of "after treatment" control technologies are cleaner low-sulfur diesel fuel, anti0idling strategies, engine replacement, diesel exhaust catalysts, and particulate filters that remove pollutants from the exhaust stream before they can escape into the atmosphere. EPA has also developed additional initiatives for reducing pollution from new diesel engines and more stringent emission standards for new nonroad diesel engines which will begin in 2008. For more information on the proposed standards, go to http://www.epa.gov/otaq/nonroad.htm.

Indoor Air Concerns

Some building materials contain chemicals that may be harmful if inhaled for extended periods of time. These materials may include:

- Paint/primers;

- Adhesives;

- Floor coatings;

- Carpet; and

- Plywood/particle board.

The most important danger from paints is from VOCs, which may include chemicals such as benzene, formaldehyde, and xylene that have been shown to cause cancer. Primer also contains many of the same chemicals found in paint. Some steps that you can take to improve air quality are to:

> **Information concerning paint can be found at http://www.epa.gov/iaq/pubs.**

- Try to find paints that have low levels of Hazardous Air Pollutants (HAPs) and VOCs;

- Allow adequate drying time before occupying the building;

- Provide proper ventilation; and

- Dispose of all paints properly.

Adhesives are a substance capable of holding materials together by surface attachment. High levels of exposure to some adhesives may cause light headiness and nausea. It is important that proper ventilation is used when applying adhesives. Appropriate protection should be used to avoid breathing in the strong fumes. During the construction phase, bonding agents such as caulks, sealants, and glue are all necessary, although particular precaution must be taken in indoor conditions when you are dealing

> **Information concerning sick building syndrome can be found at http://www.epa.gov/iaq/pubs/sbs.html.**

with large areas. Adhesives are also used as the primary backing for carpet. In order to reduce the "new carpet smell," you should air the carpet out prior to installation.

Particle board is a practical and inexpensive alternative to solid wood and has become one of the nation's leading building materials. Floors, cabinets, and doors are all examples of particle board usage. Formaldehyde and other VOCs are the primary pollutants emitted from particle board. Before installing furniture, make sure it is well laminated to avoid giving off harmful vapors. For more information on formaldehyde, go to http://www.epa.gov/iaq/formalde.html.

> **For links to state and local agencies, go to http://www.cicacenter.org/air.html**

During the construction phase, special consideration should be given to indoor air quality because many of the problems with a building will occur once it is occupied. HVAC contractors should make sure that all units are properly installed and that adequate drain pans are placed to avoid biological contaminants. Contaminants may breed in stagnant water that has accumulated in ducts, humidifiers, and drain pans.

B. Are You Responsible for the Permit?

As discussed earlier, most air permitting requirements for construction activities are at the state and local level. Therefore, either the owner, developer, contractor, or architect will need to contact the appropriate authority to determine the need for and to obtain the necessary CAA permit. To get a permit, you must submit your application to the state or local authority.

C. What Are the Penalties for Working Without the Proper Permit?

The penalties will vary from state to state. For example, in many areas, open burning of debris is not allowed at all. This activity may result in fines, or even criminal prosecution. Funding and implementation of a federal highway project in a non-attainment area can be suspended when the TIP does not conform with the SIP.

Federal environmental laws give a range of enforcement options to EPA, state agencies, and individual citizens. Most laws authorize EPA to: (1) issue an administrative order or impose an administrative penalty, (2) to file a civil action in a federal court for either injunctive relief or a civil penalty, or (3) to file a criminal action in a federal court to impose criminal sanctions.

In addition to fines, you may need to pay legal fees and face project delays. If legal action is taken against your construction site, you also may be subject to increased scrutiny at all of your other construction sites by regulatory agencies and the public.

D. Where Do You Get a Permit?

Contact your state environmental protection agency to discuss permitting requirements for sources.

E. What Questions Do You Need to Answer Before Starting Your Construction Project?

You can use the questions in Section II of Part I of this guide to start a discussion among all parties involved in the construction project and to assign tasks to ensure all environmental requirements are met. Each question has a space next to it to designate who will take the lead on each task. Note that designating a responsible party does not absolve you of your responsibility for meeting environmental requirements or liability for failing to meet these requirements.

F. Where Can You Get Additional Information?

- The Construction Industry Compliance Assistance Center (http://www.cicacenter.org/air.html) provides resources specific dust control and emission control as well as links to state and local agencies.

- The National Environmental Compliance Assistance Clearinghouse contains a search engine to help you find compliance assistance tools, contacts, and EPA-sponsored programs: http://www.epa.gov/clearinghouse/.

- EPA's web site provides links to every state environmental agency: http://www.epa.gov/air/partners.html#state. Each state agency will provide information concerning its air permitting requirements.

- The National Center for Manufacturing Sciences provides resources for highway and building construction to include air emissions data at: http://ecm.ncms.org/ERI/new/IRRconstruc.htm.

- Transportation conformity requirements can be found at: http://www.epa.gov/otaq/transp/traq-conf.htm

- Information concerning the Voluntary Diesel Retrofit Program can be found at: http://www.epa.gov/otaq/retrofit/.

- Information on State Implementation Plans can be found at: http://www.epa.gov/compliance/resources/policies/civil/caa/sipguid.html.

- Information on New Source Performance Standards can be found at: http://www.epa.gov/ttnatw01/nsps/nspstbl.html.

X. Asbestos Requirements for Construction Activities

Before beginning any demolition or renovation activities on existing buildings, you should evaluate the potential for releasing asbestos. Because exposure to asbestos can cause serious health problems such as asbestosis (diffuse fibrous scarring of the lung tissue) and certain types of cancer, EPA and the Occupational Safety and Health Administration (OSHA) have promulgated rules regulating its production, use, and disposal. These rules include the Asbestos School Hazard Abatement Reauthorization Act (ASHARA), the Asbestos Hazard Emergency Response Act (AHERA), the Asbestos Ban and Phaseout Rule, and the Asbestos National Emissions Standards for Hazardous Air Pollutants (NESHAP), promulgated under the Clean Air Act. The regulatory text discussing this program (40 CFR Part 302 and Part 763) can be found at http://ecfr.gpoaccess.gov under "Title 40 - Protection of the Environment." OSHA regulates private sector and some public sector employees' exposure to asbestos and specifies work practices and engineering controls for removing and handling asbestos. The OSHA rules can be found in Title 29 of the Code of Federal Regulations (29 CFR 1910.1001, 29 CFR 1915.100, and 29 CFR 1926.1101). The EPA

Definitions and Acronyms

Adequately Wet—Sufficiently mixed with liquid to prevent the release of particulates. If visible particles or dust are observed coming from asbestos-containing material, then that material has not been adequately wetted.

Asbestos—The name given to a number of naturally occurring fibrous silicate minerals that have been mined for their useful properties such as thermal insulation, chemical and thermal stability, and high tensile strength. The NESHAP

defines asbestos to be the asbestiform varieties of serpentine (chrysotile), riebeckite (crocidolite), cummingtonite-grunerite, anthophyllite, and actinolite-tremolite.

Friable—Asbestos that can be reduced to dust by hand pressure.

Non-friable—Asbestos that is too hard to be reduce to dust by hand.

Definitions and Acronyms

Owner or Operator of a Demolition or Renovation Activity—Any person who owns, leases, operates, controls, or supervises the facility being demolished or renovated or any person who owns, leases, operates, controls, or supervises the demolition or renovation operation, or both.

ACM—Asbestos Containing Materials

AHERA—Asbestos Hazard Emergency Response Act

ASHARA—Asbestos School Hazard Abatement Reauthorization Act

NESHAPs—National Emission Standards for Hazardous Air Pollutants

OSHA—Occupational Safety and Health Administration

RACM—Regulated Asbestos Containing Materials

TSCA—Toxic Substances Control Act

Worker Protection Rule provides identical regulations to cover certain state and local government workers who are not protected by OSHA regulations. AHERA regulates asbestos contained in schools, requires the development of management plans, specifies work practices and engineering controls for removing and handling asbestos, and sets emissions limitations in schools after an abatement activity is completed. The asbestos NESHAP regulations address the removal, disposal, and environmental fate of asbestos. This chapter discusses ONLY the NESHAP regulations because that is the most applicable regulation to the construction industry. Some states also have established asbestos requirements that extend beyond the federal requirements.

A. Could Your Construction Project Site Have Asbestos-Containing Materials (ACM) or Regulated Asbestos-Containing Materials (RACM)?

Since asbestos is strong yet flexible, does not burn, and insulates effectively, asbestos-containing materials (ACM) have been used broadly since post-World War II in building construction. ACM were used primarily in insulation, fireproofing, soundproofing, and decorative products.

Most people think that asbestos is banned in the United States; however, asbestos is still intentionally added to many building materials and occurs as a contaminant in others. Therefore, it is likely that many new building products at a construction site will contain asbestos. The most likely sources of ACMs at construction sites are:

- Insulation, including blown, rolled, and wrapped;
- Resilient floor coverings (tiles);
- Asbestos siding shingles;
- Asbestos-cement products;
- Asphalt roofing products;
- Vermiculite insulation; and
- Sand and gravel.

> **EPA Region 6 has compiled a list of suspected asbestos-containing materials at: http://www.epa.gov/Region06/6pd/ asbestos/asbmatl.htm.**

Asbestos has been detected in indoor air, where it is released from a variety of building materials including insulation and ceiling and floor tiles. It is only released, however, when these building materials are damaged or degrade to the point that they are in poor condition. Regulations governing the removal of asbestos building materials must be followed to protect both the construction workers and the public from asbestos releases.

Classifying ACM

The Asbestos NESHAP is applicable to the construction industry as it involves demolition and renovation activities, containment, transportation and disposal. It classifies ACMs into three categories: friable, Category I non-friable, and Category II non-friable. Friable ACM (defined by being able to crumble under the pressure of your hand) are always regulated ACM (RACM) under the NESHAP when being disturbed during demolition or renovation. An example of friable ACM is spray-applied asbestos fireproofing. Category I materials,

---

Vermiculite Attic Insulation:

Vermiculite attic insulation has the potential to contain contaminant asbestos fibers. Most of the world's supply of vermiculite once came from a mine near Libby, Montana, prior to its close in 1990. This mine has a natural deposit of asbestos which resulted in the vermiculite being contaminated with asbestos. Insulation produced using vermiculite ore, particularly ore that originated from the Libby mine, is known to contain asbestos fibers. Vermiculite is a slippery, light-weight pebble-like pour-in insulation product which is usually light-brown or gold in color. It is also commonly used in interstitial spaces in attics, between floors in multistory commercial buildings, and in the interstitial columnar spaces of cement block structures.

EPA and the Agency for Toxic Substances and Disease Registry (ATSDR) have produced a consumer guidance brochure which presents the current best practices for vermiculite attic insulation. You can get a copy of the brochure electronically at http://www.epa.gov/asbestos/verm.html, or you can call 1-800-471-7127. NIOSH has produced a vermiculite factsheet targeted towards workers, that can be obtained at http://www.cdc.gov/niosh/docs/2003-141/.

---

such as floor tiles, are RACM only when they "will be or have been subjected to sanding, grinding, cutting, or abrading," they are in "poor condition" and "friable," or the structure in which they are located will be demolished by burning. The applicability of the asbestos NESHAP to Category II non-friable materials, such as asbestos-cement products, is determined on a case-by-case basis. Encapsulating friable ACM does not exempt you from the Asbestos NESHAP if you are renovating or demolishing structures with ACM.

In general, cleanup activities such as loading debris onto trucks for disposal do not expose non-friable materials to sanding, grinding, cutting, or abrading, and therefore do not cause Category I or II non-friable ACM to become RACM. However, if you perform post-demolition activities involving waste consolidation and recycling in which you sand, grind, cut, or abrade Category I or II non-friable ACM, then the materials become RACM and are subject to the provisions of the asbestos NESHAP. An example of waste consolidation that falls into this category is the use of jack hammers or other mechanical devices such as grinders to break up asbestos-containing concrete.

B. Are You Responsible for Addressing ACM Wastes?

For the purpose of identifying ACM wastes, EPA defines the "generator" as being responsible for handling, storing, transporting, and disposing of RACM wastes. The "generator" is considered the party that owns the material. For most construction projects, multiple parties will be involved; all may be liable if the ACM handling and disposal requirements are not followed.

EPA has found that demolition contractors typically require that a building owner/operator accept responsibility for removing all ACM found during the building inspection prior to the start of demolition activities. Note that the Asbestos NESHAP does not require a building owner or operator to remove damaged or deteriorating ACM unless a renovation of the facility is planned that would disturb the ACM and the disturbed ACM exceeds the threshold amount. However, all OSHA requirements for worker and environmental protection will still apply.

The NESHAP regulation states that either the owner of the building or operator of the demolition or renovation operation can submit the required construction notification. You will need to decide together who will submit the notification. If neither provides adequate notice, EPA may hold either or both parties liable.

C. What Are the Penalties?

Federal environmental laws give a range of enforcement options to EPA, state agencies, and individual citizens. Most laws authorize EPA to: (1) issue an administrative order or impose an administrative penalty, (2) to file a civil action in a federal court for either injunctive relief or a civil penalty, or (3) to file a criminal action in a federal court to impose criminal sanctions.

In addition to fines, you may need to pay legal fees and face project delays. If legal action is taken against your construction site, you also may be subject to increased scrutiny at all of your other construction sites by regulatory agencies and the public.

If you do not follow the ACM management and disposal standards, you may be fined civil penalties of up to $32,500 per day per violation. You also may be fined if you release ACM waste into the environment. You can lose any existing permits for your construction site and/or need to stop work until you meet EPA requirements.

You also may face penalties or actions for past or present handling, storage, treatment, transportation, or disposal of ACM waste that may be a hazard to human health or the environment.

D. In General, What are the Removal and Disposal Requirements?

Inspection

The Asbestos NESHAP requires that you have your site inspected by a certified asbestos inspector prior to beginning any renovation or demolition activities. Owners and operators are responsible for having bulk samples of suspected ACM collected and analyzed prior to the start of construction activities.

Notification

You must submit a written notice of intent to renovate or demolish 10 working days prior to starting any construction activities. Notifications must contain certain specified information, including but not limited to, the scheduled starting and completion dates of the work, the location of the site, the names of operators or asbestos removal contractors, methods of removal and the amount of asbestos, and whether the operation is a demolition or a renovation.

You should submit the completed notification to your delegated state/local pollution control agency and your EPA Regional Office. Some EPA Regions require that both the EPA Regional Office and the local delegated agency be notified, while some require notice only to the delegated state or local agency.

Even if no asbestos is present at your site, you still must notify the appropriate regulatory agency of your intent. All demolitions and renovations are subject to the Asbestos NESHAP because you must first determine if and how much asbestos is present at the site.

> You must follow the Asbestos NESHAP regulations if your renovations or demolitions include at least 80 linear meters (260 linear feet) of RACM on pipes, 15 square meters (160 square feet) of RACM on other facility components, or at least one cubic meter (35 cubic feet) of facility components where the amount of RACM previously removed from pipes and other facility components could not be measured before stripping. These amounts are known as the "threshold" amounts.
>
> Note that the Asbestos NESHAP does not apply to residential structures with four or fewer dwellings (i.e., apartments or single family homes).

Removal and Disposal

The Asbestos NESHAP does not place specific numerical emission limitations for asbestos fibers on asbestos demolitions and removals. However, the Asbestos NESHAP does specify zero visible air emissions from construction activities. To meet the zero visible emissions requirement, the Asbestos NESHAP requires that you follow specific work practices including a requirement that you sufficiently wet any asbestos-containing materials to prevent release of fibers prior to, during, and after renovation/demolition activities and until disposal.

> **For more information, see Section 40 CFR Part 61.145(b) of the Asbestos NESHAP regulation or call EPA's Asbestos hotline at 1-800-368-5888.**

Under normal circumstances, Category I non-friable materials are not considered RACM and you will not need to remove them prior to demolition or renovation. In this case, they may also be disposed of in a landfill that accepts ordinary demolition waste. If, however, Category I materials have become friable or are in poor condition, you will have to remove them. Also, if you sand, grind, abrade, drill, cut, or chip any non-friable materials, including Category I materials, you must treat the material as RACM, if more than the threshold amount is involved.

Category II non-friable materials should be evaluated on a case-by-case basis. If category II non-friable materials are likely to become crushed, pulverized, or reduced to powder during demolition or renovation, remove them before demolition or renovation begins. For example, you should remove asbestos cement (A/C) siding on a building that is going to be demolished with a wrecking ball because it is likely that the wrecking ball will pulverize the siding.

All RACM in poor condition should be properly transported in leak-tight containers or wrapped and disposed of at an acceptable asbestos disposal site. State and local agencies that require handling or licensing procedures can supply a list of approved or licensed asbestos disposal sites upon request. Solid waste control agencies are listed in local telephone directories under state, county, or city headings.

E. What Questions Do You Need to Answer Before Starting Your Construction Project?

You can use the questions in Section II of Part I of this guide to start a discussion among all parties involved in the construction project and to assign tasks to ensure all environmental requirements are met. Each question has a space next to it to designate who will take the lead on each task. Note that designating a responsible party does not absolve you of meeting environmental requirements or liability for failing to meet these requirements.

F. Where Can You Get Additional Information?

Many tools are available to assist you with the Asbestos NESHAP permit requirements, including the following:

- The Asbestos Self-Audit Checklist in Part II of this guide;

- EPA's Asbestos Management & Regulatory Requirements web site contains links to all of the asbestos regulations: http://www.epa.gov/fedsite/cd/asbestos.html;

- The National Environmental Compliance Assistance Clearinghouse contains a search engine to help in finding compliance assistance tools, contacts, and EPA-sponsored programs: http://www.epa.gov/clearinghouse/;

- The San Joaquin Valley Air Pollution Control District Demolitions and Renovations web page contains a concise summary of the regulation and links to local notification forms: http://www.valleyair.org/busind/comply/asbestosbultn.htm;

- EPA's Region 4 asbestos web page contains links to several informative question and answer and fact sheets related to demolition and renovation: http://www.epa.gov/region04/air/asbestos/asbestos.htm;

- EPA's Region 4 demolition and renovation summary page: http://www.epa.gov/region04/air/asbestos/demolish.htm;

- EPA's Region 4 general asbestos question and answer web page contains contact phone numbers for each of the asbestos regulations: http://www.epa.gov/region04/air/asbestos/inform.htm;

- OSHA's Asbestos web page contains health and safety information related to asbestos: http://www.osha-slc.gov/SLTC/constructionasbestos/index.html;

- EPA's vermiculite web site provides information on asbestos in vermiculite: http://www.epa.gov/asbestos/verm.html;

- NIOSH's web site contains general information on vermiculite as well as recommendations for limiting potential exposures of workers to asbestos associated with vermiculite: http://www.cdc.gov/niosh/docs/2003-141/;

- The Agency for Toxic Substances and Disease Registry (ATSDR) has developed a toxicological profile for asbestos that presents general information regarding the sources and known health effects of asbestos: http://www.atsdr.cdc.gov/toxprofiles/tp61.html;

- EPA's Asbestos Ombudsman: 1-800-368-5888; and

- EPA's "Where you live" page contains links to state environmental agencies: http://www.epa.gov/epahome/whereyoulive.htm.

XI. Endangered Species Act (ESA) Requirements for Construction Activities

Before beginning any construction project, you should consider the impact of your construction activities on species listed or proposed under the Endangered Species Act (ESA) as threatened or endangered ("listed species"), and the habitat of listed species. You should assess the impacts on listed species as early as possible in the construction process to avoid delays in your project.

Definitions

Critical Habitat—The specific areas within the geographical area currently occupied by a species, at the time it is listed in accordance with the ESA, on which are found those physical or biological features essential to the conservation of the species and that may require special management considerations, and specific areas outside the geographical area occupied by a species at the time it is listed upon determination by the Secretary that such areas are essential for the conservation of the species (defined at Section 3(5) of the federal ESA).

Harass—Actions that create the likelihood of injury to listed species to such an extent as to significantly disrupt normal behavior patterns which include but may not be limited to breeding, feeding, or sheltering.

Harm—An act that actually kills or injures wildlife. Such an act may include significant habitat modification or degradation where it actually kills or injures wildlife by significantly impairing essential behavior patterns, including breeding, feeding, or sheltering.

Operator—The party (ies) that has: (1) operational control of construction project plans and has the ability to make modifications to those plans, or (2) day-to-day operational control of stormwater compliance activities.

Take—To harass, harm, pursue, hunt, shoot, wound, kill, trap, capture, or collect, or to attempt to engage in any such conduct (Section 3(18) of the federal ESA).

The ESA was passed in 1973 to protect threatened or endangered species from further harm. The U.S. Fish and Wildlife Service (FWS) and the National Marine Fisheries Services (NMFS) enforce the ESA. Under the ESA, FWS and NMFS identify the listed species and habitats, and work through consultations and permit actions to protect those species and theircritical habitat. Although ESA is not an EPA requirement, it is included as part of the EPA stormwater Construction General Permit (CGP) requirements and therefore is important to the construction industry.

The ESA has different requirements for federal activities and non-federal activities. The ESA typically applies to construction activities under three general scenarios: A) construction activities under EPA's CGP, B) activities funded or permitted by federal agencies (other than the CGP) for a construction project, or C) construction activities that impact a listed species and/or critical habitat. The requirements under these scenarios are discussed below.

Acronyms

ESA—Endangered Species Act

NMFS—National Marine Fisheries Service

NOAA—National Oceanic and Atmospheric Administration

NPDES—National Pollutant Discharge Elimination System

USFWS—U.S. Fish and Wildlife Service

A. Coverage Under the Construction General Permit

To be eligible for coverage under the CGP, discussed in Section III of Part I of this document, you must assess the potential effects of your activities on federally listed endangered and threatened species and any designated critical habitat that exists on or near your site. In making this determination, you need to consider areas beyond the immediate footprint of the construction activity and beyond the property line, including those that could be affected directly or indirectly by stormwater discharges. For coverage under the CGP, you need to complete the steps described below. Be sure to document your findings at each step of the process. For more information on these requirements, review the relevant portions of the CGP, particularly Part 1.3.C and Appendix C.

Step 1: Determine if Listed Species are Present On or Near Your Project Area

To determine whether listed species are located on or near your project area, you should:

• Determine if listed species are in your county or township. The local offices of the FWS, NMFS, and State or Tribal Heritage Centers often maintain lists of federally listed endangered or threatened species on their internet sites. Visit http://cfpub1.epa.gov/npdes/stormwater/cgp.cfm to find the appropriate site for your state or check with your local office. In most cases, these lists allow you to determine if there are listed species in your county or township.

- If there are listed species in your county or township, contact your local FWS, NMFS, or State or Tribal Heritage Center to determine if the listed species could be found on or near your project area and if any critical habitat areas have been designated that overlap or are near your project area. Critical habitat areas may be designated independently from the listed species for your county, so even if there are no listed species in your county or township, you must still contact one of the agencies mentioned above to determine if there are any critical habitat areas on or near your project area.

- If there are no listed species in your county or township, no critical habitat areas on or near your project area, or if your local FWS, NMFS, or State or Tribal Heritage Center indicates that listed species are not a concern in your part of the county or township, you may check Box A on the Notice of Intent (NOI) form (see Section III in Part I of this guide for a discussion of this form).

- If there are listed species or critical habitat, and if your local FWS, NMFS, or State or Tribal Heritage Center indicates that these could exist on or near your project area, you will need to do one or more of the following:

  — Conduct visual inspections to identify any listed species or critical habitat. This method may be particularly suitable for construction sites that are smaller in size or located in non-natural settings such as highly urbanized areas or industrial parks where there is little or no natural habitat, or for construction activities that discharge directly into municipal stormwater collection systems.

  — Conduct a formal biological survey. In some cases, particularly for larger construction sites with extensive stormwater discharges, biological surveys may be an appropriate way to assess whether species are located on or near the project area and whether there are likely to be adverse effects to such species. Biological surveys are frequently performed by environmental consulting firms. A biological survey may be useful in conjunction with Steps 2, 3, or 4 below.

  — Conduct an environmental assessment under the National Environmental Policy Act (NEPA). Such an assessment may indicate if listed species are in proximity to the project area. Note that coverage under the CGP does not trigger a requirement for a NEPA assessment. See Section XII in Part I of this guide for more information on NEPA.

If listed species or critical habitat are present in the project area, you must look at the impacts to the species and/or habitat when following Steps 2 through 4. Note that many, but not all, measures imposed to protect listed species under these steps will also protect critical habitat. Thus, meeting the eligibility requirements of the CGP may require separate measures to protect critical habitat from those to protect listed species.

Step 2: Determine if Your Construction Activities Are Likely to Adversely Affect Listed Species or Critical Habitat

To receive CGP coverage, you must assess whether your construction activities are likely to adversely affect listed species or designated critical habitat that are present on or near your project area. Potential adverse effects from stormwater discharges and stormwater discharge-related activities include:

- *Hydrological.* Stormwater discharges may cause siltation or sedimentation, or induce other changes in receiving waters such as temperature, salinity or pH. These effects will vary with the amount of stormwater discharged and the volume and condition of the receiving water. Where a stormwater discharge constitutes a minute portion of the total volume of the receiving water, adverse hydrological effects are less likely. Construction activities may also alter drainage patterns on a site where construction occurs. This can also impact listed species or critical habitat.

- *Habitat.* Excavation, site development, grading, and other surface-disturbing construction activities may adversely affect listed species or their habitat. Stormwater may drain into or inundate listed species' habitat.

- *Toxicity.* In some cases, pollutants in stormwater may have toxic effects on listed species.

The scope of effects to consider will vary with each site. If you are having difficulty determining whether your project is likely to adversely affect listed species or critical habitat, or one of the Services has already raised concerns to you, you should contact the appropriate office of the FWS, NMFS or Natural Heritage Center for assistance. If adverse effects are not likely, then you may check Box E on the NOI form and apply for coverage under the CGP. If the discharge may adversely effect listed species or critical habitat, you must follow Step 3.

Step 3: Determine if Measures Can Be Implemented to Avoid Adverse Effects

If you determine that your activities will affect listed species or critical habitat, you can still receive coverage under the CGP if you take measures to avoid or eliminate the likelihood of adverse effects prior to applying for CGP coverage. These measures may involve relatively simple changes to construction activities such as rerouting a stormwater discharge to bypass an area where species are located, relocating BMPs, or changing the "footprint" of the construction activity. Contact the FWS and/or NMFS to see what measures might be appropriate to avoid or eliminate the likelihood of adverse impacts to listed species and/or critical habitat. This can entail the initiation of informal consultation with the FWS and/or NMFS (described in more detail in Step 4).

If you adopt measures to avoid or eliminate adverse affects, you must continue to abide by those measures for the duration of the construction project and coverage under the CGP. These measures must be described in the Stormwater Pollution Prevention Plan (SWPPP) (see Section III of Part I of this guide) and are enforceable CGP conditions. If appropriate measures to avoid the likelihood of adverse effects are not available, you must follow Step 4.

Step 4: Determine if the Requirements of the CGP Can Be Met

Where adverse effects are likely, you must contact the FWS and/or NMFS. You may still be eligible for CGP coverage if any likely adverse effects can be addressed through meeting one of the following criteria as identified in Subpart 1.3.C of the CGP. Confer with FWS and/or NMFS to determine which criteria is appropriate for your project.

1. *An ESA Section 7 Consultation Is Performed for Your Activity.*

Contact FWS and/or NMFS to initiate a formal or informal ESA Section 7 consultation. The purpose of a consultation is to address the effects of your activities on listed species and critical habitat. To be eligible for coverage under the CGP, consultation must result in a "no jeopardy opinion" or a written concurrence by the Service(s) on a finding that your stormwater discharge(s) and stormwater-discharge-related activities are not likely to adversely affect listed species or critical habitat. If you receive a "jeopardy opinion," you may continue to work with the FWS and/or NMFS and your permitting authority to modify your project so that it will not jeopardize listed species or designated critical habitat.

Most consultations are "informal." By the terms of the CGP, EPA has designated operators as non-federal representatives for the purpose of conducting informal consultations. When conducting informal ESA Section 7 consultation as a non-federal representative, you must follow the procedures found in 50 CFR Part 402 of the ESA regulations. You must notify FWS and/or NMFS of your intention and agreement to conduct consultation as a non-federal representative. Consultation may also occur in the context of another federal action at the construction site (e.g., where ESA Section 7 consultation is performed for issuance of a wetlands dredge and fill permit for the project or where a NEPA review is performed for the project that incorporates a Section 7 consultation). Any terms and conditions developed through consultations to protect listed species and critical habitat must be incorporated into the SWPPP.

Whether ESA Section 7 consultation must be performed with either the FWS, NMFS or both Services depends on the listed species that may be affected by the operator's activity. In general, NMFS has jurisdiction over marine, estuaries, and anadromous species. Operators should also be aware that while formal Section 7 consultation provides protection from incidental takings liability, informal consultation does not.

2. *An Incidental Taking Permit Under Section 10 of the ESA is Issued for the Operator's Activity.*

Your construction activities can be authorized through the issuance of a permit under Section 10 of the ESA that addresses the effects of your stormwater discharge(s) and stormwater discharge-related activities on federally listed species and designated critical habitat. You must follow FWS and/or NMFS procedures when applying for an ESA Section 10 permit. Application instructions for Section 10 permits for FWS and NMFS can be obtained by accessing the FWS and NMFS web sites (http://www.fws.gov and http://www.nmfs.noaa.gov) or by contacting the appropriate FWS and NMFS regional office. More information on Section 10 requirements is provided in Section XI-C of Part I of this guide.

3. *You are Covered Under the Eligibility Certification of Another Operator for the Project Area.*

Your stormwater discharges and stormwater-discharge-related activities may already be addressed in another operator's certification of eligibility, which also included your project area. For example, a general contractor or developer may have completed and filed an NOI for the entire project area with the necessary ESA certifications. Subcontractors may then rely on that certification and must comply with any conditions resulting from that process. By certifying eligibility, you agree to comply with any measures or controls upon which the other operator's certification was based.

You must comply with any terms and conditions imposed under the eligibility requirements of the CGP to ensure that your stormwater discharges and stormwater-discharge-related activities protect listed species and/or critical habitat. Such terms and conditions must be incorporated in the project's SWPPP. If the eligibility requirements cannot be met, then you are not eligible for coverage under the CGP. In these instances, you may consider applying to EPA for an individual permit.

B. Federal Funding or Federal Permitting For a Construction Project

If a federal agency is funding (either fully or partially) a construction project, or if a federal permit (other than the CGP) is required for a construction project, the federal agency taking the action (i.e., funding or permitting) must fulfill the requirements of the ESA. Some examples that would trigger this requirement include federal highway construction projects, Section 404 permits issued by EPA, or state construction programs that receive federal funding. The federal agency may designate a state agency or contractor to fulfill the requirements of the ESA. The federal agency (or designee) needs to follow the same steps as described under Section XI-A of Part I of this guide, with the exception of requirements associated with the CGP Notice of Intent and SWPPPs. The federal agency or designee should document their findings at each step discussed under Section XI-A of Part I of this guide.

In situations where a contractor is not designated to fulfill the requirements of the ESA, the contractor should still ensure early in the process that the federal agency has fulfilled the requirements. In addition, if the agency determined that the project would impact listed species and/or critical habitat, and has developed plans to mitigate these impacts, it likely will be the obligation of the contractor to implement these plans. Failure to implement the plans can result in violation of the ESA. Therefore, you should understand the requirements of these plans up front to facilitate compliance with the ESA.

C. Construction Activities That Impact a Listed Species and/or Critical Habitat

Section 9 of the ESA generally prohibits the unauthorized "take" of a listed species and/or critical habitat. "Take" is defined in the ESA as harass, harm, pursue, hunt, shoot, wound, kill, trap, capture, or collect any threatened or endangered species. Harm may include significant habitat modification which actually kills or injures a listed species through impairment of essential behavior (e.g., nesting or reproduction). This "take" prohibition applies not only to federal agencies but to non-federal entities and citizens as well. If your construction activity is not covered by the CGP (e.g., if your stormwater permit is issued by your state), and if no federal funding or other federal permits are associated with your construction activity, you should still evaluate if your project will incidentally cause a take of a listed species and/or critical habitat. If your project will result in a take, you need to obtain an Incidental Take Permit from USFWS or NOAA-Fisheries to get authorization for the take. Such a permit, which covers non-federal activities, is issued under Section 10 of the ESA, and includes conditions that focus on efforts to minimize and mitigate the anticipated take.

To obtain an Incidental Take Permit, you need to submit a habitat conservation plan (HCP) along with your application. The HCP outlines your plans to minimize and mitigate effects of the authorized incidental take. To determine if your project will result in a take, and to obtain an Incidental Take Permit, you should complete the following steps.

Step 1: Determine if Listed Species are Present On or Near Your Project Area

You will first need to determine if listed species are present on or near your project area. Follow the steps described under Section XI-A in Step 1 (Coverage Under the Construction General Permit) above. If you find that there are not listed species present on or near your project area, document your findings and proceed with your project (you do not need an Incidental Take Permit). If listed species are present, proceed to Step 2.

Step 2: Determine if your Construction Activity Is Likely to Adversely Affect Listed Species or Critical Habitat

Follow the procedures described in Step 2 under Section XI-A to determine if your construction activity is likely to adversely affect listed species or critical habitat. Note that you need to consider all the impacts of your construction activity, not just stormwater-related impacts. If you determine that your construction activity will not adversely affect listed species or critical habitat, document your findings and proceed with your project (you do not need an Incidental Take Permit). If your construction activity will adversely affect listed species or critical habitat, proceed to Step 3.

Step 3: Obtain an Incidental Take Permit

If your construction activity will adversely affect listed species or critical habitat, you need to obtain an Incidental Take Permit. The necessary components of a permit application are: a standard application form, an HCP, an implementation agreement (if required), and, if appropriate, a draft NEPA analysis (the Service is responsible for ensuring NEPA compliance during the permitting process). General information on ESA permits can be found at http://endangered.fws.gov/permits/index.html, while the specific permit application can be found at http://forms.fws.gov/3-200-56.pdf.

You should coordinate with the FWS or NOAA-Fisheries as soon as possible for guidance in assembling a complete application package. They will inform you if you need to develop an implementation agreement or prepare a draft NEPA analysis, and will provide you the necessary guidance on how to prepare these. Before you submit an application, you may be required to conduct biological surveys to determine which species and/or habitat would be impacted by the activities covered under the permit. The surveys also provide information that can be used to develop the HCP. The HCP should include:

- An assessment of the impacts likely to result from the proposed taking of one or more federally listed species;

- Measures you will undertake to monitor, minimize, and mitigate such impacts; the funding that will be made available to implement such measures; and the procedures to deal with unforseen or extraordinary circumstances;

- Alternative actions to the take that you analyzed, and the reasons why you did not adopt such alternatives; and

- Additional measures that FWS or NOAA-Fisheries may require as necessary or appropriate.

You can find additional information on HCPs at http://endangered.fws.gov/hcp/; the Habitat Conservation Planning Handbook can be found at http://endangered.fws.gov/hcp/hcpbook.html.

D. What Are the Penalties?

The USFWS and the NMFS may impose administrative, civil, and criminal sanctions for failure to comply with the ESA. Civil penalties – imposed in a judicial proceeding – can reach $27,500 per day per violation. Stiffer penalties are authorized for criminal violations of the Act – for negligent or knowing violations – of as much as $50,000 per day, 3 years' imprisonment, or both. A fine of as much as $250,000, 15 years in prison, or both, is authorized for "knowing endangerment" violations that knowingly place another species in imminent danger of death or serious bodily injury.

Noncompliance with the requirements of the CGP is a violation of the Clean Water Act (CWA). EPA may impose administrative, civil, and criminal sanctions on a property owner and/or a contractor for failure to comply with the CWA. Administrative penalties can reach $157,500 and civil penalties – imposed in a judicial proceeding – can reach $32,500 per violation per day. Under certain circumstances, the CWA also authorizes criminal penalties. In addition, the CWA allows private citizens to bring civil actions against any person for any alleged violation of "an effluent standard or limitation." In a citizen suit, a court may issue an injunction and/or impose civil penalties, litigation costs, and attorney's fees.

In addition to fines, you may need to pay legal fees and face project delays. If legal action is taken against your construction site, you also may be subject to increased scrutiny at all of your other construction sites by regulatory agencies and the public.

E. What Questions Do You Need to Answer Before Starting Your Construction Project?

You can use the questions in Section II of Part I of this guide to start a discussion among all parties involved in the construction project and to assign tasks to ensure all environmental requirements are met. Each question has a space next to it to designate who will take the lead on each task. Note that designating a responsible party does not absolve you of meeting environmental requirements or liability for failing to meet these requirements.

F. Where Can You Get Additional Information?

Many tools are available to assist you with the ESA requirements, including the following:

- The U.S. Fish & Wildlife Service web site is the most complete source of information on ESA-listed species. This site contains valuable tools for landowners: http://endangered.fws.gov.

- The NOAA Fisheries - Office of Protected Resources provides the full text of the ESA. It also provides information on marine and anadromous species as well as recovery plans for their listed species: http://www.nmfs.noaa.gov/prot_res/overview/es.html.

- The USFWS Threatened and Endangered Species System identifies federally listed threatened and endangered species at: http://ecos.fws.gov/tess_public/TESSWebpage.

- The USFWS Threatened and Endangered Species System State and Territory Listings identifies state and territory listed threatened and endangered species at: http://ecos.fws.gov/tess_public/TESSWebpageStateLists.

- EPA's "Where you live" page contains links to state environmental agencies: http://www.epa.gov/epahome/whereyoulive.htm.

- NatureServe is a conservation organization that provides the scientific information and tools needed to help guide effective conservation action. NatureServe and its network of natural heritage programs are the leading source for information about rare and endangered species and threatened ecosystems: http://www.natureserve.org.

- The Construction Industry Compliance Assistance Center (http://www.cicacenter.org/espermits.html) provides resources specific to ESA-listed species, including state requirements and contacts.

- The National Environmental Compliance Assistance Clearinghouse contains a search engine to help you find compliance assistance tools, contacts, and EPA-sponsored programs: http://www.epa.gov/clearinghouse/.

- National and regional USFWS Endangered Species Contacts:

  — Washington D.C. Office Endangered Species, 4401 N. Fairfax Drive, Room 420, Arlington, VA 22203, http://endangered.fws.gov, Phone: (703) 358-2390,

  — Pacific Region, Eastside Federal Complex 911 N.E. 11th Avenue, Portland, OR, http://pacific.fws.gov, Phone: (503) 231-6158,

  — Southwest Region, P.O. Box 1306, Rm 4012, Albuquerque, NM 87102, http://southwest.fws.gov, Phone: (505) 248-6657,

  — Great Lakes, Big Rivers Region, Bishop Henry Federal Building One Federal Drive, Ft. Snelling, MN 55111-4056, http://midwest.fws.gov, Phone: (612) 713-5334,

  — Southeast Region, 1875 Century Boulevard Suite 200, Atlanta, GA 30345, http://southeast.fws.gov, Phone: (404) 679-7100,

  — Northeast Region, 300 Westgate Center Drive, Hadley, MA 01035-9589, http://northeast.fws.gov, Phone: (413) 253-8615,

  — Mountain Prairie Region, 134 Union Boulevard, Lakewood, CO 80228, http://mountain-prairie.fws.gov, Phone: (303) 236-7400, and

  — Alaska, 1011 E. Tudor Road, Anchorage, AK 99503-6199, http://alaska.fws.gov, Phone: (907) 786-3868.

XII. National Environmental Policy Act (NEPA)

Before beginning any construction project associated with a federal agency, you must determine the NEPA requirements that apply to your project. NEPA requires federal agencies to incorporate environmental considerations in their planning and decision making through a systematic interdisciplinary approach. Specifically, all federal agencies must prepare detailed statements assessing the environmental impact of, and alternatives to, major federal actions significantly affecting the environment. These statements are commonly referred to as environmental impact statements (EISs).

NEPA ensures that federal agencies consider environmental impacts in federal planning and decision making, and covers both construction and post-construction activities. NEPA covers the full range of potential impacts, including but not limited to water quality impacts, wetlands impacts, air quality impacts, endangered species impacts, and historic resources impacts.

NEPA applies to your construction project only if your project is considered a "federal action." Note that some states (e.g., North Carolina, Massachusetts, Washington) have requirements that are similar to the requirements established for federal agencies by NEPA. Therefore, if your construction project is entirely or partly financed, assisted, conducted, regulated, or approved by a state agency in one of these states, you should consult with state agency officials to ensure that these requirements have been met. This document addresses federal environmental requirements and does not address state requirements.

The federal agency taking the action is responsible for complying with NEPA's requirements. If NEPA requirements are applicable to your project, these requirements must be met before and during construction activities. NEPA establishes good procedural and planning practices for federal agencies and does not replace or conflict with other substantive environmental laws addressed in this document (e.g., Clean Air Act, Clean Water Act, Endangered Species Act).

The NEPA process consists of evaluating the environmental effects of a federal action including its alternatives. There are three levels of analysis depending on whether or not the construction activity or project could significantly affect the environment. These three levels are: categorical exclusion determination; preparation of an environmental assessment/finding of no significant impact (EA/FONSI); and preparation of an EIS.

At the first level, a project may be categorically excluded from a detailed environmental analysis if it meets certain criteria that a federal agency has previously determined as having no significant environmental impact. A number of agencies have developed lists of actions that are normally categorically excluded from environmental evaluation under their NEPA regulations.

At the second level of analysis, a federal agency prepares a written EA to determine whether or not a federal undertaking would significantly affect the environment. If the answer is no, the agency issues a FONSI. The FONSI may address measures that an agency will take to reduce (mitigate) potentially significant impacts.

If the EA determines that the environmental consequences of a proposed federal action may be significant, the federal agency prepares an EIS. An EIS is a more detailed evaluation of the proposed action and alternatives. The public, other federal agencies, and outside parties may provide input into the preparation of an EIS and then comment on the draft EIS when it is completed. If a federal agency anticipates that an action may significantly impact the environment, or if a project is environmentally controversial, the agency may choose to prepare an EIS without having to first prepare an EA.

After a final EIS is prepared, a federal agency will prepare a public record of its decision addressing how the findings of the EIS, including consideration of alternatives, were incorporated into the agency's decision-making process. If you perform these activities prior to the start of construction, it will help to avoid significant project delays and possible project cancellation.

You can get additional information on NEPA requirements from the following sources.

- The Council on Environmental Quality's NEPAnet web page provides the most comprehensive information about NEPA requirements: (http://ceq.eh.doe.gov/nepa/nepanet.htm);

- The Construction Industry Compliance Assistance Center provides plain language explanations of environmental rules for the construction industry, including tools to identify state-specific requirements: http://www.cicacenter.org; and

- The National Environmental Compliance Assistance Clearinghouse contains a search engine to help in finding compliance assistance tools, contacts, and EPA-sponsored programs: http://cfpub.epa.gov/clearinghouse/.

XIII. National Historic Preservation Act (NHPA)

Before beginning any construction project associated with a federal agency, you must determine whether any NHPA requirements apply to your project. NHPA is a multi-faceted statute with a variety of initiatives, including programs for identifying and listing significant historic resources; partnerships between federal agencies and federally approved state and tribal historic preservation programs; and grants. Section 106 of NHPA requires federal agencies to account for the effects of their undertakings on historic properties and to afford the Advisory Council on Historic Preservation (ACHP) a reasonable opportunity to comment with regard to such undertakings. Federal funding or permitting of a project may constitute an undertaking under the NHPA. If NHPA requirements are applicable to your project, these requirements must be met before and possibly during construction activities. The requirements of Section 106 apply prior to the approval of the expenditure of any federal funds on, or prior to the issuance of any federal license for, an undertaking.

NHPA applies to your construction project if your project constitutes an undertaking and will have a potential effect on a property that is eligible for or included in the National Register of Historic Places (NRHP). Note that many states and communities use the NRHP as the basis for their planning processes and designation criteria. In some cases, state and local ordinances may establish protections for historic preservation. To find out if your state or community has such processes in place, contact your State Historic Preservation Officer (SHPO). This guide addresses federal environmental requirements and does not address state requirements.

Under the NHPA regulations, a federal agency determines whether its action constitutes an undertaking, and, if so, whether the undertaking has the potential to affect historic properties. Historic properties include any prehistoric or historic district, site, building, structure, or object included, or eligible for inclusion, in the NRHP (which is maintained by the National Park Service), including artifacts, records, and material remains related to such a property or resource. If the undertaking has the potential to affect historic properties, the Federal agency identifies the appropriate state or tribal historic preservation officer (SHPO or THPO) and begins a consultation regarding the impacts of the undertaking. The consultation consists of the following steps: (1) identifying other appropriate consulting parties and developing plans to involve the public; (2) determining the area of potential effects of the undertaking; (3) identifying any historic properties within that area; (4) determining whether the undertaking will affect such properties and, if so, whether the effects may be adverse; and (5) resolving any identified adverse effects. Typically, measures to resolve adverse effects that are adopted as a result of Section 106 consultation are documented in memoranda of agreement or programmatic agreements that then govern the undertaking.

NHPA regulations impose procedural obligations to consider the effects of agency undertakings on historic properties, to consult with appropriate entities, and to develop and evaluate ways to minimize or mitigate any adverse effects. There is no substantive requirement to actually avoid or minimize adverse effects. Other provisions of NHPA may impose additional requirements. For instance, under NHPA Section 110(f), where a federal undertaking may directly and adversely affect a property designated as a National Historic Landmark, the agency must (prior to approving the undertaking and to the maximum extent possible) undertake such planning and actions necessary to minimize harm to such landmark. Additionally, with certain limited exceptions, federal agencies are prohibited by NHPA Section 110(k) from granting loans, loan guarantees, permits, licenses, or other assistance to any applicant who intentionally significantly adversely affected a historic property to which the assistance would relate with the intent to avoid the requirements of Section 106. If you perform these activities prior to the start of construction, it will help to avoid significant project delays and possible project cancellation.

You can get additional information on NHPA requirements from the following sources.

• The Advisory Council on Historic Preservation's web page provides the most comprehensive information about NHPA requirements (http://www.achp.gov). This web page details NHPA requirements and provides links to contact information for federal, state, and tribal historic preservation officers.

• The National Park Service's web page (http://www.cr.nps.gov/nr/) provides additional information on properties listed on the National Register of Historic Places, such as the location and historic nature of these properties (through the National Register Information System database) and details on how properties are listed.

• The Construction Industry Compliance Assistance Center provides plain language explanations of environmental rules for the construction industry, including tools to identify state-specific requirements: http://www.cicacenter.org.

• The National Environmental Compliance Assistance Clearinghouse contains a search engine to help in finding compliance assistance tools, contacts, and EPA-sponsored programs: http://cfpub.epa.gov/clearinghouse/.

XIV. Additional Sources of Information

A copy of this guide as well as a list of all of the web links listed in this document can be found on the Construction Industry Compliance Assistance Center (CICA Center) web site at http://www.cicacenter.org/links.

The construction industry includes a number of trade associations and industry organizations. A few of the trade association and organization web sites are listed below for your convenience:

- The Associated General Contractors of America (AGC): http://www.agc.org/;

- The National Association of Homebuilders (NAHB): http://www.nahb.org/;

- National Association of Demolition Contractors (NADC): http://www.demolitionassociation.com/site/index.html;

- American Road and Transportation Building Association (ARTBA): http://www.artba.org/; and

- Golf Course Builders Association of America (GCBAA): http://www.gcbaa.org/WELCOME.asp.

Other government web sites that provide information on environmental requirements and ways to protect the environment that are helpful to the construction industry include:

- The U.S. Green Building Council (USGBC): http://www.usgbc.org/;

- Energy Star: http://www.energystar.gov/;

- Rebuild America: http://www.rebuild.org/;

- U.S. Department of Energy - Energy Efficient and Renewable Energy: http://www.eere.energy.gov/;

- National Oceanic and Atmospheric Administration (NOAA): http://www.noaa.gov/;

- U.S. Fish and Wildlife Service (FWS): http://www.fws.gov/;

- The Council on Environmental Quality: http://ceq.eh.doe.gov/nepa/nepanet.htm; and

- The Advisory Council on Historic Preservation: http://www.achp.gov.

A. Map of EPA Regions

EPA has ten regional offices, each of which is responsible for several states and territories, as shown in the figure below.

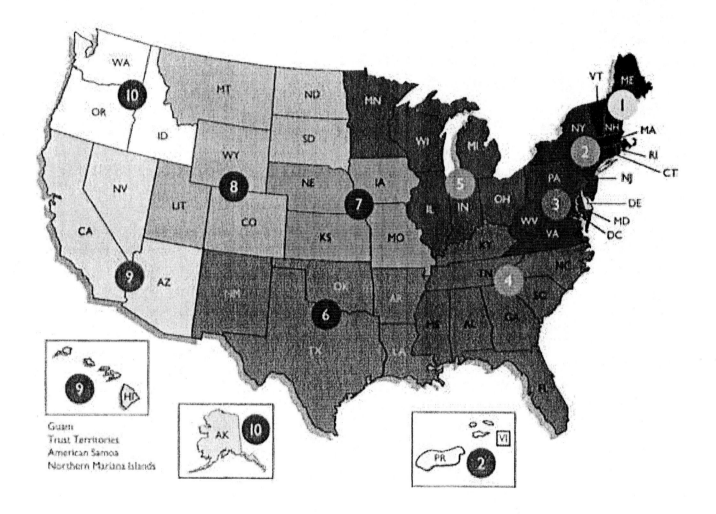

B. Glossary of Terms and Acronyms

ACM—Asbestos Containing Materials.

Adequately Wet—Sufficiently mixed with liquid to prevent the release of particulates. If visible particles or dust is observed coming from asbestos-containing material, then that material has not been adequately wetted.

AHERA—Asbestos Hazard Emergency Response Act.

Asbestos—The name given to a number of naturally occurring fibrous silicate minerals that have been mined for their useful properties such as thermal insulation, chemical and thermal stability, and high tensile strength. The NESHAP defines asbestos to be the asbestiform varieties of serpentine (chrysotile), riebeckite (crocidolite), cummingtonite-grunerite, anthophyllite, and actinolite-tremolite.

ASHARA—Asbestos School Hazard Abatement Reauthorization Act.

BMP—Best Management Practice.

Brownfield—Property where any expansion, redevelopment, or reuse may be complicated by the presence or potential presence of a hazardous substance, pollutant, or contaminant, not including sites that are part of a planned or ongoing removal action or are on the National Priorities List.

Bulk Storage Container—Any container used to store oil. These containers are used for purposes including, but not limited to, the storage of oil prior to use, while being used, or prior to further distribution in commerce. Oil-filled electrical, operating, or manufacturing equipment is not a bulk storage container. Bulk storage containers include items such as tanks, containers, drums, and mobile or portable totes.

CERCLA—Comprehensive Environmental Response, Compensation, and Liability Act.

CESQG—Conditionally Exempt Small Quantity Generators.

CFC—Chlorofluorocarbons.

CFR—Code of Federal Regulations.

CGP—Construction General Permit.

COE—Army Corps of Engineers.

Construction Activities—Can include clearing; grading; excavation; road building; construction of residential houses, office buildings, and industrial sites; and demolition.

Critical Habitat—The specific areas within the geographical area currently occupied by a species, at the time it is listed in accordance with the Endangered Species Act (ESA), on which are found those physical or biological features essential to the conservation of the species and that may require special management considerations, and specific areas outside the geographical area occupied by a species at the time it is listed upon determination by the Secretary that such areas are essential for the conservation of the species (defined at Section 3(5) of the federal ESA).

CWA—Clean Water Act.

CWA/OPA—Clean Water Act/Oil Pollution Act.

Disposal—The discharge, deposit, injection, dumping, spilling, leaking, or placing of any solid or hazardous waste into or on any land or water so that the solid or hazardous waste or any constituent may enter the environment.

DOT—Department of Transportation.

Dredged Material—Material that is excavated or dredged from waters in the United States.

EPCRA—Emergency Planning and Community Right-to-Know Act.

ESA—Endangered Species Act.

Extremely Hazardous Substances (EHSs)—Chemicals that most likely induce serious acute reactions following short-term airborne exposure (defined at 40 CFR Part 355). The list of extremely hazardous substances subject to EPCRA reporting requirements can be found in EPA's Consolidated List of Chemicals Subject to the Emergency Planning and Community Right-To-Know Act (EPCRA) and Section 112(r) of the Clean Air Act (EPA 550-B-01-003). Note that an extremely hazardous substance may also be included in the CERCLA list of hazardous substances.

Fill Material—Material placed in waters of the United States where the material has the effect of either replacing any portion of water of the United States with dry land or changing the bottom elevation of any portion of a water of the United States. Examples include rock, sand, soil, clay, plastics, construction debris, wood chips, overburden from mining or other excavation activities, and materials used to create any structure or infrastructure in waters of the United States.

Friable—Asbestos that can be reduced to dust by hand pressure.

Generator—Any person, by site, whose act or process produces hazardous waste identified or listed in RCRA Subtitle C or whose act first causes a hazardous waste to become subject to regulation. For example, an action such as unearthing soil contaminated with a hazardous substance causes the contaminated soil to be subject to RCRA regulations.

Harass—Actions that create the likelihood of injury to listed species to such an extent as to significantly disrupt normal behavior patterns which include, but may not be limited to, breeding, feeding, or sheltering.

Harm—An act that actually kills or injures wildlife. Such an act may include significant habitat modification or degradation that actually kills or injures wildlife by significantly impairing essential behavior patterns, including breeding, feeding, or sheltering.

Hazardous Substances—Defined in CERCLA Section 101(14) and includes hazardous air pollutants (designated in Section 112(b) of the Clean Air Act), radionuclides, toxic pollutants (designated in Section 307(a) of the Clean Water Act), elements and compounds that present an imminent danger to public health when discharged into waters of the United States ((designated in Section 311(b)(2)(A) of the Clean Water Act), TSCA substance that EPA has taken action against (currently none), and RCRA-listed hazardous wastes and characteristic wastes. The list of hazardous substances subject to CERCLA and EPCRA reporting requirements can be found in EPA's Consolidated List of Chemicals Subject to the Emergency Planning and Community Right-To-Know Act (EPCRA) and Section 112(r) of the Clean Air Act (EPA 550-B-01-003). Certain substances are excluded from CERCLA and/or EPCRA reporting requirements (see Section VII-F of this document for web sites and hotlines where you can obtain additional information).

Hazardous Waste—A solid waste, or combination of solid wastes, which because of its quantity, concentration, or physical, chemical, or infectious characteristics may either cause, or significantly contribute to, an increase in mortality or an increase in serious irreversible or incapacitating reversible illness; or pose a substantial present or potential hazard to human health or the environment when improperly treated, stored, transported, or disposed of, or otherwise managed.

Hot Mix Asphalt Plant—Equipment used to prepare hot aggregate and mineral filler for mixing to make hot mix asphalt.

Land Disturbance—Exposed soil due to clearing, grading, or excavation activities.

LEPC—Local Emergency Planning Committee.

LQG—Large Quantity Generators.

NESHAPs—National Emission Standards for Hazardous Air Pollutants.

NMFS—National Marine Fisheries Service.

NOAA—National Oceanic and Atmospheric Administration.

NOI—Notice of Intent.

Non-friable—Asbestos that is too hard to be reduce to dust by hand.

NOT—Notice of Termination.

NPDES—National Pollutant Discharge Elimination System.

NPL—National Priorities List. The list of national priorities among the known releases or threatened releases of hazardous substances, pollutants, or contaminants throughout the United States and its territories. The NPL is intended primarily to guide EPA in determining which sites warrant further investigation.

Oil—Oil of any kind or in any form, including, but not limited to: petroleum; fuel oil; sludge; oil refuse; oil mixed with wastes other than dredged spoil; fats, oils or greases of animal, fish, or marine mammal origin; vegetable oils, including oil from seeds, nuts, fruits, or kernels; and other oils and greases, including synthetic oils and mineral oils.

Operator—The party(ies) that has: (1) operational control of construction project plans and has the ability to make modifications to those plans, or (2) day-to-day operational control of stormwater compliance activities.

OSHA—Occupational Safety and Health Administration.

Owner or Operator of a Demolition or Renovation Activity—Any person who owns, leases, operates, controls, or supervises the facility being demolished or renovated or any person who owns, leases, operates, controls, or supervises the demolition or renovation operation, or both.

Polychlorinated Biphenyls (PCB)—Mixtures of synthetic organic chemicals with the same basic chemical structure and similar physical properties ranging from oily liquids to waxy solids. For regulatory purposes, PCBs are defined as any chemical substance that is limited to the biphenyl molecule that has been chlorinated to varying degrees or any combination of substances which contains such substance. Due to their non-flammability, chemical stability, high boiling point and electrical insulating properties, PCBs were used in hundreds of industrial and commercial applications including electrical, heat transfer, and hydraulic equipment; as plasticizers in paints, plastics and rubber products; in pigments, dyes and carbonless copy paper; and many other applications.

Portland Cement Plant—Any manufacturing facility producing Portland cement by either the wet or dry process.

RACM—Regulated Asbestos Containing Materials.

RCRA—Resource Conservation and Recovery Act.

Release—Any spilling, leaking, pumping, pouring, emitting, emptying, discharging, injecting, escaping, leaching, dumping, or disposing into the environment, including abandonment or discarding of barrels, containers, and other closed receptacles containing any hazardous substance.

Reportable Quantity—Amount of hazardous substance (or extremely hazardous substance) released into the environment within a 24-hour period that must be met or exceeded before emergency release notification requirements are triggered. Reportable quantities are listed in EPA's Consolidated List of Chemicals Subject to the Emergency Planning and Community Right-To-Know Act (EPCRA) and Section 112(r) of the Clean Air Act (EPA 550-B-01-003).

Rock Crushing Plant—All activities to crush or grind nonmetallic minerals that include the crusher, grinding mill, screening, bucket elevator, conveyer, bagging, storage bin, and loading.

SERC—State Emergency Response Commission.

Sick Building Syndrome—Condition in which building occupants experience acute health and comfort effects that appear to be linked to indoor air quality and time spent in a buildings.

SIP—State Implementation Plan.

SPCC—Spill Prevention Control and Countermeasures.

SQG—Small Quantity Generators.

Storage—When used in connection with hazardous waste, means the containment of hazardous waste, either on a temporary basis or for a period of years, in such a manner as not to constitute disposal of such hazardous waste.

Storage Capacity—The shell capacity of the container (i.e., the maximum volume of the storage container used to store oil, not the actual amount of product stored in the container).

Stormwater—Stormwater runoff, snow melt runoff, and surface runoff and drainage.

SWPPP—Stormwater Pollution Prevention Plan.

Take—To harass, harm, pursue, hunt, shoot, wound, kill, trap, capture, or collect, or to attempt to engage in any such conduct (Section 3(18) of the federal ESA).

TIP—Transportation Improvement Plan.

TSCA—Toxic Substances Control Act.

TSDF—Treatment, Storage, and Disposal Facility.

Universal Waste—Federal Universal Wastes are batteries such as nickel-cadmium (Ni-Cd) and small sealed lead-acid batteries, agricultural pesticides that are recalled under certain conditions and unused pesticides that are collected and managed as part of a waste pesticide collection program, thermostats which can contain as much as 3 grams of liquid mercury, and lamps which are the bulb or tube portion of electric lighting devices that have a hazardous component.

USFWS—U.S. Fish and Wildlife Service.

VOC—Volatile Organic Compound.

Waters of the United States—All waters currently used, or were used in the past, or may be susceptible to use in interstate or foreign commerce, including all waters which are subject to ebb and flow of the tide. Waters of the United States include, but are not limited to all interstate waters and intrastate lakes, rivers, streams (including intermittent streams), mudflats, sandflats, wetlands, sloughs, prairie potholes, wet meadows, playa lakes, or natural ponds. See 40 CFR Part 122.2 for the complete definition.

Wetlands—Areas inundated or saturated by surface or ground water at a frequency and duration sufficient to support, and that under normal circumstances do support, a prevalence of vegetation typically adapted for life in saturated soil conditions. Wetlands generally include swamps, marshes, bogs, and similar areas.

Part II

Managing Your Environmental Responsibilities:

Self-Audit Checklists

This Page Is Intentionally Left Blank

TABLE OF CONTENTS FOR PART II

This Page Is Intentionally Left Blank

I.   STORMWATER SELF-AUDIT CHECKLIST

This section contains a self audit checklist for the specific stormwater requirements in the EPA Construction General Permit (CGP) for construction activities. In addition, this section contains background information on the U.S. Environmental Protection Agency's (EPA) stormwater requirements. It is best to review this checklist prior to construction to ensure that you are aware of the steps required to comply with the environmental requirements. You can also use this checklist to conduct self audits during construction. The current CGP was issued in 2003 by EPA Headquarters, and applies to construction activities in:

- Indian Country in certain states;
- U.S. Territories (except the Virgin Islands);
- Federal facilities in certain states;
- Alaska;

- Idaho;
- Massachusetts;
- New Hampshire;
- New Mexico;
- Certain industry discharges in Oklahoma and Texas; and
- Washington, D.C.

For a detailed list of areas, see Attachment A of this checklist. For a copy of the complete CGP, go to http://www.epa.gov/npdes/pubs/cgp2003_entirepermit.pdf. The CGP requirements apply to all stormwater discharges associated with the construction activity unless operators of the construction site choose to apply for either an individual permit or an alternative general permit.

Construction activities in areas not listed in Attachment A may be subject to state or local requirements that are different from the CGP requirements. The EPA Region or state in which the construction activity is located will have more information on stormwater requirements that apply (or go to http://www.cicacenter.org/swp2.html).

Section III of Part I of this guide contains a more detailed discussion on stormwater requirements.

CHECKLIST FOR EPA'S CONSTRUCTION GENERAL PERMIT (CGP) REQUIREMENTS FOR CONSTRUCTION AREAS

BACKGROUND INFORMATION

Name of Auditor: _____

Date of Audit: _____

Name of Project/Site: _____

This CGP checklist has two parts. The first part allows users to audit their compliance with the paperwork requirements. The second part covers the implementation of the field requirements. This second part can be removed from the rest of the checklist and used in the field.

A "notes" area is provided at the end of each section of this checklist. For every "No" answer, enter a description of the missing information and the action required to bring the site into compliance in the "notes" area.

CGP - NOTICE OF INTENT (NOI)

Yes	No	
		1. Does the NOI include the following information:
❏	❏	Name, address, and telephone number of the operator who submitted the NOI?
❏	❏	Whether the operator is a federal, state, tribal, other public, or private entity?
❏	❏	Name (or other identifier), address, county, and latitude/longitude of the construction project or site?
❏	❏	Whether the project or site is located on Indian Country lands?
❏	❏	Name of the water body (e.g., stream, lake) that receives stormwater runoff from the construction site?
❏	❏	Estimated start and completion dates for the project?
❏	❏	Estimated number of acres on the site on which soil will be disturbed?
❏	❏	Confirmation that a Stormwater Pollution Prevention Plan (SWPPP) was developed prior to commencing construction activities?
❏	❏	Confirmation that the SWPPP complies with applicable local sediment and erosion control plans?
❏	❏	Indication of where the SWPPP can be reviewed and the name and telephone number of a contact person who can schedule a review?

Yes	No	
❏	❏	2. Does the NOI indicate whether any listed or proposed threatened or endangered species or designated critical habitat are in proximity to the stormwater discharges or stormwater-discharge-related activities covered by the permit?
❏	❏	3. Does the NOI contain information concerning preservation of historic properties? (This is optional.)
❏	❏	4. Was the NOI signed by the appropriate person (e.g., for a partnership by a general partner)?

NOTES / ACTIONS NEEDED TO BRING SITE INTO COMPLIANCE: _____

_____

_____

_____

_____

_____

_____

_____

_____

CGP - STORMWATER POLLUTION PREVENTION PLAN (SWPPP)

Yes	No	
		General Items
		5. Is a notice with the following information posted near the main entrance of the construction site?
❏	❏	The permit number for the project or a copy of the NOI if a permit number has not been assigned.
❏	❏	The name and telephone number of a local contact person.
❏	❏	A brief description of the project.
❏	❏	The location of the SWPPP if the site is inactive or does not have an on-site location to store the plan.

<u>**Yes**</u>   <u>**No**</u>

		SWPPP Requirements
❏	❏	6. Does the SWPPP identify the name and NPDES permit number of the operator who has control over construction plans and specifications (including the ability to make modifications in the plans and specifications) and indicate the areas of the project for which the operator has control?
❏	❏	7. Does the SWPPP contain measures to ensure all other permittees impacted by a modification to the plans and specifications are notified of a modification in a timely manner?
❏	❏	8. Does the SWPPP indicate the portions of the project for which each operator has control over day-to-day activities?
❏	❏	9. For each portion of the project, does the SWPPP indicate the name and permit number of the parties with day-to-day operational control of those activities necessary to ensure compliance with the SWPPP or other permit conditions?
❏	❏	10. Was the SWPPP signed by the appropriate official (e.g., the responsible officer for a corporation)?
		11. Does the SWPPP contain the following information?
❏	❏	A description of the potential sources of pollutants.
❏	❏	A description of the nature of the construction activity.
❏	❏	A description of the intended sequence of major activities that disturb soils for major portions of the site (e.g., grubbing, excavation, grading, utilities, and infrastructure installation).
❏	❏	Estimates of the total area of the site and the total area of the site that is expected to be disturbed by excavation, grading, or other activities including use of off-site borrow and fill areas.
❏	❏	An estimate of the runoff coefficient of the site for both the pre-construction and post-construction conditions and data describing the soil or the quality of any discharge from the site.
		A general location map and a site map that indicate the following:
❏	❏	Drainage patterns and approximate slopes anticipated after major grading activities.
❏	❏	Areas of soil disturbance.
❏	❏	Areas that will not be disturbed.

Yes	No	
❑	❑	Locations of major structural and nonstructural controls identified in the SWPPP.
❑	❑	Locations where stabilization practices are expected to occur.
❑	❑	Locations of off-site material, waste, borrow, or equipment storage areas.
❑	❑	Surface waters (including wetlands).
❑	❑	Locations where stormwater discharges to a surface water.
❑	❑	Location and description of any discharge associated with industrial activity other than construction, including stormwater discharges from dedicated asphalt plants and dedicated concrete plants covered by the CGP. A description of controls and measures implemented at those areas to minimize pollutant discharges.
❑	❑	The name of the receiving water(s) and the areal extent and description of wetlands or other special aquatic sites at or near the site that will be disturbed or that will receive discharges from disturbed areas of the project.
❑	❑	A copy of the permit requirements.
❑	❑	Information on whether listed endangered or threatened species, or critical habitat are found in proximity to the construction activity and whether such species may be affected by the site's stormwater discharges or stormwater-discharge-related activities.
		Inspections (Also See the Field Checklist)
❑	❑	12. Are inspections by the permittee being performed: At least once every seven calendar days? OR At least once every 14 calendar days and within 24 hours of a storm event (≥ 0.5 inches)? *Inspection frequency may be reduced – see Section 3.10 of the CGP for more details.*
❑	❑	13. Are inspection reports signed and certified by an authorized person?
❑	❑	14. Are the inspections being performed by a qualified person (and are the qualifications listed in the SWPPP)?

Yes	No	
		SWPPP Control Measures
		15. Does the SWPPP contain the following information for the major activities (e.g., grubbing) that disturb soils for major portions of the site?
❑	❑	A description of the appropriate measures to control pollutants in stormwater discharges (e.g., best management practices (BMPs)) and the general timing (sequence) during the construction process for implementing the control measures.
❑	❑	The permittee responsible for implementing the control measures.
		16. Does the description in the SWPPP of the appropriate measures to control pollutants in stormwater discharges address the following with respect to erosion and sediment?
❑	❑	Designing the construction-phase erosion and sediment controls to retain sediment on site to the extent practicable.
❑	❑	Properly selecting control measures, and installing and maintaining the measures in accordance with the manufacturer's specifications and good engineering practices.
❑	❑	Removing off-site accumulations of sediment that escape the construction site at a frequency sufficient to minimize the impact of the accumulations (e.g., fugitive sediment in a street could be washed into storm sewers by the next rain or pose a safety hazard to users of a public street).
❑	❑	Removing sediment in sediment traps or sedimentation ponds when design capacity is reduced by 50 percent.
❑	❑	Preventing litter, construction debris, and construction chemicals exposed to stormwater from becoming a pollutant source for the stormwater.
❑	❑	Managing off-site material storage areas (e.g., stockpiles of dirt and borrow areas) used solely for the permitted project in the SWPPP.
❑	❑	17. Does the SWPPP include a description of the interim and permanent stabilization practices for a site (e.g., sod stabilization and vegetative buffer strips) and an implementation schedule for the practices?
❑	❑	18. Does the SWPPP indicate the date when major grading activities will occur, the dates when construction activity on each portion of a site will temporarily or permanently cease, and the date when stabilization measures will be initiated?

Yes	No	
❑	❑	19. Does the SWPPP include a description of the structural practices (e.g., earth dikes and drainage swales) used to divert flows from exposed soils, to store flows, or to otherwise limit runoff and the discharge of pollutants from exposed areas of the site?
❑	❑	20. For common drainage locations, does the SWPPP include the requirement for: Temporary or permanent sediment basin(s) with a capacity to store either 3,600 cubic feet of runoff per acre drained, or the volume of runoff from a 2-year, 24-hour storm from each disturbed acre drained until final stabilization of the site (applicable to any size site)? OR For less than 10 acres, silt fences, vegetative buffer strips, or equivalent sediment controls for all down slope boundaries (and side slope boundaries, as appropriate) of the construction area?
❑	❑	21. Does the SWPPP include a description of the measures that will be used to manage stormwater during the construction activity and explain why a particular measure was selected? Example measures include stormwater detention structures, stormwater retention structures, and velocity dissipation devices placed at discharge locations and along the length of any outfall channel.
❑	❑	22. Does the SWPPP describe how solid material, including building material, is prevented from being discharged to waters of the United States, except as authorized in a permit issued under Section 404 of the Clean Water Act (CWA)?
❑	❑	23. Does the SWPPP describe how off-site vehicle tracking of sediments and generation of dust is minimized?
❑	❑	24. Does the SWPPP state it is consistent with applicable state, tribal, and local waste disposal, sanitary sewer, and septic tank system regulations to the extent these are located within the permitted area?
❑	❑	25. Does the SWPPP include a description of construction and waste materials expected to be stored on site; a description of controls to reduce the discharge of pollutants from these materials, including storage practices to minimize exposure of the materials to stormwater; and a description of spill prevention and response measures?
❑	❑	26. Does the SWPPP include a description of measures necessary to protect listed endangered or threatened species or critical habitat?
❑	❑	27. Is the SWPPP consistent with the requirements in applicable sediment and erosion site plans or site permits, or stormwater management site plans or site permit approved by state, tribal, or local officials?

Yes	No	
❏	❏	28. Does the SWPPP identify the sources of non-stormwater that are combined with stormwater discharges associated with construction activities, and does the SWPPP identify and ensure implementation of pollution prevention measures for the non-stormwater component of a discharge from the construction site?

SWPPP Updates

Yes	No	
		29. Did the permittee amend the SWPPP whenever:
❏	❏	There was a change in the project design, construction, operation, or maintenance that had a significant effect on the discharge of pollutants to waters of the United States?
❏	❏	Results of inspections or investigations indicated that the SWPPP is not achieving the general objectives of controlling pollutants in stormwater discharges associated with construction activities?
❏	❏	There was a release of a hazardous substance or oil in an amount equal to or in excess of a reportable quantity (including date, description, and circumstances of the release) within 14 days of the release? The SWPPP must identify measures to prevent the reoccurrence of a release and to respond to a release.

Recordkeeping

Yes	No	
		30. Does the SWPPP include the following documentation required by the CGP?
❏	❏	Permit eligibility related to the Endangered Species Act (See Section 3.7 of the CGP).
❏	❏	Permit eligibility related to Total Maximum Daily Loads (TMDL) (See Section 3.14 of the CGP).
❏	❏	NOI.
❏	❏	NOI receipt/confirmation from EPA.
❏	❏	Permit requirements (i.e., CGP).
❏	❏	Inspection reports.
		Sites must maintain the records for three years past expiration of permit (or completion of project).

NOTES / ACTIONS NEEDED TO BRING SITE INTO COMPLIANCE: _____

_____

_____

_____

_____

CGP - NOTICE OF TERMINATION (NOT)

<u>Yes</u>	<u>No</u>	
		31. Does the NOT contain the following information?
❑	❑	Permit number for the stormwater discharge.
❑	❑	Reason for termination (see CGP Requirements).
❑	❑	Name, address, and telephone number of the permittee submitting the NOT.
❑	❑	Name of the project and street address (or description of the location if no street address is available) for the construction site for which the NOT is submitted.
❑	❑	32. Was the NOT signed (certified) by the appropriate official (e.g., for a State, the principal executive officer or ranking elected official)?

NOTES / ACTIONS NEEDED TO BRING SITE INTO COMPLIANCE: _____

_____

_____

_____

_____

_____

_____

This Page Is Intentionally Left Blank

SELF-AUDIT FIELD CHECKLIST FOR STORMWATER REQUIREMENTS

Date of Audit/Self-Audit: _____

Auditor (name, title, qualifications): _____

Name & Location of Project/Site: _____

Areas Audited: _____

Weather (since last inspection): _____

Name of Receiving Water: _____

For each of the questions below, please identify the area audited, any relevant observations, corrective actions that are needed, and the date that the corrective action is completed.

1. As described in the SWPPP, are the appropriate measures in place to control pollutants in stormwater discharges (e.g., BMPs as silt fencing)? List the control measures and observations below:

Control Measures and Observations:_____

_____

_____

_____

Corrective Actions Needed/Expected Completion Date:_____

_____

_____

2. As described in the SWPPP, are the structural practices (e.g., earth dikes and drainage swales) in place to divert flows from exposed soils, to store flows, or to otherwise limit runoff and the discharge of pollutants from exposed areas?

Structural Practices and Observations:_____

_____

_____

_____

Corrective Actions Needed/Expected Completion Date:_____

_____

_____

3. Are there any additional BMPs that need to be used (e.g., for any exposed areas)?

Areas and Observations:_____

_____

_____

_____

Corrective Actions Needed/Expected Completion Date:_____

_____

_____

4. As described in the SWPPP, are the site practices in place to prevent stored materials (including solid, building, and waste materials) from being discharged into waters of the United States (except as authorized in the Section 404 permit)?

Material Storage Areas and Observations:_____

_____

_____

_____

Corrective Actions Needed/Expected Completion Date:_____

_____

_____

5. Are the site practices listed in the SWPPP in place to minimize off-site vehicle tracking of sediments and generation of dust?

Practices and Observations:_____

_____

_____

_____

Corrective Actions Needed/Expected Completion Date:_____

_____

_____

6. Are roadways clear of debris (e.g., no off-site vehicle tracking)?

Areas and Observations:_____

_____

_____

_____

Corrective Actions Needed/Expected Completion Date:_____

_____

_____

7. Is there any exposed litter, debris or chemicals? Check the following areas: equipment washing, maintenance, concrete washout, and site drainage locations.

Areas and Observations:_____

_____

_____

Corrective Actions Needed/Expected Completion Date:_____

_____

_____

8. As described in the SWPPP, are the appropriate measures in place to control pollutants in stormwater discharges with respect to erosion and sediment?

Erosion and Sediment Controls and Observations:_____

_____

_____

_____

Corrective Actions Needed/Expected Completion Date:_____

_____

_____

BACKGROUND ON STORMWATER REQUIREMENTS FOR CONSTRUCTION ACTIVITIES

DEFINITIONS

- **Construction Activities or Construction-Related Activities.** Refers to the actual earth disturbing construction activities and those activities supporting the construction project such as construction materials or equipment storage or maintenance (e.g., fill piles, borrow area, concrete truck washout, fueling), measures used to control the quality for storm water associated with construction activity, or other industrial storm water directly related to the construction process (e.g., concrete or asphalt batch plants). It does not refer to construction activities unrelated to earth disturbing activities such as interior remodeling, completion of interiors of structures, etc. "Construction" does not include routine earth disturbing activities that are part of the normal day-to-day operation of a completed facility (e.g., daily cover for landfills, maintenance of gravel roads or parking areas, landscape maintenance, etc). Also, it does not include activities under a State or Federal reclamation program to return an abandoned property into an agricultural or open land use.

- **Final Stabilization.** All soil disturbing activities at the site have been completed and a uniform perennial vegetative cover with a density of at least 70 percent of the native background vegetative cover for the area has been established on all unpaved areas and areas not covered by permanent structures, or equivalent permanent stabilization measures (such as the use of riprap, gabions, or geotextiles) have been employed. See "final stabilization" definition in Appendix A of the Construction General Permit for further guidance where background native vegetation covers less than 100 percent of the ground, in arid or semi-arid areas, for individual lots in residential construction, and for construction projects on land used for agricultural purposes.

- **Land Disturbance.** Exposed soil due to clearing, grading, or excavation activities. This is also commonly referred to as ground disturbing activities.

- **Larger Common Plan of Development or Sale**. A contiguous area where multiple separate and distinct construction activities occur under one plan (e.g., construction is being done on 10 one-half acre lots in a six-acre development).

- **Operator.** The party (ies) that has: (1) operational control of construction project plans and specifications, including the ability to make modifications to those plans and specifications, or (2) day-to-day operational control of those activities necessary to ensure compliance with a stormwater pollution prevention plan or other permit conditions.

- **Plan**. Any announcement or piece of documentation (e.g., sign, public notice or hearing, sales pitch, advertisement, drawing, permit application, zoning request, or computer design) or physical demarcation (e.g., boundary signs, lot stakes, or surveyor markings) indicating that construction activities may occur on a specific plot.

- **Stormwater**. Stormwater runoff, snow melt runoff, and surface runoff and drainage.

- **Waters of the United States.** All waters currently used, or used in the past, or may be susceptible to use in interstate or foreign commerce, including all waters that are subject to ebb and flow of the tide. Waters of the United States include, but are not limited to, all interstate waters and intrastate lakes, rivers, streams (including intermittent streams), mudflats, sandflats, wetlands, sloughs, prairie potholes, wet meadows, play lakes, or natural ponds. See 40 CFR Part 122.2 for the complete definition.

ACRONYMS

- BMP - Best Management Practice
- CGP - Construction General Permit
- CWA - Clean Water Act
- NOI - Notice of Intent
- NOT - Notice of Termination
- NPDES - National Pollutant Discharge Elimination System
- SWPPP - Stormwater Pollution Prevention Plan

APPLICABILITY

EPA's CGP for construction activities applies to stormwater discharges from:[2]

- A construction activity that disturbs one or more acres of land.

- A construction activity that disturbs less than one acre of land, but is part of a larger common plan of development or sale that disturbs one or more acre of land.

---

[2]Except when the stormwater discharges associated with the construction activity are covered by either an individual permit or an alternative general permit.

- Construction related activities (e.g., concrete or asphalt batch plants, equipment staging yards, and material storage areas) for a local project an operator currently is involved with (e.g., a concrete batch plant providing concrete to several different highway projects in the same county) if: (1) the support activity is directly related to the construction site required to have NPDES permit coverage for discharges of stormwater associated with construction activity; (2) the support activity is not a commercial operation serving multiple, unrelated construction projects and does not operate beyond the completion of the last related construction project it serves; and (3) appropriate controls are identified in a SWPPP for the stormwater discharges from the construction support activities.

- Non-stormwater discharges that include:
  — Discharges from fire-fighting activities,
  — Fire hydrant flushings,
  — Waters used to wash vehicles where detergents are not used,
  — Water used to control dust,
  — Potable water including uncontaminated water line flushings,
  — Routine external building wash down that does not use detergents,
  — Pavement wash waters where spills or leaks of toxic or hazardous materials have not occurred (unless all spilled material has been removed) and where detergents are not used,
  — Uncontaminated air conditioning or compressor condensate,
  — Uncontaminated ground water or spring water,
  — Foundation or footing drains where flows are not contaminated with process materials such as solvents,
  — Uncontaminated excavation dewatering, and
  — Landscape irrigation.

CGP REQUIREMENTS

- The CGP requires, among other things, an operator to submit a **NOI** to be covered by the permit for a construction activity, to prepare a **SWPPP** for the construction activity, and to submit a **NOT** when the construction activity is completed. Either a hard copy or electronic version of the notices can be submitted. If the construction activity is covered by the CGP, the notices can be submitted to the following addresses:

<u>Regular U.S. Mail Delivery</u>
Stormwater Notice of Intent
U.S. EPA - Ariel Rios Building
Mail Code 4203M
U.S. EPA
1200 Pennsylvania Ave., NW
Washington, DC 20460

<u>Overnight/Express Mail Delivery</u>
Stormwater Notice of Intent
U.S. EPA - East Building, Room 7420
U.S. EPA
1201 Constitution Ave., NW
Washington, DC 20004

To complete an electronic NOI (eNOI), follow the instructions on the following EPA web site: http://cfpub.epa.gov/npdes/stormwater/enoi.cfm.

• A **SWPPP** must be developed for each construction project and it must be prepared prior to submitting the NOI. The SWPPP must identify all potential sources of stormwater pollution and the practices that will be used to reduce that pollution. Samples of construction SWPPPs can be found at: http://www.cicacenter.org/swppp.html.

• Construction activities (i.e., the initial disturbance of soils associated with clearing, grading, excavation activities, or other construction activities) may not begin until seven days after the completed **NOI** is posted on EPA's web site at http://cfpub.epa.gov/npdes/stormwater/noi/noisearch.cfm. Therefore, the certifying official should submit the electronic NOI form at http://cfpub.epa.gov/npdes/stormwater/enoi.cfm approximately 10 days prior to the scheduled start of construction activities. (When submitting by mail, allow additional time for EPA receipt and review.) The certifying official may be either the site owner or operator. The site operator is defined above.

• The NOI form includes Endangered Species Act information that also must be completed prior to NOI submission. If there are concerns about endangered or threatened species, EPA may delay the authorization of the CGP permit coverage (and therefore the construction start) until the concerns are addressed.

• Operators must follow the pollution prevention practices outlined in the SWPPP, including inspection and maintenance of control structures.

• Operators should keep records together by attaching the following to the SWPPP: a copy of the NOI, the EPA NOI receipt/confirmation, inspection reports, and plan amendments.

• Operators must submit a **NOT** (found in Appendix F of the CGP and on-line at http://www.epa.gov/npdes/pubs/cgp_appendixf.pdf) to EPA within 30 days after one or more of the following:

— Final stabilization has been achieved on all portions of the site for which the permittee is responsible,

— Another operator/permittee assumes control over all areas of the site that have not received final stabilization,

— Coverage has been obtained under an individual or alternative NPDES permit, or

— For residential construction only, temporary stabilization has been completed and the residence has been transferred to the homeowner.

Attachment A. States, Indian Country, and Territories Where the EPA Construction General Permit (CGP) Applies

State or Territory Name	Is EPA the Permitting Authority (a,b)?	Areas Where EPA is the Permitting Authority / Permit Number	Additional Permit Conditions (c)?	State-Specific Stormwater Links
Alabama	For Indian Country only	Indian Country construction activities in Region 4 must use the Region 4 Construction General Permit. (http://www.epa.gov/npdes/pubs/cgp-reg4.pdf).	No	http://www.cicacenter.org/swrl.cfm ?st=AL
Alaska	Yes	The State of Alaska (except Indian Country) Permit number: AKR100000 Indian Country within the State of Alaska Permit Number: AKR10000I	Yes	http://www.cicacenter.org/swrl.cfm ?st=AK
American Samoa	Yes	The Island of American Samoa Permit Number: ASR100000	Yes	
Arizona	For Indian Country only	Indian country within the State of Arizona, as well as Navajo Reservation lands in New Mexico and Utah Permit Number: AZR10000I	Yes	http://www.cicacenter.org/swrl.cfm ?st=AZ
Arkansas	No	The State of Arkansas is the NPDES Permitting Authority for all regulated discharges.	No	http://www.cicacenter.org/swrl.cfm ?st=AR
California	For Indian Country only	Indian Country within the State of California Permit Number: CAR10000I	No	http://www.cicacenter.org/swrl.cfm ?st=CA
Colorado	For Indian Country and federal facilities only	Indian Country within the State of Colorado, as well as the portion of the Ute Mountain Reservation located in New Mexico Permit Number: COR10000I Federal facilities in the State of Colorado, except those located on Indian Country Permit Number: COR10000F	No	http://www.cicacenter.org/swrl.cfm ?st=CO
Connecticut	For Indian Country only	Indian Country in the State of Connecticut Permit Number: CTR10000I	No	http://www.cicacenter.org/swrl.cfm ?st=CT
Delaware	For federal facilities only	Federal facilities in the State of Delaware Permit Number: DER10000F	No	http://www.cicacenter.org/swrl.cfm ?st=DE
District of Columbia	Yes	The District of Columbia Permit Number: DCR100000	No	http://www.cicacenter.org/swrl.cfm ?st=DC

Attachment A. States, Indian Country, and Territories Where the EPA Construction General Permit (CGP) Applies (Continued)

State or Territory Name	Is EPA the Permitting Authority (a,b)?	Areas Where EPA is the Permitting Authority / Permit Number	Additional Permit Conditions (c)?	State-Specific Stormwater Links
Florida	For Indian Country only	Indian Country construction activities in Region 4 must use the Region 4 Construction General Permit. (http://www.epa.gov/npdes/pubs/cgp-reg4.pdf).	No	http://www.cicacenter.org/swrl.cfm ?st=FL
Georgia	No	The State of Georgia is the NPDES Permitting Authority for all regulated discharges.	No	http://www.cicacenter.org/swrl.cfm ?st=GA
Guam	Yes	The Island of Guam Permit Number: GUR100000	No	
Hawaii	No	The State of Hawaii is the NPDES Permitting Authority for all regulated discharges.	No	http://www.cicacenter.org/swrl.cfm ?st=HI
Idaho	Yes	The State of Idaho (except Indian Country) Permit Number: IDR100000 Indian Country within the State of Idaho, except Duck Valley Reservation lands Permit Number: IDR100000I Duck Valley Reservation lands are covered under the Nevada permit NVR100000I.	Yes	http://www.cicacenter.org/swrl.cfm ?st=ID
Illinois	No	The State of Illinois is the NPDES Permitting Authority for all regulated discharges.	No	http://www.cicacenter.org/swrl.cfm ?st=IL
Indiana	No	The State of Indiana is the NPDES Permitting Authority for all regulated discharges.	No	http://www.cicacenter.org/swrl.cfm ?st=IN
Iowa	For Indian Country only	Indian Country within the State of Iowa Permit Number: IAR100000I	No	http://www.cicacenter.org/swrl.cfm ?st=IA
Johnston Atoll	Yes	The Island of Johnston Atoll Permit Number: JAR100000	No	
Kansas	For Indian Country only	Indian Country within the State of Kansas Permit Number: KSR100000I	No	http://www.cicacenter.org/swrl.cfm ?st=KS

Attachment A. States, Indian Country, and Territories Where the EPA Construction General Permit (CGP) Applies (Continued)

State or Territory Name	Is EPA the Permitting Authority (a,b)?	Areas Where EPA is the Permitting Authority / Permit Number	Additional Permit Conditions (c)?	State-Specific Stormwater Links
Kentucky	No	The State of Kentucky is the NPDES Permitting Authority for all regulated discharges.	No	http://www.cicacenter.org/swrl.cfm ?st=KY
Louisiana	For Indian Country only	Indian Country within the State of Louisiana Permit Number: LAR15000I	No	http://www.cicacenter.org/swrl.cfm ?st=LA
Maine	No	The State of Maine is the NPDES Permitting Authority for all regulated discharges.	No	http://www.cicacenter.org/swrl.cfm ?st=ME
Maryland	No	The State of Maryland is the NPDES Permitting Authority for all regulated discharges.	No	http://www.cicacenter.org/swrl.cfm ?st=MD
Massachusetts	Yes	Commonwealth of Massachusetts (except Indian Country) Permit Number: MAR100000 Indian Country within the Commonwealth of Massachusetts Permit Number: MAR10000I	Yes	http://www.cicacenter.org/swrl.cfm ?st=MA
Michigan	For Indian Country only	Indian Country within the State of Michigan Permit Number: MIR10000I	No	http://www.cicacenter.org/swrl.cfm ?st=MI
Midway Islands	Yes	The Islands of Midway Island and Wake Island Permit Number: MWR100000	No	
Minnesota	For Indian Country only	Indian Country within the State of Minnesota Permit Number: MNR10000I	No	http://www.cicacenter.org/swrl.cfm ?st=MN
Mississippi	For Indian Country only	Indian Country construction activities in Region 4 must use the Region 4 Construction General Permit. (http://www.epa.gov/npdes/pubs/cgp-reg4.pdf).	No	http://www.cicacenter.org/swrl.cfm ?st=MS
Missouri	No	The State of Missouri is the NPDES Permitting Authority for all regulated discharges.	No	http://www.cicacenter.org/swrl.cfm ?st=MO
Montana	For Indian Country only	Indian Country within the State of Montana Permit Number: MTR10000I	Yes	http://www.cicacenter.org/swrl.cfm ?st=MT

Attachment A. States, Indian Country, and Territories Where the EPA Construction General Permit (CGP) Applies (Continued)

State or Territory Name	Is EPA the Permitting Authority (a,b)?	Areas Where EPA is the Permitting Authority / Permit Number	Additional Permit Conditions (c)?	State-Specific Stormwater Links
Nebraska	For Indian Country only	Indian Country within the State of Nebraska, except Pine Ridge Reservation lands Permit Number: NER100001 The Pine Ridge Reservation lands are covered under the South Dakota Permit SDR100001.	No	http://www.cicacenter.org/swrl.cfm ?st=NE
Nevada	For Indian Country only	Indian Country within the State of Nevada, as well as the Duck Valley Reservation in Idaho, the Fort McDermitt Reservation in Oregon and the Goshute Reservation in Utah Permit Number: NVR100001	No	http://www.cicacenter.org/swrl.cfm ?st=NV
New Hampshire	Yes	State of New Hampshire Permit Number: NHR100000	Yes	http://www.cicacenter.org/swrl.cfm ?st=NH
New Jersey	No	The State of New Jersey is the NPDES Permitting Authority for all regulated discharges.	No	http://www.cicacenter.org/swrl.cfm ?st=NJ
New Mexico	Yes	The State of New Mexico (except Indian Country) Permit Number: NMR150000 Indian Country within the State of New Mexico, except Navajo Reservation Lands that are covered under Arizona permit AZR100001 and Ute Mountain Reservation Lands that are covered under Colorado permit COR100001 Permit Number: NMR150001	No	http://www.cicacenter.org/swrl.cfm ?st=NM
New York	For Indian Country only	Indian Country within the State of New York Permit Number: NYR100001	Yes	http://www.cicacenter.org/swrl.cfm ?st=NY
North Carolina	For Indian Country only	Indian Country construction activities in Region 4 must use the Region 4 Construction General Permit. (http://www.epa.gov/npdes/pubs/cgp-reg4.pdf).	No	http://www.cicacenter.org/swrl.cfm ?st=NC

Attachment A. States, Indian Country, and Territories Where the EPA Construction General Permit (CGP) Applies (Continued)

State or Territory Name	Is EPA the Permitting Authority (a,b)?	Areas Where EPA is the Permitting Authority / Permit Number	Additional Permit Conditions (c)?	State-Specific Stormwater Links
North Dakota	For Indian Country only	Indian Country within the State of North Dakota, as well as that portion of the Standing Rock Reservation located in South Dakota (except for the portion of the lands within the former boundaries of the Lake Traverse Reservation, which is covered under South Dakota permit SDR10000I listed below) Permit Number: NDR10000I	No	http://www.cicacenter.org/swrl.cfm ?st=ND
Northern Mariana Islands	Yes	Commonwealth of the Northern Mariana Islands Permit Number: NIR100000	Yes	
Ohio	No	The State of Ohio is the NPDES Permitting Authority for all regulated discharges.	No	http://www.cicacenter.org/swrl.cfm ?st=OH
Oklahoma	For Indian Country and specific discharges only	Indian Country within the State of Oklahoma Permit Number: OKR15000I Discharges in the State of Oklahoma that are not under the authority of the Oklahoma Department of Environmental Quality, including activities associated with oil and gas exploration, drilling, operations, and pipelines (includes SIC Groups 13 and 46, and SIC codes 492 and 5171), and point source discharges associated with agricultural production, services, and silviculture (includes SIC Groups 01, 02, 07, 08, 09) Permit Number: OKR15000F	No	http://www.cicacenter.org/swrl.cfm ?st=OK
Oregon	For Indian Country only	Indian Country within the State of Oregon, except Fort McDermitt Reservation lands Permit Number: ORR10000I Fort McDermitt Reservation lands are covered under the Nevada Permit NVR10000I.	Yes	http://www.cicacenter.org/swrl.cfm ?st=OR

Attachment A. States, Indian Country, and Territories Where the EPA Construction General Permit (CGP) Applies (Continued)

State or Territory Name	Is EPA the Permitting Authority (a,b)?	Areas Where EPA is the Permitting Authority / Permit Number	Additional Permit Conditions (c)?	State-Specific Stormwater Links
Pennsylvania	No	The State of Pennsylvania is the NPDES Permitting Authority for all regulated discharges.	No	http://www.cicacenter.org/swrl.cfm ?st=PA
Puerto Rico	Yes	The Commonwealth of Puerto Rico Permit Number: PRR100000	No	
Rhode Island	For Indian Country only	Indian Country within the State of Rhode Island Permit Number: RIR10000I	No	http://www.cicacenter.org/swrl.cfm ?st=RI
South Carolina	No	The State of South Carolina is the NPDES Permitting Authority for all regulated discharges.	No	http://www.cicacenter.org/swrl.cfm ?st=SC
South Dakota	For Indian Country only	Indian Country within the State of South Dakota, as well as the portion of the Pine Ridge Reservation located in Nebraska and the portion of the lands within the former boundaries of the Lake Traverse Reservation located in North Dakota (except for the Standing Rock Reservation, which is covered under North Dakota permit NDR100001 listed above) Permit Number: SDR10000I	No	http://www.cicacenter.org/swrl.cfm ?st=SD
Tennessee	No	The State of Tennessee is the NPDES Permitting Authority for all regulated discharges.	No	http://www.cicacenter.org/swrl.cfm ?st=TN
Texas	For Indian Country and specific discharges only	Indian Country within the State of Texas Permit Number: TXR15000I Discharges in the State of Texas that are not under the authority of the Texas Commission on Environmental Quality (formerly TNRCC), including activities associated with the exploration, development, or production of oil or gas or geothermal resources, including transportation of crude oil or natural gas by pipeline Permit Number: TXR15000F	No	http://www.cicacenter.org/swrl.cfm ?st=TX

Attachment A. States, Indian Country, and Territories Where the EPA Construction General Permit (CGP) Applies (Continued)

State or Territory Name	Is EPA the Permitting Authority (a,b)?	Areas Where EPA is the Permitting Authority / Permit Number	Additional Permit Conditions (c)?	State-Specific Stormwater Links
Utah	For Indian Country only	Indian Country within the State of Utah, except Goshute and Navajo Reservation lands Permit Number: UTR100001. Goshute Reservation lands are covered under the Nevada Permit NVR100001. Navajo Reservation lands are covered under the Arizona Permit AZR100001.	No	http://www.cicacenter.org/swrl.cfm ?st=UT
Vermont	For federal facilities only	Federal facilities in the State of Vermont Permit Number: VTR10000F	No	http://www.cicacenter.org/swrl.cfm ?st=VT
Virgin Islands	No	The Virgin Islands is the NPDES Permitting Authority for all regulated discharges.	No	
Virginia	No	The State of Virginia is the NPDES Permitting Authority for all regulated discharges.	No	http://www.cicacenter.org/swrl.cfm ?st=VA
Wake Island	Yes	The Islands of Midway Island and Wake Island Permit Number: MWR100000	No	
Washington	For Indian Country and federal facilities only	Federal facilities in the State of Washington, except those located on Indian country Permit Number: WAR10000F Indian country within the State of Washington Permit Number: WAR100001	Yes	http://www.cicacenter.org/swrl.cfm ?st=WA
West Virginia	No	The State of West Virginia is the NPDES Permitting Authority for all regulated discharges.	No	http://www.cicacenter.org/swrl.cfm ?st=WV
Wisconsin	For Indian Country only	Indian Country within the State of Wisconsin, except the Sokaogon Chippewa (Mole Lake) Community Permit Number: WIR100001	No	http://www.cicacenter.org/swrl.cfm ?st=WI

Attachment A. States, Indian Country, and Territories Where the EPA Construction General Permit (CGP) Applies (Continued)

State or Territory Name	Is EPA the Permitting Authority (a,b)?	Areas Where EPA is the Permitting Authority / Permit Number	Additional Permit Conditions (c)?	State-Specific Stormwater Links
Wyoming	For Indian Country only	Indian Country within the State of Wyoming Permit Number: WYR10000I	No	http://www.cicacenter.org/swrl.cfm ?st=WY

(a) For updates to the CGP coverage, go to: http://cfpub.epa.gov/npdes/stormwater/authorizationstatus.cfm.

(b) Permit information for areas where EPA is *not* the permitting authority is available at: http://www.cicacenter.org/swp2.html.

(c) See Part 9 of the CGP for additional permit conditions (http://www.epa.gov/npdes/pubs/cgp2003_entirepermit.pdf).

This Page Is Intentionally Left Blank

II.   DREDGE AND FILL/WETLANDS (SECTION 404) SELF-AUDIT CHECKLIST

This section contains a self-audit checklist and associated background information related to dredge and fill (Section 404) environmental requirements for construction projects. The United States Army Corps of Engineers (COE) and U.S. Environmental Protection Agency (EPA) regulate discharges of dredged or fill material into waters of the United States under Section 404 of the Clean Water Act (CWA). Owners, developers, architects, contractors, and subcontractors can use the checklist to identify who will be responsible for addressing each requirement, and to conduct a self-audit. The checklist also can be used by compliance inspectors to conduct an inspection of a construction site.

When preparing for any construction project, it must be determined if dredged material (i.e., material excavated from waters) or fill materials (i.e., material placed in waters such that dry land replaces any portion of water or the bottom elevation of waters is changed) will be discharged into waters of the United States.

A permit may be needed if the construction activity impacts a water of the United States. Impacts include the discharge of dredged material, discharge of fill material, and disturbance of hydrological support to wetlands (i.e., cut off of water supply). Specific activities impacting wetlands that require a permit include, but are not limited to, placement of dredged or fill material in a water of the United States, ditching activities when excavated material is sidecast, levee and dike construction, mechanized land clearing, land leveling, road construction, dam construction, and draining wetlands. Depending on the impacts, a Section 404 permit may be required prior to performing any construction activities. A waiting period of 45 days or more after permit application may be required before the construction project can start, depending on the type of permit necessary.

Background on the Section 404 regulation, including definitions, applicability, and permit process requirements, follows the checklist. Attachment A includes the application for individual permits.

Section IV in Part I of this guide contains a more detailed discussion on Section 404 requirements.

CHECKLIST FOR DREDGE AND FILL (SECTION 404) PERMITS FOR CONSTRUCTION PROJECTS

BACKGROUND INFORMATION

Name of Auditor: _____

Date of Audit: _____

Name of Project/Site: _____

A "notes" area is provided at the end of each section of this checklist. For every "No" answer, enter a description of the missing information and the action required to bring the site into compliance in the "notes" area.

SECTION 404 - GETTING A PERMIT

Yes	No	
❑	❑	1. Are construction activities being performed in waters of the United States (see *Background* following the checklist for definition)? If yes, a permit may be required.
❑	❑	2. Is there a wetland in the proposed construction area (see the Recognizing Wetlands Checklist included in this checklist)? If yes, a wetland delineation should be performed by trained personnel. The delineation may need to be submitted to the COE District Office for review.
❑	❑	3. Will dredged or fill material be discharged into waters of the United States? If yes, a permit is required. *Note that EPA and COE assume a discharge will occur for any mechanized land clearing in United States waters unless it is documented that only incidental fallback will occur.*
❑	❑	4. Is the construction project exempt from federal permit requirements? (see 33 CFR 323.4, available on-line at: http://www.usace.army.mil/inet/functions/cw/cecwo/reg/33cfr323.htm) If yes, a federal permit is not required. If no, either a general or individual permit is required.
❑	❑	5. Is state authorization needed (Section 401 certification) for the construction activity (i.e., the state has not already granted certification for general permits in your area)? Contact the state environmental department for further information.

<u>Yes</u>   <u>No</u>

		Nationwide Permits
❑	❑	6. Is the construction activity currently covered by a Nationwide Permit (NWP)? Refer to the COE web site for details at: http://www.usace.army.mil/inet/functions/cw/cecwo/reg/nationwide_permits.htm .If no, skip to the Individual Permits section of this checklist.
❑	❑	7. Is a Preconstruction Notification (PCN) required? *The individual application form (see Attachment A) can be used as the PCN, as long as it is clearly marked that it is a PCN.*
❑	❑	8. If required by the NWP, was a wetland delineation in the PCN?
❑	❑	9. If required by the NWP, were mitigation plans submitted to the COE District Engineer?
❑	❑	10. Have all regional requirements for the NWP been complied with?
❑	❑	11. If a PCN was submitted, has the site received authorization to begin construction? (Authorization is granted by the COE District Engineer or is assumed to have been granted if notification is not received within 45 days after submission of the PCN).
❑	❑	12. If a PCN was submitted, has the site received notification from the COE District Engineer that an individual permit was required?
		Individual Permits
❑	❑	13. Was an application for an Individual Permit (see Attachment A) submitted to the COE and/or the state? Note that only a single application submitted to either the state or COE may be required.
❑	❑	14. Was authorization to begin construction received from the COE District Engineer?

NOTES / ACTIONS NEEDED TO BRING SITE INTO COMPLIANCE: _____

_____

_____

_____

_____

SECTION 404 - MEETING PERMIT REQUIREMENTS

<u>Yes</u>   <u>No</u>

Nationwide Permits

Yes	No	
❏	❏	15. Were all of the general conditions required in the NWP met, including proper maintenance of any structure or fill, soil erosion and sediment controls, and removal of temporary fills?
❏	❏	16. Were special conditions that were required in the NWP authorization from the COE District Engineer met?
❏	❏	17. Was wetlands mitigation performed as required in the permit?
❏	❏	18. If authorization from the COE District Engineer was received, was a signed compliance certification to COE submitted once the construction was complete?

Individual Permits

Yes	No	
❏	❏	19. Were all conditions that were required in the permit met?
❏	❏	20. Were all special conditions required in the permit met (e.g., keeping a copy of the COE-issued permit on the vessel used to transport and dispose of dredge materials or advise the COE District Office at least two weeks prior to starting maintenance dredging activities)?
❏	❏	21. Was wetlands mitigation performed if required in the permit?
❏	❏	22. Was a signed compliance certification submitted to COE once the construction was complete?

NOTES / ACTIONS NEEDED TO BRING SITE INTO COMPLIANCE: _____

_____

_____

_____

_____

_____

_____

_____

This Page Is Intentionally Left Blank

CHECKLIST FOR RECOGNIZING WETLANDS

The following checklist provides some general questions that can help determine if a wetland is present at the construction site. For more specific details, see the COE *Wetlands Delineation Manual* (http://www.saj.usace.army.mil/permit/documents/87manual.pdf). If the answer to any of these questions is yes, seek assistance from a wetlands expert to determine if a wetland is present.

Yes	No	
☐	☐	1. Is the site in a flood plain or otherwise has low spots in which water stands at or above the soil surface during the growing season?
☐	☐	2. Does the site have plant communities that commonly occur in areas having standing water for part of the growing season (e.g., cypress-gum swamps, cordgrass marshes, cattail marshes, bulrush and tule marshes, and sphagnum bogs)?
☐	☐	3. Does the site have soils called peats or mucks?
☐	☐	4. Is the site periodically flooded by tides, even if only by strong, wind-driven, or spring tides?
		If the response to any of the following questions is "yes," then one or more of the wetland indicators (vegetation, soil, and hydrology) are present in the site, and you should seek assistance from the COE District Office or a wetlands expert to determine if a wetland is present.
☐	☐	5. Are any of the wetland vegetation indicators growing on the site? See the COE *Wetlands Delineation Manual* for a list of indicators.
☐	☐	6. Are any of the wetland soil indicators found on the site? See the COE *Wetlands Delineation Manual* for a list of indicators.
☐	☐	7. Are any of the wetland hydrology indicators identified on the site? See the COE *Wetlands Delineation Manual* for a list of indicators.

NOTES/ACTION ITEMS: _____

_____

_____

_____

_____

This Page Is Intentionally Left Blank

BACKGROUND ON DREDGE AND FILL/WETLANDS REQUIREMENTS
FOR CONSTRUCTION ACTIVITIES

DEFINITIONS

- **Dredged Material.** Material that is excavated or dredged from waters of the United States.

- **Fill Material.** Material placed in waters of the United States where the material has the effect of:

    — Replacing any portion of a water of the United States with dry land, or

    — Changing the bottom elevation of any portion of a water of the United States.

    Examples of fill material include rock, sand, soil, clay, plastics, construction debris, wood chips, overburden from mining or other excavation activities, and materials used to create any structure or infrastructure in waters of the United States. The term "fill material" does not include trash or garbage.

- **Incidental Fallback.** Redeposit of small volumes of dredged material that is incidental to excavation activity in waters of the United States when such material falls back to substantially the same place as the initial removal. Examples of incidental fallback include soil that is disturbed when dirt is shoveled and the back-spill from a bucket falls into substantially the same place from which it was initially removed.

- **Waters of the United States (United States Waters).** See 40 CFR Part 122.2 for the complete definition. Waters include, but are not limited to:

    — All waters that are currently used, or were used in the past, or may be susceptible to use in interstate or foreign commerce, including all waters which are subject to ebb and flow of the tide,

    — All interstate waters including interstate wetlands, and

    — All other waters such as intrastate lakes, rivers, streams (including intermittent streams), mudflats, sandflats, wetlands, sloughs, prairie potholes, wet meadows, playa lakes, or natural ponds, the use, degradation or destruction of which could affect interstate or foreign commerce.

- **Wetlands.** Areas inundated or saturated by surface or ground water at a frequency and duration sufficient to support, and that under normal circumstances do support, a prevalence of vegetation typically adapted for life in saturated soil conditions. Wetlands generally include swamps, marshes, bogs, and similar areas.

ACRONYMS

- COE - United States Army Corps of Engineers
- CWA - Clean Water Act
- NWP - Nationwide Permit
- PCN - Preconstruction Notification

APPLICABILITY

COE defines discharges of dredged material at 33 CFR 323. These discharges, which require permits under Section 404 of the CWA, include:

- The addition of dredged material to a specified discharge site located in waters of the United States;

- The runoff or overflow from a contained land or water disposal area; and

- Any addition, including redeposit other than incidental fallback, of dredged material, including excavated material, into waters of the United States that is incidental to any activity, including mechanized land clearing, ditching, channelization, or other excavation.

COE also defines discharges of fill material at 33 CFR 323. These discharges, which require permits under Section 404 of the CWA, include:

- Placement of fill necessary for the construction of any structure or infrastructure in a water of the United States;

- Building of any structure, infrastructure, or impoundment in waters of the United States requiring rock, sand, dirt, or other material for its construction;

- Site-development fills in waters of the United States for recreational, industrial, commercial, residential, or other uses;

- Causeways or road fills, dams and dikes, artificial islands, beach nourishment, levees, and artificial reefs;

- Property protection and/or reclamation devices such as rip rap, groins, seawalls, breakwaters, and revetments;

- Fill for structures such as sewage treatment facilities;

- Intake and outfall pipes associated with power plants and subaqueous utility lines;

- Placement of fill material in waters of the United States for construction or maintenance of any liner, berm, or other infrastructure associated with solid waste landfills; and

- Placement of overburden, slurry, or tailings or similar mining-related materials in waters of the United States.

Contact the state environmental or permitting office and the COE District Office to determine whether permits are required for the construction project.

SECTION 404 PERMIT PROCESS REQUIREMENTS

Section 404 requires that no discharge of dredged or fill material be permitted if a practicable alternative exists that is less damaging to the aquatic environment or if the nation's waters would be significantly degraded. When applying for a permit, a wetlands mitigation must be performed to show that the project:

- Avoided wetland impacts where practicable;

- Minimized potential impacts to wetlands; and

- Will provide compensation for any remaining, unavoidable impacts through activities to restore or create wetlands.

COE may issue permits, after notice and opportunity for public hearings, for the discharge of dredged or fill material into waters of the United States at specified disposal sites. Prior to issuing Section 404 permits, state approval must also be obtained (Section 401 certification).

There are two types of Section 404 permits: general permits and individual permits. For discharges that have only minimal adverse effects, COE issues general permits. General permits may be issued on a nationwide, regional, or state basis for particular categories of activities. Attachment C includes a list of current Nationwide Permits (NWPs). Individual permits are usually required for activities with potentially significant impacts.

General Permit Process. An NWP may require that the COE District Engineer (DE) of the construction activity be notified in a preconstruction notification (PCN). If required, the PCN should be submitted as early as possible. Within 30 days, the DE will determine whether the PCN is complete and may request additional information. The PCN review process will not begin until all required information is submitted. Construction activity may not begin until one of the following occurs:

(1)   Notification that the activity may proceed is received from the DE. This notification may include special conditions imposed on the specific construction activity.

(2)   Notification that an individual permit is required is received from the DE, and the individual permit is issued.

(3)   Forty-five days have passed since the DE received the complete PCN and no written notice has been received from the DE.

The text of the NWPs should be reviewed to assess whether a particular NWP applies to the construction project (see 67 FRN 2020 or the on-line guide at http://www.usace.army.mil/inet/functions/cw/cecwo/reg/nationwide_permits.htm). Some items to check include:

•   NWP use limits (e.g., NWP 19 Minor Dredging only applies if the site dredges less than 25 cubic yards); and

•   Applicable waters (e.g., NWP 13 Bank Stabilization does not apply to special aquatic sites (i.e., sanctuaries and refuges, wetlands, mud flats, vegetated shallows, coral reefs, and riffle and pool complexes)).

If the construction activity is covered under an NWP, the site must comply with the general conditions listed for the permit. The COE District Office or state environmental department should be contacted for information on regional and state general permits.

Individual Permit Process. The following steps need to be completed to obtain an individual permit:

•   **Application.** To receive a Section 404 individual permit, operators must complete an *Application for Department of Army Permit* (available on line at:

http://www.usace.army.mil/inet/functions/cw/cecwo/reg/eng4345a.pdf), included in Attachment D. COE requires, among other things, that permit applicants describe the project and its purpose, the reasons for discharging dredged or fill material, types of material being discharged (and volume of each type in cubic yards), and the surface area of wetlands or other waters filled (in acres). Applicants must also submit one set of drawings showing location and character of proposed activity. The application is submitted to the DE having jurisdiction over the location of the proposed activity. (Note that states may contact the COE in conjunction with granting state approval for the project. The application process varies by state; contact the state and COE District Office for details.)

- **Public Notice.** COE will issue a public notice once the complete permit application has been received. The notice includes the proposed activity, location, and potential environmental impacts.

- **Comment Period.** The public comment period lasts between 15-30 days, depending on the proposed activity. The application and comments are reviewed by the COE and other interested federal and state agencies, organizations, and individuals. COE also determines whether an Environmental Impact Statement is necessary.

- **Public Hearing.** Citizens may request that COE conduct a public hearing; however, public hearings are not usually held.

- **Permit Evaluation.** COE, along with states and other federal agencies, evaluates the permit application, taking into account the comments received.

- **Permit Award or Denial.** Based on the steps above, COE may either approve or deny the application.

- **Environmental Assessment and Statement of Findings.** The *Statement of Finding* document explains how the permit decision was made. This document is made available to the public.

The above steps are a basic example of the requirements to obtain an individual permit. The process may require additional steps such as a pre-application meeting with the COE district engineer or state officials or negotiation of mitigation plans.

Attachment A. Application for Individual Permit

The following information was taken from
www.usace.army.mil/inet/functions/cw/cecwo/reg/eng4345a.pdf. Note this form expired in
2004. However, a revised form was not available at the time of publication.

APPLICATION FOR DEPARTMENT OF THE ARMY PERMIT *(33 CFR 325)*	OMB APPROVAL NO. 0710-0003
	Expires December 31, 2004

The public reporting burden for this collection of information is estimated to average 10 hours per response, although the majority of applications should require 5 hours or less. This includes the time for reviewing instructions, searching existing data sources, gathering and maintaining the data needed, and completing and reviewing the collection of information. Send comments regarding this burden estimate or any other aspect of this collection of information, including suggestions for reducing this burden, to Department of Defense, Washington Headquarters Service Directorate of Information Operations and Reports, 1215 Jefferson Davis Highway, Suite 1204, Arlington, VA 22202-4302; and to the Office of Management and Budget, Paperwork Reduction Project (0710-0003), Washington, DC 20503. Respondents should be aware that notwithstanding any other provision of law, no person shall be subject to any penalty for failing to comply with a collection of information if it does not display a currently valid OMB control number. Please DO NOT RETURN your form to either of those addresses. Completed applications must be submitted to the District Engineer having jurisdiction over the location of the proposed activity.

PRIVACY ACT STATEMENT

Authorities: Rivers and Harbors Act, Section 10, 33 USC 403; Clean Water Act, Section 404, 33 USC 1344; Marine Protection, Research, and Sanctuaries Act, Section 103, 33 USC 1413. Principal Purpose: Information provided on this form will be used in evaluating the application for a permit. Routine Uses: This information may be shared with the Department of Justice and other federal, state, and local government agencies. Submission of requested information is voluntary, however, if information is not provided, the permit application cannot be processed nor can a permit be issued. One set of original drawings or good reproducible copies which show the location and character of the proposed activity must be attached to this application (see sample drawings and instructions) and be submitted to the District Engineer having jurisdiction over the location of the proposed activity. An application that is not completed in full will be returned.

(ITEMS 1 THRU 4 TO BE FILLED BY THE CORPS)

1. APPLICATION NO.	2. FIELD OFFICE CODE	3. DATE RECEIVED	4. DATE APPLICATION COMPLETED

(ITEMS BELOW TO BE FILLED BY APPLICANT)

5. APPLICANT'S NAME	8. AUTHORIZED AGENT'S NAME AND TITLE *(an agent is not required)*
6. APPLICANT'S ADDRESS	9. AGENT'S ADDRESS
7. APPLICANT'S PHONE NUMBERS WITH AREA CODE	10. AGENT'S PHONE NUMBERS WITH AREA CODE
a. Residence	a. Residence
b. Business	b. Business

11.	STATEMENT OF AUTHORIZATION

I hereby authorize _____ to act in my behalf as my agent in the processing of this application and to furnish, upon request, supplemental information in support of this permit application.

APPLICANT'S SIGNATURE	DATE

NAME, LOCATION AND DESCRIPTION OF PROJECT OR ACTIVITY

12. PROJECT NAME OR TITLE *(see instructions)*

13. NAME OF WATERBODY, IF KNOWN *(if applicable)*	14. PROJECT STREET ADDRESS *(if applicable)*
15. LOCATION OF PROJECT	
COUNTY STATE	

16. OTHER LOCATION DESCRIPTIONS, IF KNOWN *(see instructions)*

17. DIRECTIONS TO THE SITE

ENG FORM 4345. Jul 97 EDITION OF SEP 94 IS OBSOLETE (Proponent: CECW-OR)

18. Nature of Activity *(Description of project, include all features)*

19. Project Purpose *(Describe the reason or purpose of the project, see instructions)*

USE BLOCKS 20-22 IF DREDGED AND/OR FILL MATERIAL IS TO BE DISCHARGED

20. Reason(s) for Discharge

21. Type(s) of Material Being Discharged and the Amount of Each Type in Cubic Yards

22. Surface Area in Acres of Wetlands or Other Waters Filled *(see instructions)*

23. Is Any Portion of the Work Already Complete?	Yes	No	IF YES, DESCRIBE THE COMPLETED WORK

24. Addresses of Adjoining Property Owners, Lessees, etc., Whose Property Adjoins the Waterbody *(if more than can be entered here, please attach a supplemental list).*

25. List	of Other Certifications or Approvals/Denials Received from other Federal, State, or Local Agencies for Work Described in This Application					
	AGENCY APPROVED	TYPE APPROVAL* DATE DENIED	IDENTIFICATION NUMBER		DATE APPLIED	DATE

*Would include but is not restricted to zoning, building and flood plain permits.

26. Application is hereby made for a permit or permits to authorize the work described in this application. I certify that the information in this application is complete and accurate. I further certify that I possess the authority to undertake the work described herein or am acting as the duly authorized agent of the applicant.

SIGNATURE OF APPLICANT   DATE   SIGNATURE OF AGENT   DATE

The application must be signed by the person who desires to undertake the proposed activity (applicant) or it may be signed by a duly authorized agent if the statement in block 11 has been filled out and signed.

18 U.S.C. Section 1001 provides that: Whoever, in any manner within the jurisdiction of any department or agency of the United States, knowingly and willfully falsifies, conceals, or covers up any trick scheme, or disguises a material fact or makes any false, fictitious or fraudulent statements or representations or makes or uses any false writing or document knowing same to contain any false, fictitious or fraudulent statements or entry, shall be fined not more than $10,000 or imprisoned not more than five years or both.

Instructions for Preparing a
Department of the Army Permit Application

Blocks 1 through 4. To be completed by Corps of Engineers.

Block 5. Applicant's Name. Enter the name of the responsible party or parties. If the responsible party is an agency, company, corporation, or other organization, indicate the responsible officer and title. If more than one party is associated with the application, please attach a sheet with the necessary information marked Block 5.

Block 6. Address of Applicant. Please provide the full address of the party or parties responsible for the application. If more space is needed, attach an extra sheet of paper marked Block 6.

Block 7. Applicant Telephone Number(s). Please provide the number where you can usually be reached during normal business hours.

Blocks 8 through 11. To be completed, if you choose to have an agent.

Block 8. Authorized Agent's Name and Title. Indicate name of individual or agency, designated by you, to represent you in this process. An agent can be an attorney, builder, contractor, engineer, or any other person or organization. Note: An agent is not required.

Blocks 9 and 10. Agent's Address and Telephone Number. Please provide the complete mailing address of the agent, along with the telephone number where he/she can be reached during normal business hours.

Block 11. Statement of Authorization. To be completed by applicant, if an agent is to be employed.

Block 12. Proposed Project Name or Title. Please provide name identifying the proposed project, e.g., Landmark Plaza, Burned Hills Subdivision, or Edsall Commercial Center.

Block 13. Name of Waterbody. Please provide the name of any stream, lake, marsh, or other waterway to he directly impacted by the activity. If it is a minor (no name) stream, identify the waterbody the minor stream enters.

Block 14. Proposed Project Street Address. If the proposed project is located at a site having a street address (not a box number), please enter it here.

Block 15. Location of Proposed Project. Enter the county and state where the proposed project is located. If more space is required, please attach a sheet with the necessary information marked Block 15.

Block 16. Other Location Descriptions. If available, provide the Section, Township, and Range of the site and / or the latitude and longitude. You may also provide description of the proposed project location, such as lot numbers, tract numbers, or you nay choose to locate the proposed project site from a known point (such as the right descending bank of Smith Creek, one mile downstream from the Highway 14 bridge). If a large river or stream, include the river mile of the proposed project site if known.

Block 17. Directions to the Site. Provide directions to the site from a known location or landmark. Include highway and street numbers as well as names. Also provide distances from known locations and any other information that would assist in locating the site.

Block 18. Nature of Activity. Describe the overall activity or project. Give appropriate dimensions of structures such as wingwalls, dikes (identify the materials to be used in construction, as well as the methods by which the work is to be done), or excavations (length, width, and height). Indicate whether discharge of dredged or fill material is involved. Also, identify any structure to be constructed on a fill, piles, or float-supported platforms.

The written descriptions and illustrations are an important part of the application. Please describe, in detail, what you wish to do. If more space is needed, attach an extra sheet of paper marked Block 18.

Block 19. Proposed Project Purpose. Describe the purpose and need for the proposed project. What will it be used for and why? Also include a brief description of any related activities to be developed as the result of the proposed project. Give the approximate dates you plan to both begin and complete all work.

Block 20. Reasons for Discharge. If the activity involves the discharge of dredged and/or fill material into a wetland or other waterbody, including the temporary placement of material, explain the specific purpose of the placement of the material (such as erosion control).

Block 21. Types of Material Being Discharged and the Amount of Each Type in Cubic Yards. Describe the material to be discharged and amount of each material to be discharged within Corps jurisdiction. Please be sure this description will agree with your illustrations. Discharge material includes: rock, sand, clay, concrete, etc.

Block 22. Surface Areas of Wetlands or Other Waters Filled. Describe the area to he filled at each location. Specifically identify the surface areas, or part thereof, to be filled. Also include the means by which the discharge is to be done (backhoe, dragline, etc.). If dredged material is to be discharged on an upland site, identify the site and the steps to be taken (if necessary) to prevent runoff from the dredged material back into a waterbody. If more space is needed, attach an extra sheet of paper marked Block 22.

Block 23. Is Any Portion of the Work Already Complete`? Provide any background on any part of the proposed project already completed. Describe the area already developed, structures completed, any dredged or fill material already discharged, the type of material, volume in cubic yards, acres filled, if a wetland or other waterbody (in acres or square feet). If the work was done under an existing Corps permit, identity the authorization, if possible.

Block 24. Names and Addresses of Adjoining Property Owners, Lessees, etc., Whose Property Adjoins the Project Site. List complete names and full mailing addresses of the adjacent property owners (public and private) lessees. etc., whose property adjoins the waterbody or aquatic site where the work is being proposed so that they may be notified of the proposed activity (usually by public notice). If more space is needed, attach an extra sheet of paper marked Block 24.

Information regarding adjacent landowners is usually available through the office of the tax assessor in the county or counties where the project is to be developed.

Block 25. Information about Approvals or Denials by Other Agencies. You may need the approval of other federal, state, or local agencies for your project. Identify any applications you have submitted and the status, if any (approved or denied) of each application. You need not have obtained all other permits before applying for a Corps permit.

Block 26. Signature of Applicant or Agent. The application must be signed by the owner or other authorized party (agent). This signature shall be an affirmation that the party applying for the permit possesses the requisite property rights to undertake the activity applied for (including compliance with special conditions, mitigation, etc.).

DRAWINGS AND ILLUSTRATIONS

General Information.

Three types of illustrations are needed to properly depict the work to be undertaken. These illustrations or drawings are identified as a Vicinity Map, a Plan View or a Typical Cross-Section Map. Identify each illustration with a figure or attachment number.

Please submit one original, or good quality copy, of all drawings on 8'/z x I 1 inch plain white paper (tracing paper or film may be substituted). Use the fewest number of sheets necessary for your drawings or illustrations.

Each illustration should identify the project, the applicant, and the type of illustration (vicinity map, plan view, or cross section). **While illustrations need not be professional (many small, private project illustrations are prepared by hand), they should be clear, accurate, and contain all necessary information.**

III.   OIL SPILL PREVENTION SELF-AUDIT CHECKLIST

This section contains a checklist and associated background information on the U.S. Environmental Protection Agency's (EPA) oil spill requirements for construction activities, developed under Section 311 of the Clean Water Act (CWA). If a construction site consumes, stores, transfers, or otherwise handles oils, appropriate preparation will need to be taken to prevent oil spills, and to take action in case of a spill.

For oil spill prevention and response, construction sites must follow EPA's Spill Prevention Control and Countermeasures Plan (SPCC Plan) requirement. A construction project must meet SPCC requirements if it meets the following three criteria:

1.   The site stores, uses, transfers, or otherwise handles oil;

2.   The site has a maximum aboveground storage *capacity* greater than 1,320 gallons of oil (which includes both bulk and operational storage volumes) OR total underground storage *capacity* greater than 42,000 gallons of oil; AND

3.   There is a reasonable expectation (based on location of the site) that an oil spill would reach navigable waters or adjoining shorelines of the United States.

The Background discussion following the checklist and Section V of Part I of this Guide provide more detailed information on SPCC program requirements including instructions on calculating aboveground storage volume. Attachment A to this checklist includes information on the August 2002 updates to the SPCC rule. The current compliance dates for the new rule are as follows:

• February 17, 2006: Facilities must prepare and certify (using a Professional Engineer, or P.E.) an SPCC Plan in accordance with the new SPCC rule.

• August 18, 2006: The revised SPCC Plan must be implemented.

Affected facilities that start operations between August 16, 2002 and August 18, 2006 must prepare and implement an SPCC Plan by August 18, 2006. Affected facilities that become operational after August 18, 2006 must prepare and implement an SPCC Plan before starting operations.

CHECKLIST FOR OIL SPILL REQUIREMENTS AT CONSTRUCTION ACTIVITIES

BACKGROUND INFORMATION

Name of Auditor: _____

Date of Audit: _____

Name of Project/Site: _____

There are three parts to this checklist. The first part covers the spill prevention control and countermeasure (SPCC) written requirements. The second part is a field checklist for inspecting oil storage areas. The third part is a checklist for determining whether requirements are met following an on-site oil spill.

A "notes" area is provided at the end of each section of this checklist. For every "No" answer, enter a description of the missing information and the action required to bring the site into compliance into the "notes" area.

WHAT REQUIREMENTS APPLY?

Yes	No	
		1. Does the construction site meet the following requirements?
❑	❑	Stores, uses, transfers, or otherwise handles oil.
❑	❑	Has a maximum aboveground storage capacity greater than 1,320 gallons of oil OR total underground storage capacity greater than 42,000 gallons of oil[1].
❑	❑	Reasonable expectation (based on location of site) that an oil spill would reach navigable waters or adjoining shorelines of the U.S.
		If yes to all of the above, the site must meet the requirements of EPA's SPCC program.

---

[1] The following items are exempt from SPCC calculations and requirements: completely buried tanks subject to all the technical requirements of the underground storage tank regulation (40 CFR Part 280/281), storage tanks with less than 55-gallon capacity, and permanently closed tanks.

<u>**Yes**</u>   <u>**No**</u>

❑	❑	2. Does the construction site meet the following requirements for "substantial harm" sites?
		
		    Transfers oil over water and has a total oil storage capacity of 42,000 gallons, OR
		
		    Total oil storage capacity greater than one million gallons.
		
		If yes to either of the above, the site must meet Facility Response Plan requirements. See http://www.epa.gov/oilspill/frps/index.htm.

SPCC Plan Requirements

❑	❑	3. Is the SPCC Plan up to date?
❑	❑	4. Does the SPCC Plan include a Professional Engineer certification?
❑	❑	5. Does the SPCC plan follow the format listed in the rule OR cross-reference the requirements in 40 CFR Part 112.7?
❑	❑	6. Does the SPCC plan include a site diagram that identifies the location and contents of each container (including underground storage tanks that are otherwise exempt from the SPCC requirements)?
❑	❑	7. For each container, does the SPCC Plan include the type of oil stored and storage capacity?
❑	❑	8. Does the SPCC plan include site procedures for preventing oil spills (discharge prevention measures and oil handling procedures)?
❑	❑	9. Does the SPCC Plan include oil spill predictions, including direction, flow rate, and total quantity that could be discharged as a result of a major equipment failure?
❑	❑	10. Does the SPCC Plan include site drainage?
❑	❑	11. Does the SPCC plan include site inspection documentation?
❑	❑	12. Does the SPCC Plan include site security?
❑	❑	13. Does the SPCC Plan include management approval?
❑	❑	14. Does the SPCC Plan include requirements for mobile, portable containers (e.g., totes, drums, or fuel vehicles)?
❑	❑	15. Does the SPCC plan identify secondary containment or diversionary structures?

Yes **No**

Yes	No	
❑	❑	16. Does the SPCC plan identify secondary containment for fuel transfer?
❑	❑	17. Does the SPCC plan include personnel training records and oil spill briefings?
❑	❑	18. Does the SPCC Plan include tank integrity testing?
❑	❑	19. Does the SPCC Plan include bulk storage container compliance?
❑	❑	20. Does the SPCC Plan include transfer procedures and transfer equipment information (including piping)?
❑	❑	21. If construction lasts five years, does the SPCC plan include the five-year plan review?

Meeting Oil Spill Requirements

Yes	No	
❑	❑	22. Is the site following the SPCC Plan site security procedures?
❑	❑	23. Is the site following the SPCC Plan requirements for mobile, portable containers (e.g., totes, drums, or fuel vehicles)?
❑	❑	24. Is the site following the SPCC Plan requirements for tank integrity testing?
❑	❑	25. Is the site following the SPCC Plan requirements for bulk storage container compliance?
❑	❑	26. Is the site following the SPCC Plan transfer (loading and unloading) procedures and maintaining transfer equipment (e.g., piping)?
❑	❑	27. Is the site regularly inspecting the oil storage containers to check for spills and leaks?
❑	❑	28. Is the site following the procedures outlined in the SPCC Plan to prevent oil spills?
❑	❑	29. Are the appropriate secondary containment or diversionary structures in place?
❑	❑	30. Are the secondary containment practices for fuel transfer in place?
❑	❑	31. Are all employees trained on how to prevent oil spills and what to do in the event of an oil spill?
❑	❑	32. Do the SPCC records include written inspection procedures?
❑	❑	33. Do the SPCC records include inspection reports and any corrective actions taken based on the inspection? These records must be maintained for three years.

NOTES / ACTIONS NEEDED TO BRING SITE INTO COMPLIANCE: _____

_____

_____

_____

_____

_____

_____

_____

This Page Is Intentionally Left Blank

SELF-AUDIT FIELD CHECKLIST: SPCC REQUIREMENTS

Date of Audit/Self-Audit: _____

Auditor (name, title, qualifications): _____

Name & Location of Project/Site: _____

Oil Storage Area: _____

1. Is the site following the SPCC Plan transfer (loading and unloading) procedures and maintaining transfer equipment (e.g., piping)?

Transfer Procedures and Observations:_____

_____

_____

_____

Corrective Actions Needed/Expected Completion Date:_____

_____

_____

2. Are there any spills or leaks at the oil storage containers?

Container Locations and Observations:_____

_____

_____

_____

Corrective Actions Needed/Expected Completion Date:_____

_____

_____

3. Are the appropriate secondary containment or diversionary structures in place?

Containment Locations and Observations:_____

_____

_____

_____

Corrective Actions Needed/Expected Completion Date:_____

_____

_____

4. Are the secondary containment practices for fuel transfer in place?

Containment Practices and Observations:_____

_____

_____

_____

Corrective Actions Needed/Expected Completion Date:_____

_____

_____

SELF-AUDIT CHECKLIST: SPCC REQUIREMENTS FOLLOWING AN OIL SPILL

Date of Spill: _____

Description/Location of Spill: _____

Name & Location of Project/Site: _____

Yes	No	
		1. If a spill resulting in a discharge to navigable waters or adjoining shorelines of the United States has occurred, did the site notify the following?
❑	❑	Site Emergency Coordinator and any client representatives.
❑	❑	National Response Center (1-800-424-8802) - if oil discharge meets the "sheen rule" (see Appendix A).
❑	❑	State Emergency Response Commission - if spill may potentially harm people off site.
❑	❑	Local Emergency Planning Committee or local fire department - if spill may potentially harm people off site.
❑	❑	2. If a spill has occurred, were the necessary response actions, as outlined in the SPCC Plan, performed?
❑	❑	3. Was EPA notified of any spills over 1,000 gallons or of any two spills over 42 gallons within a 12-month period?
❑	❑	4. For any reportable oil spills, did the site add a copy of the report with oil spill details to the SPCC Plan documentation? The oil spill details should include corrective actions taken, cause of discharge, and additional preventive measures taken.

NOTES / ACTIONS NEEDED TO BRING SITE INTO COMPLIANCE: _____

_____

_____

_____

_____

_____

This Page Is Intentionally Left Blank

BACKGROUND ON OIL SPILL PREVENTION REQUIREMENTS FOR CONSTRUCTION ACTIVITIES

DEFINITIONS

- **Bulk Storage Container**. Any container used to store oil. These containers are used for purposes including, but not limited to, the storage of oil prior to use, while being used, or prior to further distribution in commerce. Oil-filled electrical, operating, or manufacturing equipment is not a bulk storage container. Bulk storage containers include items such as tanks, containers, drums, and mobile or portable totes.

- **Oil.** Oil of any kind or in any form, including, but not limited to: petroleum; fuel oil; sludge; oil refuse; oil mixed with wastes other than dredged spoil; fats, oils or greases of animal, fish, or marine mammal origin; vegetable oils, including oil from seeds, nuts, fruits, or kernels; and other oils and greases, including synthetic oils and mineral oils.

- **Storage Capacity.** The shell capacity of the container (i.e., the maximum volume of the storage container used to store oil, not the actual amount of product stored in the container).

APPLICABILITY

The construction project must adhere to SPCC program requirements if it meets the following three criteria:

1. Stores, uses, transfers, or otherwise handles oil;

2. Has a maximum aboveground storage *capacity* greater than 1,320 gallons of oil (which includes both bulk and operational storage volumes) OR total underground storage *capacity* greater than 42,000 gallons of oil; AND

3. There is a reasonable expectation (based on location of the site) that an oil spill would reach navigable waters or adjoining shorelines of the United States.

CALCULATING STORAGE CAPACITY

To calculate the maximum aboveground storage capacity at the site, add together the capacity of the following:

- Aboveground oil storage tanks;

- Fuel/fluid tanks on mobile equipment; and

- Fuel/fluid tanks on other operation/construction equipment (e.g., fuel tanks on bulldozers, cranes, and backhoes).

For storage capacity calculations, do not include the following oil tanks: completely buried tanks subject to all the technical requirements of the underground storage regulation, tanks (aboveground or underground, including mobile and operation/construction equipment tanks) with storage capacity less than 55 gallons, and permanently closed tanks.

If the site's storage capacity exceeds 1,320 gallons, it must meet the SPCC requirements.

OIL SPILL REQUIREMENTS

If the site meets the storage capacity criteria, it must prepare and follow spill prevention plans to avoid oil spills into navigable waters or adjoining shorelines of the United States. The plan must identify operating procedures in place and control measures installed to prevent oil spills, and countermeasures to contain, clean up, or mitigate the effects of any oil spills that occur. The plan must be updated as conditions change at the construction site. Specific items in the SPCC plan include the following:

- Professional Engineer certification;

- For plans not following the format listed in the rule (e.g., plans developed for a combined Stormwater Pollution Prevention Plan and SPCC Plan), cross-references to the requirements in 40 CFR Part 112.7;

- Site diagram that identifies the location and contents of each container (including completely buried tanks that are otherwise exempted from the SPCC requirements);

- For each container, the type of oil stored and the storage capacity;

- Discharge prevention measures, including procedures for oil handling;

- Predictions of direction, flow rate, and total quantity of oil that could be discharged from the site as a result of a major equipment failure;

- Site drainage;

- Site inspections;

- Site security;

- Five-year plan review (if construction lasts five years);

- Management approval;

- Requirements for mobile, portable containers (e.g., totes, drums, or fuel vehicles that remain on the construction site);

- Appropriate secondary containment or diversionary structures;

- Secondary containment for fuel transfer;

- Personnel training and oil spill prevention briefings;

- Tank integrity testing;

- Bulk storage container compliance; and

- Transfer procedures and equipment (including piping).

Spill Response Requirements

If a spill occurs, the site must follow the spill response procedures outlined in the SPCC Plan. These procedures should include identifying the spilled material, preventing (or restricting) additional leaks from the container, confining the spill area with absorbent materials or dikes, beginning cleanup (remediation and decontamination) of the spill areas, and notifying all of the appropriate parties.

In the event of an oil spill, the construction site Emergency Coordinator and any client representatives should be notified. If the oil spill results in a discharge, the National Response Center must be notified at 1-800-424-8802. 40 CFR Part 110 defines an oil discharge as a quantity that:

- Violates applicable water quality standards;

- Causes a film or "sheen" upon, or discoloration of, the surface water or adjoining shorelines; or

- Causes a sludge or emulsion to be deposited beneath the surface of the water or upon adjoining shorelines.

This is referred to as the "sheen rule." If the oil spill has the potential to harm people off site, the State Emergency Response Commission and Local Emergency Planning Committee (or local fire department) must also be notified.

Facility Response Plans

In addition to SPCC requirements, the Clean Water Act/Oil Pollution Act (CWA/OPA) requires Facility Response Plans for "substantial harm" sites. Substantial harm sites include:

- Sites that transfer oil over water AND have a total oil storage capacity of 42,000 gallons or more; or

- Sites with a total oil storage capacity greater than one million gallons.

Construction sites are not expected to meet the definition of "substantial harm"; however, if the site does meet one of the definitions above, the Facility Response Plan requirements should be reviewed at http://www.epa.gov/oilspill/frps/index.htm.

Attachment A. August 2002 Update of the SPCC Rule

This attachment highlights how the August 2002 update of the SPCC rule may affect the construction site.

What Are the Major Changes to the SPCC Rule?

- Individual aboveground tanks with storage capacity greater than 660 gallons of oil are no longer regulated unless the total site capacity is greater than 1,320 gallons of oil.

- The following are exempt from the storage capacity calculations and SPCC requirements:

    — Completely buried storage tanks subject to all of the technical requirements of the underground storage tank (UST) regulations (40 CFR Parts 280 or 281), and

    — Tanks with a storage capacity of 55 gallons or less.

- Sites do not need to report oil spills to EPA unless the site has:

    — Two discharges (over 42 gallons) in any 12-month period, or
    — A single discharge of more than 1,000 gallons.

- The rule allows deviations from most provisions (with the exception of secondary containment requirements) when equivalent environmental protection is provided.

- The rule provides for a flexible plan format, but requires a **cross-reference** showing that all regulatory requirements are met.

- The rule clarifies applicability to the storage and operational use of oil.

When Do I Need to Meet the New SPCC Rule Requirements?

On July 16, 2002, EPA promulgated a revised final SPCC regulation, which became effective August 17, 2002. EPA subsequently extended the regulatory compliance schedule included in the new SPCC rule.

The current compliance dates for the new rule are as follows:

- February 17, 2006: Facilities must prepare and certify (using a Professional Engineer, or P.E.) an SPCC Plan in accordance with the new SPCC rule.

- August 18, 2006: The revised SPCC Plan must be implemented.

Affected facilities that start operations between August 16, 2002 and August 18, 2006 must prepare and implement an SPCC Plan by August 18, 2006. Affected facilities that become operational after August 18, 2006 must prepare and implement an SPCC Plan before starting operations.

IV.   HAZARDOUS WASTE SELF-AUDIT CHECKLIST

This section contains a checklist and associated background information on the U.S. Environmental Protection Agency's (EPA) hazardous waste requirements for construction projects. Hazardous wastes are regulated under Subtitle C of the Resource Conservation and Recovery Act (RCRA), 40 CFR Parts 260 - 279. EPA may authorize states to take the lead on RCRA Subtitle C programs. EPA also authorizes states to establish regulatory programs for solid wastes, using federal guidelines provided in Subtitle D of RCRA. In addition, states regulate construction and demolition (C&D) debris.

This document includes a checklist for Subtitle C requirements for generators of **hazardous waste**. Operators of construction projects can use the checklist to identify who will be responsible for addressing each requirement, and to conduct a self-audit of their construction site. The checklist also can be used by compliance inspectors to conduct an inspection of a construction project.

Construction projects may be subject to state or local regulations under RCRA Subtitle C. Check with the EPA Region or state in which the construction project is located to determine the hazardous and non-hazardous solid waste handling requirements that apply to the site.

Background information on federal hazardous waste requirements follows the checklist. Attachment A provides a list of materials at construction sites that may be covered by the RCRA Subtitle C requirements. Attachment B lists exclusions for hazardous wastes. Attachment C includes a list of the hazardous wastes regulated by RCRA Subtitle C.

This checklist applies to hazardous waste requirements only. For non-hazardous solid waste and construction and demolition waste requirements, check with the state or local regulatory agency.

Section VI in Part I of this guide contains a more detailed discussion on hazardous and non-hazardous solid waste requirements.

CHECKLIST FOR HAZARDOUS WASTE REQUIREMENTS FOR CONSTRUCTION PROJECTS

BACKGROUND INFORMATION

Name of Auditor: _____
Date of Audit: _____
Name of Project/Site: _____

There are three parts to this checklist. The first part covers identifying hazardous waste, determining generator size, and meeting the hazardous waste storage requirements. The second part is a field checklist for inspecting hazardous waste storage areas. The last part is a field checklist for transporting hazardous waste.

A "notes" area is provided at the end of each section of this checklist. For every "No" answer, enter a description of the missing information and the action required to bring the site into compliance in the "notes" area.

IDENTIFYING HAZARDOUS WASTES (40 CFR Part 261)

Photocopy this page as many times as necessary to capture information on each of the hazardous wastes present at the site.

Name of Material/Waste: _____

Yes	No	
❏	❏	1. Is the material a solid waste (for RCRA Subtitle C purposes) - see the definition in *Background* (following the checklist)?
❏	❏	2. Is the material excluded from the definition of solid waste or hazardous waste - see Attachment B? If yes, the state should be contacted for any applicable requirements. *State Contact*: _____ *Applicable Requirements*: _____
❏	❏	3. Is the material a listed or characteristic hazardous waste - see Attachment C?
❏	❏	4. Is the waste a universal waste (i.e., hazardous waste batteries, hazardous waste pesticides (either recalled or collected through waste pesticide collection programs), hazardous waste thermostats, and hazardous waste lamps)? Specific RCRA requirements apply to these wastes.

REQUIREMENTS FOR HAZARDOUS WASTE GENERATORS (40 CFR Part 262)

Yes	No	
❏	❏	5. Does the site generate ≤100 kilograms (220 pounds) of hazardous waste per month and store ≤1,000 kilograms (2,200 pounds) of hazardous waste? If yes, the site is a **Conditionally Exempt Small Quantity Generator** (CESQG) and should answer the applicable questions below. *Note: Some state hazardous waste management regulations do not recognize this generator status.*
❏	❏	6. Does the site generate between 100 and 1,000 kilograms (220 - 2,200 pounds) of hazardous waste per month and store ≤6,000 kilograms (13,200 pounds) of hazardous waste? If yes, the site is a **Small Quantity Generator** (SQG) and should answer the applicable questions below.
❏	❏	7. Does the site generate 1,000 kilograms (2,200 pounds) or more of hazardous waste per month OR store more than 6,000 kilograms (13,200 pounds) of hazardous waste? If yes, the site is a **Large Quantity Generator** (LQG) and should answer the applicable questions below.

Conditionally Exempt Small Quantity Generators (CESQG)

CESQGs are exempt from requirements listed in 40 CFR Parts 262 through 270 if they meet the requirements in 40 CFR Part 261.5.

Yes	No	
❏	❏	8. Did the site get an EPA Identification Number (i.e., a RCRA Hazardous Waste Generator Number)[1]? *EPA Identification Number (if applicable):* _____
❏	❏	9. Is the waste properly accumulated in containers or tanks[1]?
❏	❏	10. Are the hazardous waste containers closed, marked as "Hazardous Waste," and marked with the date when accumulation began[1]?
❏	❏	11. Does the site have specified emergency responses[1]?
❏	❏	12. Is the site's basic safety information readily accessible[1]?
❏	❏	13. Are site personnel familiar with proper handing of hazardous waste and site emergency procedures[1]?
❏	❏	14. Does the site store greater than 2,200 pounds of hazardous waste? If yes, the site must start meeting the requirements for SQGs (see the checklist below).

---

[1]This is an optional federal requirement (40 CFR Part 261.5), but may be required by the state.

Yes   No

		Small Quantity Generators (SQG)
❑	❑	15. Did the site get an EPA Identification Number (i.e., a RCRA Hazardous Waste Generator Number)? *EPA Identification Number (if applicable):* _____
❑	❑	16. Is the waste properly accumulated in containers or tanks (*also see the Self-Audit Field Checklist: RCRA Waste Storage Areas*)?
❑	❑	17. Are the hazardous waste containers closed, marked as "Hazardous Waste," and marked with the date when accumulation began (*also see the Self-Audit Field Checklist: RCRA Waste Storage Areas*)?
❑	❑	18. Does the site have specified emergency responses? (Note: a written contingency plan is not required.)
❑	❑	19. Is the site's basic safety information readily accessible?
❑	❑	20. Are site personnel familiar with proper handing of hazardous waste and site emergency procedures?
❑	❑	21. Does the site store hazardous waste for longer than 180 days? If yes, a RCRA permit is required (see 40 CFR Part 270).
❑	❑	22. If stored for less than 180 days, does the site have documentation showing the waste was shipped off site within 180 days?
		Large Quantity Generators (LQG)
❑	❑	23. Did the site get an EPA Identification Number (i.e., a RCRA Hazardous Waste Generator Number)? *EPA Identification Number (if applicable):* _____
❑	❑	24. Is the waste properly accumulated in containers, tanks, drip pads, or containment buildings (*also see the Self-Audit Field Checklist: RCRA Waste Storage Areas*)?
❑	❑	25. Are the hazardous waste containers closed, marked as "Hazardous Waste," and marked with the date when accumulation began (*also see the Self-Audit Field Checklist: RCRA Waste Storage Areas*)?

<u>Yes</u>   <u>No</u>

❏	❏	26. Does the site store hazardous waste for longer than 90 days? If yes, a RCRA permit is required (see 40 CFR Part 270).
❏	❏	27. If stored for less than 90 days, does the site have documentation showing the waste was shipped off site within 90 days?
❏	❏	28. Does the site have an established personnel training program to educate workers on the proper handling of hazardous waste?
❏	❏	29. Were the state and local authorities contacted to identify any additional requirements for LQGs? *Contact Name/Department*: _____ *Date Contacted*: _____

RCRA Waste Storage Requirements (LQG & SQG)

❏	❏	30. Is there a secure location to store the hazardous waste containers? *Location(s)*: _____
❏	❏	31. Do site personnel perform weekly inspections of the hazardous waste containers?
❏	❏	32. Does the site have secondary containment around the hazardous waste storage area (*also see the Self-Audit Field Checklist: RCRA Waste Storage Areas)*?
❏	❏	33. Does the site have fire suppression equipment in the hazardous waste storage area (*also see the Self-Audit Field Checklist: RCRA Waste Storage Areas)*?
❏	❏	34. Does the site have radio or telephone communication available in the hazardous waste storage area (*also see the Self-Audit Field Checklist: RCRA Waste Storage Areas)*?
❏	❏	35. Is an emergency coordinator on site or on call at all times? *Emergency Coordinator(s)*: _____ _____ *How to Contact*: _____

NOTES / ACTIONS NEEDED TO BRING SITE INTO COMPLIANCE: _____

_____

_____

_____

_____

_____

_____

_____

SELF-AUDIT FIELD CHECKLIST: RCRA WASTE STORAGE AREAS

Date of Audit/Self-Audit: _____

Auditor (name, title, qualifications): _____

Name & Location of Project/Site: _____

Name of Hazardous Waste Storage Area: _____

1. Is the waste properly accumulated in containers, tanks, drip pads, or containment buildings?

Accumulation Areas and Observations:_____

_____

_____

_____

Corrective Actions Needed/Expected Completion Date:_____

_____

_____

2. Are the hazardous waste containers closed, marked as "Hazardous Waste," and marked with the date when accumulation began?

Accumulation Areas and Observations:_____

_____

_____

_____

Corrective Actions Needed/Expected Completion Date:_____

_____

_____

3. Is adequate secondary containment in place?

Accumulation Areas and Observations:_____

_____

_____

Corrective Actions Needed/Expected Completion Date:_____

_____

_____

4. Is fire suppression equipment available and working in the storage area?

Accumulation Areas and Observations:_____

_____

_____

Corrective Actions Needed/Expected Completion Date:_____

_____

_____

5. Is the radio or telephone communication available and working in the storage area?

Accumulation Areas and Observations:_____

_____

_____

Corrective Actions Needed/Expected Completion Date:_____

_____

_____

SELF-AUDIT FIELD CHECKLIST: TRANSPORTING HAZARDOUS WASTES

Date of Transport: _____

Auditor (name, title, qualifications): _____

Name & Location of Project/Site: _____

Type/Name Hazardous Waste: _____

Yes	No	
		Preparation for Transport (LQG, SQG, & CESQG)
❑	❑	1. Is the site using a licensed hazardous waste hauler for transport? *Hauler Name*: _____ *License Information*: _____
❑	❑	2. Has the site properly packaged the hazardous waste to prevent leakage by following Department of Transportation (DOT) requirements?
❑	❑	3. Is the hazardous waste properly labeled and marked?
❑	❑	4. Does the transporter have the proper placards to identify the characteristics and dangers associated with the waste?
❑	❑	5. Has the site completed and signed the Uniform Hazardous Waste Manifest? (See checklist below.)

Uniform Hazardous Waste Manifest Requirements
(EPA Form 8700-22, Appendix to 40 CFR Part 262)
Note this is an optional federal requirement for CESQGs, but may be required by the state.

Yes	No	
❑	❑	6. Does the manifest include the name, address, and EPA ID number of the hazardous waste generator (the site), transporter, and designated treatment, storage, and disposal facility (TSDF)?
❑	❑	7. Does the manifest include a description of the waste's hazards as required by DOT rules?
❑	❑	8. Did the site provide the quantities of the waste being transported and the types of containers?
❑	❑	9. Did the site complete the certification?

Yes	**No**	
❑	❑	10. Did the site receive a copy of the signed and dated manifest from the designated TSDF (within 45 days of shipment for LQG or within 60 days for SQG)? If no, did the site submit an "exception report" to EPA and the state? *Date of Exception Report Submittal (if applicable):* _____

NOTES / ACTIONS NEEDED TO BRING SITE INTO COMPLIANCE: _____

_____

_____

_____

_____

_____

_____

_____

BACKGROUND ON HAZARDOUS WASTE REQUIREMENTS
FOR CONSTRUCTION PROJECTS

DEFINITIONS

- **Construction and Demolition (C&D) Debris.** Waste material that is produced in the process of construction, renovation, or demolition of structures. Structures include buildings of all types (both residential and nonresidential), roads, and bridges. Materials considered C&D debris include concrete, asphalt, wood, metals, gypsum wall board, and roofing.

- **Disposal.** The discharge, deposit, injection, dumping, spilling, leaking, or placing of any solid waste or hazardous waste into or on any land or water so that such solid waste or hazardous waste or any constituent may enter the environment (e.g., emitted into the air or discharged into any waters, including ground water).

- **Generator.** Any person, by site, whose act or process produces hazardous waste identified or listed in Part 261 (i.e., RCRA Subtitle C) or whose act first causes a hazardous waste to become subject to regulation. Note that the generator may not necessarily produce the waste. Generators fall under three size classes: 1) large quantity generators (LQG); 2) small quantity generators (SQG); and 3) conditionally exempt small quantity generators (CESQG). Most construction activities are considered conditionally exempt small quantity generators.

  CESQGs generate:

  — ≤ 220 pounds of hazardous waste per month,
  — ≤ 2.2 pounds of acute hazardous waste, or
  — ≤ 220 pounds of contaminated soil, waste, or debris from the cleanup of an acute hazardous waste spill.

  Acute hazardous wastes are denoted with the hazard code "H" or are P-listed wastes.

  SQGs generate between 220 and 2,200 pounds of hazardous waste per month.

  LQGs generate:

  — ≥ 2,200 pounds of hazardous waste per month,

  — > 2.2 pounds of acute hazardous waste per month, or

—   > 220 pounds of contaminated soil, waste, or debris from the cleanup of an acute hazardous waste spill.

• **Hazardous Waste.** A solid waste, or combination of solid wastes, which because of its quantity, concentration, or physical, chemical, or infectious characteristics may either cause, or significantly contribute to an increase in mortality or an increase in serious irreversible or incapacitating reversible illness; or pose a substantial present or potential hazard to human health or the environment when improperly treated, stored, transported, or disposed of, or otherwise managed.

• **Hazardous Waste Management.** The systematic control of the collection, source separation, storage, transportation, processing, treatment, recovery, and disposal of hazardous wastes.

• **Solid Waste under RCRA Subtitle C.** Discarded material by being either:

—   Abandoned (i.e., disposed of, burned, or incinerated),

—   Inherently waste-like (i.e., materials that pose a threat to human health and the environment, such as certain dioxin-containing wastes),

—   Military munition, or

—   Recycled (e.g., accumulated for speculative recycle).

• **Solid Waste under RCRA Subtitle D.** Any garbage; refuse; sludge from a waste treatment plant, water supply treatment plant, or air pollution control facility; nonhazardous industrial wastes; and other discarded material including solid, liquid, semisolid, or contained gaseous material resulting from industrial, commercial, mining, agricultural, and community activities.

• **Storage.** When used in connection with hazardous waste, means the containment of hazardous waste, either on a temporary basis or for a period of years, in such a manner as not to constitute disposal of such hazardous waste.

• **Treatment.** When used in connection with hazardous waste, means any method, technique, or process, including neutralization, designed to change the physical, chemical, or biological character or composition of any hazardous waste so as to neutralize such waste or to render such waste nonhazardous, safer for transport, amenable for recovery, amenable for storage, or reduced in volume. This includes any activity or processing designed to change the physical form or chemical composition of hazardous waste so as to render it nonhazardous.

APPLICABILITY

RCRA Subtitle C applies to:

- Generators of hazardous waste;

- Transporters of hazardous waste; and

- Treatment, storage, and disposal facilities for hazardous waste (typically not applicable to construction sites).

RCRA Subtitle C requirements do not apply to CESQGs except for ensuring proper disposal of hazardous wastes and getting a RCRA permit for storage of more than 2,200 pounds of hazardous wastes. Note that states may regulate hazardous wastes differently. For example, some states require CESQGs to meet the same requirements as small quantity generators. Therefore, the state environmental department should be contacted to determine the site's hazardous waste requirements.

RCRA Subtitle D provides guidelines for states to develop their own solid waste programs. These can vary from state to state; therefore, the state should be contacted for the applicable requirements (e.g., recycling standards, types of wastes prohibited from disposal in RCRA Subtitle D landfills).

RCRA SUBTITLE C REQUIREMENTS

RCRA Subtitle C has several requirements:

- Preliminary notification to EPA of the generation, transportation, treatment, storage, or disposal of hazardous waste. Notify EPA within 90 days of this activity. The notification includes site location, description of construction activity, and the hazardous waste being handled. The notification form and instructions can be found on line at: http://www.epa.gov/epaoswer/ hazwaste/notify/notiform.pdf and http://www.epa.gov/epaoswer/hazwaste/ notify/noti-ins.pdf.

- EPA may require owners/operators of a construction site to perform monitoring, analysis, and testing if there is a substantial hazard to human health or the environment. For example, if waste containers are uncovered during construction activities, the site may need to analyze the waste to determine the extent of the hazard.

• Large and small quantity generators must perform the following:

— Identify and determine the amount of hazardous waste generated each month (this determines generator status),

— Get an EPA identification (ID) number,

— Comply with accumulation and storage requirements (including training, contingency planning, and emergency arrangements),

— Prepare waste for transportation,

— Track the shipment and receipt of such waste, and

— Meet recordkeeping and reporting requirements.

• A treatment, storage, and disposal facility (TSDF) permit is required if the site stores hazardous waste:

— Greater than 90 days for large quantity generators,

— Greater than 180 days for small quantity generators, and

— In quantities of 2,200 pounds or more for conditionally exempt small quantity generators.

• Conditionally exempt small quantity generators are only required to perform the following:

— Identify hazardous waste,
— Comply with storage limit requirements, and
— Ensure proper hazardous waste treatment or disposal (on site or off site).

• Transporters of hazardous waste must follow recordkeeping, labeling, manifest, and transportation requirements.

• Sites cannot apply waste, used oil, or any other contaminated material as a dust suppressant.

- Sites cannot perform underground injection of hazardous wastes into any drinking water source.

Attachment A. Potential Hazardous Wastes at Construction Sites (RCRA Subtitle C)

- Ignitable wastes (flashpoint of less than 140 degrees) such as paint thinners, paints, paint and varnish strippers, epoxy resins, adhesives degreasers, and spent cleaning solvents.

- Corrosive wastes (acids with pH less than 2 or bases with pH greater than 12.5) such as rust removers, cleaning fluids, and battery acids.

- Reactive wastes (can explode or violently react) such as cyanide, plating waste, bleaches, waste oxidizers.

- Toxic wastes (meeting certain concentrations) such as materials containing metals (e.g., mercury, cadmium, or lead) or solvents (e.g., carbon tetrachloride or methyl ethyl ketone). Materials may include adhesives, paints, coatings, polishes, varnishes, thinners, and treated woods.

- Spent solvents listed under RCRA (hazardous waste code F).

- Discarded commercial chemical products containing listed chemicals under RCRA (hazardous waste codes P and U).

- Mercury-containing wastes (e.g., fluorescent bulbs, broken mercury switches, batteries, or thermostats).

- Lead-based paints (note that lead-based paint debris from homes and residences is not covered by hazardous waste requirements).

- Used oil and hydraulic fluid.

- Soil contaminated with toxic or hazardous pollutants.

To identify hazardous wastes at the construction site:

— Refer to the RCRA regulations at 40 CFR Part 261,

— Review the list of commonly reported hazardous wastes in EPA's *Notification of Regulated Waste Activities: Instructions and Forms* (available on-line at http://www.epa.gov/epaoswer/hazwaste/data/ form8700/8700-12.pdf), and

—   Contact the state or EPA Region for assistance (EPA's *Notification of Regulated Waste Activities: Instructions and Forms* includes a list of state contacts).

Attachment B. RCRA Subtitle C Hazardous Waste Exclusions

RCRA Subtitle C hazardous waste exclusions applicable to the construction industry include:

Exclusions from the definition of solid waste. Hazardous wastes must meet the definition of solid wastes. Exclusions applicable to the construction industry include the following:

- Radioactive waste;
- Spent sulfuric acid;
- Spent wood preservatives;
- Fuels comparable to pure or virgin fuels;
- Processed scrap metal;
- Shredded circuit boards; and
- Zinc fertilizers made from recycled hazardous secondary materials.

Exclusions from the definition of hazardous waste. Exclusions applicable to the construction industry include the following:

- Household hazardous waste;
- Wood treated with arsenic;
- Petroleum-contaminated media and debris from underground storage tanks;
- Spent chlorofluorocarbon refrigerants; and
- Used oil filters.

Exclusions for waste generated in raw material, product storage, or manufacturing units. This exclusion applies while the waste remains in the unit (e.g., tanks, vehicles). This exclusion does **not** apply to surface impoundments. Once the unit temporarily or permanently ceases operation for 90 days, the waste is considered generated and subject to RCRA Subtitle C provisions.

Exclusions for laboratory samples and waste treatability study samples. These samples are small, discrete amounts of hazardous waste that are essential to ensure accurate characterization and proper treatment of hazardous wastes.

Exclusions for dredged material regulated under the Marine Protection Research and Sanctuaries Act of the Clean Water Act (CWA). Dredge materials subject to Section 404 of the CWA or Section 103 of the Marine Protection, Research, and Sanctuaries Act are excluded from the definition of hazardous waste.

Exclusion for Lead-Based Paint Debris from Homes and Residences. EPA classifies lead-based paint debris generated by contractors in households as "household waste" and excludes this debris from RCRA Subtitle C hazardous waste regulations.

Attachment C. Hazardous Wastes Regulated Under RCRA Subtitle C

Characteristic Wastes

1.   *Ignitable waste.* Waste having one of the following properties:

   - Liquid, other than an aqueous solution containing less than 24 percent alcohol by volume, with a flash point of less than 60°C (140 °F);

   - Not a liquid and is capable, under standard temperature and pressure, of causing fire through friction, absorption of moisture or spontaneous chemical changes and, when ignited, burns so vigorously and persistently that it creates a hazard;

   - Ignitable compressed gas; or

   - An oxidizer.

2.   *Corrosive waste.* Waste having one of the following properties:

   - Aqueous solution with pH < 2 or pH >12.5; or

   - Liquid that corrodes steel at a rate of > 6.35 millimeters (0.250 inch) per year at a test temperature of 55 °C (130 °F).

3.   *Reactive waste.* Waste having one of the following properties:

   - Can explode or violently react when exposed to water or under normal handling conditions;

   - Can create toxic fumes or gases when exposed to water or under normal handling conditions;

   - Meets the criteria for classification as an explosive under DOT rules; or

   - Generates toxic levels of sulfide or cyanide gas when exposed to a pH range of 2 through 12.5.

4.   *Toxic waste.* Waste where the listed toxic chemical concentration exceeds the regulatory level when sampled using the Toxicity Characteristic Leaching Procedure (TCLP). The following table lists wastes (and potential toxic chemicals) that may be generated at

construction sites and the corresponding hazardous waste regulatory level. See 40 CFR Part 261.24 for a complete list of toxic chemicals and their regulatory level.

Construction Waste	Potential Toxic Pollutant	Regulatory Level (mg/L) (a)	EPA Hazardous Waste Number
Painting operation waste	Chromium	5.0	D007
	Lead	5.0	D008
Cleaning fluids	Carbon tetrachloride	0.5	D019
	Methyl ethyl ketone (MEK)	200.0	D035
Contaminated soil	*depends on the site*		

(a) If the waste generated has any toxic chemical exceeding the regulatory level, the waste must be handled as a RCRA Subtitle C regulated hazardous waste.

Listed Wastes

1. *The F List*. Wastes from nonspecific sources. Potential F List wastes for construction sites are spent solvent wastes and dioxin-bearing wastes.

2. *The K List*. Wastes from specific sources. Not applicable to construction sites.

3. *The P List*. Discarded commercial chemical products. The waste must contain one of the chemicals on the P List and the chemical in the waste must be unused and in the form of a commercial chemical product (i.e., either 100 percent pure, technical (or commercial) grade, or the sole active ingredient in a chemical formulation).

4. *The U List*. Discarded commercial chemical products. The waste must contain one of the chemicals on the U List and the chemical in the waste must be unused and in the form of a commercial chemical product (i.e., either 100 percent pure, technical (or commercial) grade, or the sole active ingredient in a chemical formulation).

The complete list of RCRA-listed wastes can be found in 40 CFR Part 261 Subpart D, which can be found electronically at http://ecfr.gpoaccess.gov/ under "Title 40 - Protection of Environment."

This Page Is Intentionally Left Blank

V.   HAZARDOUS SUBSTANCES (SUPERFUND LIABILITY) SELF-AUDIT CHECKLIST

This section contains a checklist and associated background information on the U.S. Environmental Protection Agency's (EPA) hazardous substance requirements. These requirements fall under the Comprehensive Environmental Response, Compensation, and Liability Act (CERCLA, also known as "Superfund") and the Emergency Planning and Community Right-to-Know Act (EPCRA). The requirements of Superfund and EPCRA include emergency planning and release reporting requirements.

The construction site may be affected by Superfund if:

- The site is listed on the National Priorities List (NPL);

- The site is a brownfield site;

- Soil, surface water, or groundwater tests indicate the presence of a hazardous substance, as defined by CERCLA; or

- A hazardous substance, as defined by CERCLA, is discovered during construction or demolition activities.

If the site meets any of the above, site personnel should work with EPA to clean up any hazardous substances. If site personnel discover a hazardous substance at the site, they must notify the National Response Center (1-800-424-8802).

If a CERCLA-listed hazardous substance is released, the site may be subject to reporting requirements. Notify the National Response Center (1-800-424-8802) when there is a hazardous substance release in an amount equal to or greater than the reportable quantity for that substance (CERCLA Section 103(a)).

The construction site may be affected by EPCRA emergency planning requirements if it stores an extremely hazardous substance (EHS) as defined by EPCRA, or any substance regulated by state or local authorities, and stores the substance above the designated Threshold Planning Quantity, which varies by substance. Planning requirements include providing information to State Emergency Response Commissions (SERC) and Local Emergency Planning Committees (LERC).

If a hazardous substance (defined by EPCRA) or an EHS release occurs, the site may be subject to reporting requirements under EPCRA Section 304. However, EPA has found that most construction sites do not produce, use, or store EPCRA-listed hazardous substances or EHS and are not subject to the requirements of EPCRA. Therefore, this guide provides only a brief discussion and checklist on EPCRA requirements.

The list of hazardous substances subject to CERCLA and EPCRA reporting requirements (and the respective reportable quantities) can be found in EPA's *Consolidated List of Chemicals Subject to the Emergency Planning and Community Right-To-Know Act (EPCRA) and Section 112(r) of the Clean Air Act* (EPA 550-B-01-003, http://yosemite.epa.gov/oswer/ceppoweb.nsf/vwResourcesByFilename/title3.pdf/$File/title3.pdf).

Section VII in Part 1 of this guide and the Background section following the checklist provide more details on the Superfund and EPCRA program requirements.

CHECKLIST OF SUPERFUND REQUIREMENTS FOR CONSTRUCTION ACTIVITIES

BACKGROUND INFORMATION

Name of Auditor: _____

Date of Audit: _____

Name of Project/Site: _____

A "notes" area is provided at the end of each section of this checklist. For every "No" answer, enter a description of the missing information and the action required to bring the site into compliance in the "notes" area.

PRE-PLANNING ISSUES/APPLICABILITY

Yes	No	
❑	❑	1. Prior to bidding on a construction project, was the site researched to determine if it is a Superfund site or National Priorities List (NPL) site? EPA's database is located at: http://cfpub.epa.gov/supercpad/cursites/srchsites.cfm.
❑	❑	2. Was a historical review of the construction site conducted to determine the possible presence of hazardous substances? The review should include the following: Historical records to determine site's previous uses. Historical aerial photographs to identify potential areas of contamination. State/local files to identify past environmental concerns.
❑	❑	3. If the site is a Superfund or brownfield property, was it determined whether there are specific issues associated with the site (e.g., are there ongoing or remaining cleanup or long-term maintenance obligations associated with the site)?
❑	❑	4. Have any hazardous substances been discovered during construction or demolition activities?
❑	❑	5. If hazardous substances are suspected, was the soil, surface water, or groundwater sampled and analyzed?

NOTES / ACTIONS NEEDED TO BRING SITE INTO COMPLIANCE: _____

_____

_____

_____

_____

_____

_____

_____

SUPERFUND REQUIREMENTS

Yes	No	
		Brownfield Requirements
❑	❑	6. Did the site follow the steps of the Brownfields Program if the construction site is a brownfield site? More information is available at the following web site: http://www.epa.gov/swerosps/bf/index.html.
		If a Hazardous Substance Is Found at the Site
❑	❑	7. Was the National Response Center (1-800-424-8802) contacted?
❑	❑	8. Did the site coordinate with EPA regarding any necessary site cleanup activities?
❑	❑	9. Did the site properly handle, store, transport, and dispose of the discovered (i.e., generated) waste?
❑	❑	10. Are the documents/records containing hazardous substance information maintained?
		If a Hazardous Substance Is Released at the Site
❑	❑	11. Did the amount of hazardous substance released meet or exceed the reportable quantity (RQ)?

Yes	No	
		12. If the RQ has been met, did the site notify the:
❏	❏	National Response Center (1-800-424-8802)?
❏	❏	State Emergency Response Commission - if the release may potentially affect off-site persons?
❏	❏	Local Emergency Planning Committee - if the release may potentially affect off-site persons?
❏	❏	13. Did the site properly clean up the release (or arrange for proper cleanup)?
❏	❏	14. Did the site provide notice in local newspapers serving the affected area?
❏	❏	15. Are the documents/records about the hazardous substance release maintained?

NOTES / ACTIONS NEEDED TO BRING SITE INTO COMPLIANCE: _____

_____

_____

_____

_____

_____

_____

_____

This Page Is Intentionally Left Blank

CHECKLIST OF EPCRA REQUIREMENTS FOR CONSTRUCTION ACTIVITIES

BACKGROUND INFORMATION

Name of Auditor: _____
Date of Audit: _____
Name of Project/Site: _____

Yes	No	
❑	❑	1. Does the site produce, use, or store hazardous substances or extremely hazardous substances (EHS), as defined by EPCRA?
❑	❑	2. If the site produces, uses, or stores hazardous substances or EHS, was the information provided to the State Emergency Response Commission (SERC) and Local Emergency Planning Committee (LEPC) for planning purposes?
❑	❑	3. If a hazardous substance release occurred, did the release meet the reportable quantity and have the potential to affect off-site persons? If yes, were the SERC and LEPC notified?
❑	❑	4. If a release has occurred, were the necessary response actions performed?
❑	❑	5. Are the documents/records about the hazardous substance release maintained?

NOTES / ACTIONS NEEDED TO BRING SITE INTO COMPLIANCE: _____

_____

_____

_____

_____

_____

_____

This Page Is Intentionally Left Blank

BACKGROUND ON HAZARDOUS SUBSTANCES REQUIREMENTS FOR CONSTRUCTION ACTIVITIES

DEFINITIONS

- **Brownfield.** A property where any expansion, redevelopment, or reuse may be complicated by the presence or potential presence of a hazardous substance, pollutant, or contaminant, not including sites that are part of a planned or ongoing removal action or are on the National Priorities List.

- **Extremely Hazardous Substances (EHSs).** Chemicals that most likely induce serious acute reactions following short-term airborne exposure (defined at 40 CFR Part 355). The list of extremely hazardous substances subject to EPCRA reporting requirements can be found in EPA's *Consolidated List of Chemicals Subject to the Emergency Planning and Community Right-To-Know Act (EPCRA) and Section 112(r) of the Clean Air Act* (EPA 550-B-01-003). Note that an extremely hazardous substance may also be included in the CERCLA list of hazardous substances.

- **Hazardous Substances.** Defined in CERCLA Section 101(14) and includes hazardous air pollutants (designated in Section 112(b) of the Clean Air Act), radionuclides, toxic pollutants (designated in Section 307(a) of the Clean Water Act), elements and compounds that present an imminent danger to public health when discharged into waters of the United States (designated in Section 311(b)(2)(A) of the Clean Water Act), TSCA substance that EPA has taken action against (currently none), RCRA-listed hazardous wastes and characteristic wastes. The list of hazardous substances subject to CERCLA and EPCRA reporting requirements can be found in EPA's *Consolidated List of Chemicals Subject to the Emergency Planning and Community Right-To-Know Act (EPCRA) and Section 112(r) of the Clean Air Act* (EPA 550-B-01-003). Certain substances are excluded from CERCLA and/or EPCRA reporting requirements.

- **National Priorities List (NPL).** The list of national priorities among the known releases or threatened releases of hazardous substances, pollutants, or contaminants throughout the United States and its territories. The NPL is intended primarily to guide EPA in determining which sites warrant further investigation.

- **Release.** Any spilling, leaking, pumping, pouring, emitting, emptying, discharging, injecting, escaping, leaching, dumping, or disposing into the environment, including abandonment or discarding of barrels, containers, and other closed receptacles containing any hazardous substance.

- **Reportable Quantity.** Amount of hazardous substance (or extremely hazardous substance) released into the environment within a 24-hour period that must be met or exceeded before emergency release notification requirements are triggered. Reportable quantities are listed in EPA's *Consolidated List of Chemicals Subject to the Emergency Planning and Community Right-To-Know Act (EPCRA) and Section 112(r) of the Clean Air Act* (EPA 550-B-01-003).

SUPERFUND APPLICABILITY

The construction site may be affected by Superfund and federal cleanup activities if it is a brownfield site, listed on the NPL, or CERCLA-defined hazardous substances are present at the site. If a CERCLA-listed hazardous substance is discovered during construction/demolition activities or based on soil, air, or water test results, the National Response Center (1-800-424-8802) must be notified.

If a hazardous substance is released into the environment, the site may be subject to reporting requirements. Notify the National Response Center (1-800-424-8802) when there is a hazardous substance release in an amount equal to or greater than the reportable quantity for that substance (CERCLA Section 103(a)). Depending on the substance, the reportable quantity may be 1, 10, 100, 1,000, or 5,000 pounds within a 24-hour period.

EPA uses these notifications to identify sites that require federal response (i.e., cleanup). CERCLA was originally enacted to address hazardous substances at inactive or abandoned sites. The Superfund program is administered by EPA in cooperation with individual states and tribal governments. The program includes a revolving Trust Fund used by EPA and other agencies to clean up hazardous waste sites where no responsible party can be identified. Site personnel should work with EPA to clean up any discovered or released hazardous substances.

Responsibility for the cleanup of hazardous waste usually falls on the "generator" (i.e., person whose activity first produces the waste). However, if soils containing a hazardous substance (e.g., waste pesticides) are excavated or spread, site personnel may be responsible under CERCLA as an operator, arranger, or transporter. For example:

- Site personnel may be an operator if they spread soil that contains a hazardous substance on the land.

- Site personnel may be an arranger if they dispose of a hazardous substance or arrange to have it removed from the construction site. For example, if soil that contains pollutants buried by a previous owner is excavated and spread, the person who spread the soil may be liable for disposal of a hazardous substance.

- Site personnel may be a transporter if they move a hazardous substance from one location to another. For example, they may be liable if they transport dioxin-contaminated soil even if they did not know the soil contained dioxin.

SUPERFUND REQUIREMENTS

Hazardous Substance Discoveries

If hazardous materials or contaminated soil, surface water, or groundwater are discovered at the construction site, the National Response Center must be notified at 1-800-424-8802. The site may be entered into the Comprehensive Environmental Response, Compensation, and Liability Information System (CERCLIS), EPA's computerized inventory of potential hazardous substance release sites. When this happens, the responsible parties should work with EPA to evaluate the severity of the problem and develop remedies. The evaluation includes determining the potential for a release of hazardous substances from the site through these steps in the Superfund cleanup process:

- Preliminary Assessment/Site Inspection (PA/SI) - Investigate the site conditions;

- Hazard Ranking System (HRS) Scoring - Based on the results of the PA/SI, rate the site and determine if it should be placed on the NPL; and

- NPL Site Listing Process - Based on the HRS score, EPA lists the most serious of the sites for further investigation and possible long-term cleanup.

If the construction site is placed on the NPL, the responsible parties must work with EPA to conduct several steps to clean up the site, including:

- Remedial Investigation/Feasibility Study (RI/FS) - Investigate the NPL site to determine the nature and extent of contamination as well as the potential treatment options;

- Records of Decision (ROD) - Use the results of the RI/FS to explain which cleanup alternatives will be used at the NPL site;

- Remedial Design/Remedial Action (RD/RA) - Design the cleanup technology and begin the site cleanup process;

- Construction Completion - Complete any required construction activities or remove the site from the NPL; and

- Postconstruction Completion - Once construction is complete, begin cleanup and maintenance programs that will provide for the long-term protection of human health and the environment.

Superfund Release Reporting

If there is a hazardous substance release exceeding the reportable quantity for CERCLA at the site, the National Response Center must be notified immediately at 1-800-424-8802. The State Emergency Response Commission (SERC) and Local Emergency Planning Committee (LEPC) should also be notified if the release may affect off-site persons. In addition to these notifications, a notice must be published to potentially injured parties in local newspapers serving the affected area.

The CERCLA definition of release specifically excludes emissions from engine exhaust of a motor vehicle, rolling stock, aircraft, vessel, or pipeline pumping station engines; certain releases of nuclear materials; the normal application of fertilizers in accordance with product instructions; and application of pesticide products registered under the Federal Insecticide, Fungicide, and Rodenticide Act (FIFRA).

Federally permitted releases are also excluded from the CERCLA (and EPCRA) notification requirements, including releases regulated by National Pollutant Discharge Elimination System (NPDES) permits, Dredge and Fill (Clean Water Act Section 404) permits, RCRA-permitted units, clean dumping and incineration permits, Clean Air Act permits, publicly owned treatment works (POTW) pretreatment agreements, and nuclear materials under the Atomic Energy Act.

EPCRA PLANNING AND REPORTING APPLICABILITY

The construction site may be affected by EPCRA emergency planning requirements if it stores an extremely hazardous substance (EHS), or any substance regulated by the state or local authority, and stores the substance above the designated Threshold Planning Quantity, which varies by substance. Planning requirements include providing information to SERCs and LERCs. EHSs are defined at http://yosemite.epa.gov/oswer/ceppoweb.nsf/content/chemicalinfo.htm, Threshold Planning Quantities can be found at http://yosemite.epa.gov/oswer/ceppoweb.nsf/vwResourcesByFilename/title3.pdf/$File/title3.pdf.

To trigger EPCRA Section 304 reporting requirements, the construction site must:

- Release a hazardous substance or EHS (as defined by EPCRA) with the potential to affect off-site persons; AND

- Release the hazardous substance or EHS in an amount that meets or exceeds the reportable quantity within a 24-hour period; AND

- Produce, use, or store the hazardous substance or EHS.

EPCRA PLANNING AND REPORTING REQUIREMENTS

If EPCRA applies to the construction project, the SERC/LEPC may require information on the presence of hazardous chemicals and their releases (accidental or routine). In addition, the SERC/LEPC may have additional requirements. EPA has found that most construction sites are not subject to EPCRA requirements.

If the site produces, uses, or stores a hazardous substance or EHS defined by EPCRA, it may be subject to reporting requirements. Notify the SERC and LEPC when there is a release in an amount equal to or greater than the reportable quantity for that substance (EPCRA Section 304(a)) and the release may potentially affect off-site persons. The notice to the SERC and LEPC must include:

- The chemical name or identity of any released substance;

- Indication of whether the substance is an EHS;

- Estimate of amount released into the environment;

- Time and duration of the release;

- Medium or media into which the release occurred;

- Any known or anticipated acute or chronic health risks associated with the emergency, and, where appropriate, advice regarding medical attention necessary for exposed individuals;

- Proper precautions to take as a result of the release (unless already readily available to the community emergency coordinator); and

- Contact names and numbers.

Federally permitted releases are excluded from the EPCRA notification requirements, including releases regulated by NPDES permits, Dredge and Fill (Clean Water Act Section 404) permits, RCRA-permitted units, clean dumping and incineration permits, Clean Air Act permits, POTW pretreatment agreements, and nuclear materials under the Atomic Energy Act.

This Page Is Intentionally Left Blank

VI.   POLYCHLORINATED BIPHENYL (PCB) SELF-AUDIT CHECKLIST

This section contains a checklist and associated background information on the U.S. Environmental Protection Agency's (EPA) PCB processing and use prohibitions for construction projects. PCBs are regulated under 40 CFR Part 761 as a part of the Toxic Substances Control Act (TSCA). The PCB regulations and requirements apply to both PCB waste materials and PCBs still in use. States and the Federal Government regulate the use, storage, and disposal of equipment containing PCBs, depending upon the concentration of PCBs present. EPA's Office of Prevention, Pesticides and Toxic Substances provides interpretive guidance on PCB waste regulations including the *PCB Questions and Answers Manual* at http://www.epa.gov/pcb/guidance.html.

Because they are regulated under TSCA, PCBs are not considered *hazardous wastes* under Subtitle C of the Resource Conservation and Recovery Act (RCRA). PCB wastes can become *hazardous wastes* if they are mixed with a listed hazardous waste (regulated under the RCRA mixture rule) or they exhibit a characteristic of hazardous waste (regulated under RCRA). Under 40 CFR Part 261.8, the disposal of PCB-containing dielectric fluids regulated under TSCA, that are hazardous only for the toxicity characteristic, is exempt from RCRA. If hazardous debris is also a waste PCB and covered by both RCRA and TSCA, the debris is covered by the most stringent requirement. Refer to the *Hazardous Solid Waste Self-Audit Checklist* (Section IV, Part II of this guide) for more information on RCRA Subtitle C requirements.

This section includes a checklist for TSCA requirements for generators of **PCB waste**. Operators of construction projects can use the checklist to identify who will be responsible for addressing each requirement, and to conduct a self-audit of their construction site. The checklist also can be used by compliance inspectors to conduct an inspection of a construction project.

Construction projects may be subject to state or local regulations. Check with the EPA Region or state in which the construction project is located to determine the PCB-handling requirements that apply to the site.

More information on PCB waste requirements can be found in Section VIII in Part I of this guide and in the Background section following the checklist. Attachment A provides a list of potential PCB-containing wastes at construction sites. Attachment B lists PCB trade names and other synonyms to help the site identify PCB-containing equipment. Attachment C includes PCB concentration assumptions for use (for equipment manufactured prior to July 2, 1979).

CHECKLIST FOR PCB REQUIREMENTS FOR CONSTRUCTION PROJECTS

BACKGROUND INFORMATION

Name of Auditor: _____
Date of Audit: _____
Name of Project/Site: _____

A "notes" area is provided at the end of each section of this checklist. For every "No" answer, enter a description of the missing information and the action required to bring the site into compliance in the "notes" area.

IDENTIFYING PCB MATERIALS

Yes	No	
		Prior to Demolition
❑	❑	1. Do the construction activities involve demolition of a building or structure constructed prior to July 2, 1979? If so, PCB-containing materials may be present.
❑	❑	2. Were the building and structures inspected to determine if any materials containing PCBs are present at the site prior to demolition? (See Attachments A and B for additional information to use in identifying PCBs.)
❑	❑	3. Are there any PCB transformers registered for this structure? PCB transformers located within a commercial building, including those in storage for reuse, and any PCB transformer within 30 meters of a commercial building must be registered with the building owner.
❑	❑	4. Are there any facility records such as annual records required by 40 CFR Part 761.180(a) for PCB articles in storage?
❑	❑	5. Are there any inspection logs for PCB transformers or PCB voltage regulators?

PCB Wastes Identified:

_____

_____

<u>Yes</u>	<u>No</u>	
		During Demolition or Construction
❑	❑	6. If unidentified, potentially hazardous, or PCB-containing materials were discovered during construction or demolition, were the proper parties (e.g., construction manager and property owner) informed?
		Material Identification
❑	❑	7. If the contractor/developer/owner could not determine if materials containing PCBs are present, was a company specializing in PCB identification and remediation services hired?
❑	❑	8. If materials containing PCBs were found, were the concentrations of PCBs determined? Concentrations can be estimated using the EPA assumptions provided in Appendix C, through laboratory testing of the PCB-containing material, or through use of the "worst case" assumption that the materials are above the regulated concentration of 50 ppm.
❑	❑	9. Was a record kept of all regulated PCB-containing materials found at the site and was a Notification of PCB Activity Form completed prior to storage or disposal? (A copy of the form can be found at http://www.epa.gov/pcb/data.html.)

NOTES / ACTIONS NEEDED TO BRING SITE INTO COMPLIANCE: _____

_____

_____

_____

_____

_____

_____

_____

PCB MATERIAL LABELING, STORAGE, AND TRANSFER

Yes	No	
❑	❑	10. Is the PCB-containing material labeled as required[1]?
❑	❑	11. Is the material labeled with either a large mark (M_L) label (square from 6 inch by 6 inch to 2 inch by 2 inch) or a small mark (M_s) label (rectangular from 1 inch by 2 inch to 0.4 inch by 0.8 inch) that has letters and striping on a white or yellow background and is sufficiently durable to exceed the life of the PCB item it is marking?
❑	❑	12. Is the site inspected for old spills or leaks from PCB-containing equipment?
❑	❑	13. Are materials prepared properly for storage or disposal?
❑	❑	14. Are nonleaking and structurally undamaged large PCB capacitors and PCB-contaminated electrical equipment containing free flowing dielectric fluid stored on pallets in a storage facility? This is only allowed if the storage facility contains available storage equivalent to 10 percent of the volume of equipment stored on the pallet. If the equipment is drained of dielectric fluid, there is no available storage requirement.
❑	❑	15. Is PCB waste in storage for disposal marked with the date removed from service?
❑	❑	16. Is a permanent storage facility used for materials stored for more than 30 days?

[1] The following items must be labeled: PCB containers; large PCB transformers, PCB low and high voltage capacitors, and equipment containing these transformers or capacitors at the time of removal from use if not already marked; large PCB high voltage capacitors at the time of manufacture, at the time of distribution in commerce if not already marked, and at the time of removal from use if not already marked; electric motors using PCB coolants; hydraulic systems using PCB hydraulic fluid; heat transfer systems (other than PCB transformers) using PCBs; PCB article containers containing articles or equipment that must be marked; and each storage area used to store PCBs and PCB items for disposal.

Yes   No

Temporary Storage

Yes	No	
		17. Does the temporary storage for disposal area meet the following requirements?
❑	❑	Marked with a PCB M_L label.
❑	❑	Have a roof and walls to protect the materials from rain or snow.
❑	❑	Have impermeable floor with six-inch curbing and no drains.
❑	❑	Have containment volume equal to at least two times the volume of the largest PCB article or 25 percent of the total volume of all PCB articles, whichever is greater.
❑	❑	Not located in a 100-year flood plain.
❑	❑	Have all leaking equipment stored in a nonleaking PCB container with absorbents and have nonleaking equipment on pallets.
❑	❑	18. If PCB material is stored in a RCRA-permitted facility, has a Notification of PCB Activity Form been completed?
❑	❑	19. Is the waste storage area inspected every 30 days and records of the inspections maintained?

Transportation and Disposal

Yes	No	
❑	❑	20. Is the manifest complete and signed? The manifest is complete if it contains the following information:
		For each bulk load of PCBs, the identity of the PCB waste, the earliest date of removal from service for disposal, and the weight in kilograms of the PCB waste.
		For each PCB article container or PCB container, the unique identifying number, type of PCB waste, earliest date of removal from service for disposal, and weight in kilograms of the PCB waste contained.
		For each PCB article not in a PCB container or PCB article container, the serial number if available or other identification if there is no serial number, the date of removal from service for disposal, and weight in kilograms of the PCB waste in each PCB article.

Yes	No	
❑	❑	21. Are all of the records including the activity form, the manifest, the certification of disposal, and any on-site inspection reports being kept? A copy of each signed manifest must be kept until the generator receives a signed copy from the designated commercial storage or disposal facility that received the PCB waste. The copy signed by the commercial storer or disposer shall be retained for at least three years from the date the PCB waste was accepted by the initial transporter.
❑	❑	22. Did the site hire an approved PCB waste disposal company?
❑	❑	23. Will the transporter properly dispose of PCB waste?
❑	❑	24. Were the labeled items and transport vehicles inspected to ensure that the markings are visible and contain all of the necessary information?
❑	❑	25. Was a signed copy of the manifest received from the operator of the designated disposal site within 35 days of the date the waste was accepted by the initial transporter? If not, was the transporter and/or the owner or operator of the designated disposal site contacted to determine the status of the waste shipment?
❑	❑	26. Was a copy of the waste shipment record, signed by the owner or operator of the designated waste disposal site, received within 45 days of the date the waste was accepted by the initial transporter? If not, was an Exception Report submitted to the EPA Regional Administrator? If not, did this report include a copy of the manifest for which a confirmation of delivery was not received and a cover letter signed by the waste generator explaining the efforts taken to locate the PCB waste shipment and the results of those efforts?

NOTES / ACTIONS NEEDED TO BRING SITE INTO COMPLIANCE: _____

_____

_____

_____

_____

_____

_____

PCB REMEDIATION WASTES

Yes	No	
		27. Did the person in charge of the cleanup or the owner of the property where the PCB remediation waste is located notify, in writing, the proper agencies 30 days prior to startup of remediation? The notice is complete if it contains the following:
❑	❑	The nature of the contamination, including kinds of materials contaminated.
❑	❑	A summary of the procedures used to sample contaminated and adjacent areas and a table or cleanup site map showing PCB concentrations measured in all precleanup characterization samples.
❑	❑	The location and extent of the identified contaminated area, including topographic maps with sample collection sites cross-referenced to the sample identification numbers in the data summary.
❑	❑	A cleanup plan for the site, including schedule, disposal technology, and approach.
❑	❑	A written certification signed by the owner of the property where the cleanup site is located and the party conducting the cleanup. The certification must state that all sampling plans, sample collection procedures, sample preparation procedures, extraction procedures, and instrumental/chemical analysis procedures used to assess or characterize the PCB contamination at the cleanup site, are on file at the location designated in the certificate, and are available for EPA inspection. *Notice Submittal Date(s)*: _____
❑	❑	28. Does the area meet the cleanup levels specified in 40 CFR Part 761 Subpart 61?

NOTES / ACTIONS NEEDED TO BRING SITE INTO COMPLIANCE: _____

_____

_____

_____

_____

_____

_____

_____

PCB SPILLS

Date of Spill: _____

Name & Location of Project/Site: _____

PCB Waste/Material: _____

Yes	No	
❏	❏	29. Did the site contact the EPA Regional Administrator, the Director of the state or tribal environmental protection agency, and the Director of the county or local environmental protection agency as soon as possible once a spill is discovered, as required?
❏	❏	30. Did the site call a PCB waste remediation company to clean up any existing (more than 72 hours old) spills? (If the sites chose to cleanup the remediation waste, see the Remediation Waste section above.)
❏	❏	31. Where a spill directly contaminates surface water, sewers, drinking water supplies, grazing lands, or vegetable gardens, or for releases more than 10 pounds of PCBs, did the site notify the appropriate EPA Regional office and the Office of Prevention, Pesticides and Toxic Substances Branch and obtain guidance for appropriate cleanup measures in the shortest possible time after discovery, but in no case later than 24 hours after discovery?
❏	❏	32. Did the site contact the National Response Center [(800) 424-8802] and the state and local agencies if the spill involved 10 pounds or more by weight of PCBs as required?

<u>Yes</u>	<u>No</u>	
		33. For <u>high concentration spills</u> (defined as 500 ppm or greater of PCBs, or low concentration spills involving more than one pound of PCBs by weight, or more than 270 gallons of untested material) within 24 hours of the spill or within 48 hours for spills involving PCB transformers did the site:
❑	❑	Notify the National Response Center at (800) 424-8802 if the spill involved 10 pounds or more by weight of PCBs?
❑	❑	Notify local environmental agencies?
❑	❑	Notify local authorities immediately if there was a fire?
❑	❑	Restrict and label the visible spill area?
❑	❑	Record and document the extent of PCB contamination of the estimated spill area?
❑	❑	Immediately begin cleanup of the visible spill area and then, once the concentration level of the PCB spill was determined, begin the appropriate cleanup depending upon the release location, exposure risk, PCB concentration, and future use of the site?
❑	❑	Test the area to confirm that the PCB concentration met EPA-specified levels?
		34. For <u>low concentration spills</u> (defined as less than 500 ppm PCB, or less than one pound of PCBs by weight, or less than 270 gallons of untested material) did the site:
❑	❑	Double wash/rinse all contaminated surfaces within 48 hours of the spill?
❑	❑	Collect a standard wipe test sample from smooth surfaces, using hexane wipe samples to detect PCB contamination and confirm that the concentration is not more than 10 micrograms per 100 square centimeters?

Yes	No	
		35. At the completion of cleanup, did the site properly document the cleanup with records and certification of decontamination? The records and certification must be maintained for a period of five years. The records are complete if they contain the following:
❏	❏	Identification of the source of the spill (e.g., type of equipment).
❏	❏	Estimated or actual date and time of the spill.
❏	❏	The date and time cleanup was completed or terminated (if cleanup was delayed by emergency or adverse weather: the nature and duration of the delay).
❏	❏	A brief description of the spill location.
❏	❏	Precleanup sampling data used to establish the spill boundaries if required.
❏	❏	A brief description of the sampling methodology used to establish the spill boundaries.
❏	❏	A brief description of the solid surfaces cleaned and of the double wash/rinse method used.
❏	❏	Approximate depth of soil excavation and the amount of soil removed.
❏	❏	A certification statement signed by the responsible party stating that the cleanup requirements have been met and that the information contained in the record is true to the best of his/her knowledge.

NOTES / ACTIONS NEEDED TO BRING SITE INTO COMPLIANCE: _____

_____

_____

_____

_____

_____

_____

BACKGROUND ON PCB WASTE REQUIREMENTS FOR
CONSTRUCTION PROJECTS

DEFINITIONS

- **Capacitor.** Device for accumulating and holding a charge of electricity and consisting of conducting surfaces separated by a dielectric. Types of capacitors are as follows:

  — Small capacitor means a capacitor which contains less than 1.36 kg (3 lbs) of dielectric fluid. The following assumptions may be used if the actual weight of the dielectric fluid is unknown. A capacitor whose total volume is less than 1,639 cubic centimeters (100 cubic inches) may be considered to contain less than 1.36 kgs (3 lbs) of dielectric fluid and a capacitor whose total volume is more than 3,278 cubic centimeters (200 cubic inches) must be considered to contain more than 1.36 kg (3 lbs) of dielectric fluid. A capacitor whose volume is between 1,639 and 3,278 cubic centimeters may be considered to contain less then 1.36 kg (3 lbs) of dielectric fluid if the total weight of the capacitor is less than 4.08 kg (9 lbs).

  — Large high voltage capacitor means a capacitor which contains 1.36 kg (3 lbs) or more of dielectric fluid and which operates at 2,000 volts (a.c. or d.c.) or above.

  — Large low voltage capacitor means a capacitor which contains 1.36 kg (3 lbs) or more of dielectric fluid and which operates below 2,000 volts (a.c. or d.c.).

- **Chemical Waste Landfill.** Landfill at which protection against risk of injury to health or the environment from migration of PCBs to land, water, or the atmosphere is provided from PCBs and PCB items deposited therein by locating, engineering, and operating the landfill as specified in 40 CFR Part 761.75.

- **Commercial Storer of PCB Waste.** Owner or operator of each facility that is subject to the PCB storage unit standards of 40 CFR Part 761.65(b)(1) or (c)(7) or meets the alternate storage criteria of 40 CFR Part 761.65(b)(2), and who engages in storage activities involving either PCB waste generated by others or that was removed while servicing the equipment owned by others and brokered for disposal. The receipt of a fee or any other form of compensation for storage services is not necessary to qualify as a commercial storer of PCB waste. A generator who only stores its own waste is subject to the storage requirements of 40 CFR Part 761.65, but is not required to obtain approval as a commercial storer. If a facility's storage of PCB waste generated by others at no time exceeds a total of 500 gallons of liquid and/or nonliquid material containing PCBs at regulated levels, the owner or operator is a commercial storer but is not required to seek EPA approval as a commercial storer of PCB waste. Storage of one company's PCB waste by a related company is not considered commercial storage. A "related company" includes, but is not limited to: a parent company and its subsidiaries; sibling companies owned by the same parent company; companies owned by a common holding company; members of electric cooperatives; entities within the same executive agency as defined at 5 U.S.C. 105; and a company having a joint ownership interest in a facility from which PCB waste is generated (such as a jointly owned electric power generating station) where the PCB waste is stored by one of the co-owners of the facility. A "related company" does not include another voluntary member of the same trade association. Change in ownership or title of a generator's facility, where the generator is storing PCB waste, does not make the new owner of the facility a commercial storer of PCB waste.

- **Disposal.** Intentionally or accidentally to discard, throw away, or otherwise complete or terminate the useful life of PCBs and PCB items. Disposal includes spills, leaks, and other uncontrolled discharges of PCBs as well as actions related to containing, transporting, destroying, degrading, decontaminating, or confining PCBs and PCB items.

- **Distribute in Commerce and Distribution in Commerce.** When used to describe an action taken with respect to a chemical substance, mixture, or article containing a substance or mixture means to sell, or the sale of, the substance, mixture, or article in commerce; to introduce or deliver for introduction into commerce, or the introduction or delivery for introduction into commerce of the substance, mixture, or article; or to hold or the holding of, the substance, mixture, or article after its introduction into commerce.

- **Double Wash/Rinse.** Solid surfaces must be cleaned two times with an appropriate solvent or other material in which PCBs are at least 5 percent soluble by weight. The cleanser must cover the contaminated surface completely in both wash/rinses. The runoff must be contained and disposed of properly.

- **EPA Identification Number.** 12-digit number assigned to a facility by EPA upon notification of PCB waste activity under 40 CFR Part 761.205.

- **Generator of PCB Waste.** Any person whose act or process produces PCBs that are regulated for disposal under Subpart D of this part, or whose act first causes PCBs or PCB items to become subject to the disposal requirements of Subpart D of this part, or who has physical control over the PCBs when a decision is made that the use of the PCBs has been terminated and therefore is subject to the disposal requirements of Subpart D of this part. Unless another provision of this part specifically requires a site-specific meaning, ''generator of PCB waste'' includes all of the sites of PCB waste generation owned or operated by the person who generates PCB waste.

- **In or Near Commercial Buildings.** Within the interior of, on the roof of, attached to the exterior wall of, in the parking area serving, or within 30 meters of a nonindustrial nonsubstation building. Commercial buildings are typically accessible to both members of the general public and employees, and include: (1) public assembly properties, (2) educational properties, (3) institutional properties, (4) residential properties, (5) stores, (6) office buildings, and (7) transportation centers (e.g., airport terminal buildings, subway stations, bus stations, or train stations).

- **Leak or Leaking.** Any instance in which a PCB article, PCB container, or PCB equipment has any PCBs on any portion of its external surface.

- **Manifest.** Shipping document EPA Form 8700–22 and any continuation sheet attached to EPA Form 8700–22, originated and signed by the generator of PCB waste in accordance with the instructions included with the form and Subpart K of this part.

- **Mineral Oil PCB Transformer.** Any transformer originally designed to contain mineral oil as the dielectric fluid and which has been tested and found to contain 500 ppm or greater PCBs.

- **PCB and PCBs.** Any chemical substance that is limited to the biphenyl molecule that has been chlorinated to varying degrees or any combination of substances which contains such substance. Refer to 40 CFR Part 761.1(b) for applicable concentrations of PCBs. PCB and PCBs as contained in PCB items are defined in 40 CFR Part 761.3. For any purposes under this part, inadvertently generated non-Aroclor PCBs are defined as the total PCBs calculated following division of the quantity of monochlorinated biphenyls by 50 and dichlorinated biphenyls by 5. PCB article means any manufactured article, other than a PCB container, that contains PCBs and whose surface(s) has been in direct contact with PCBs. ''PCB article'' includes capacitors, transformers, electric motors, pumps, pipes and any other manufactured item (1) which is formed to a specific shape or design during manufacture, (2) which has end use function(s) dependent in whole or in part upon its shape or design during end use, and (3) which has either no change of chemical composition during its end use or only those changes of composition which have no commercial purpose separate from that of the PCB article.

- **PCB Bulk Product Waste.** Waste derived from manufactured products containing PCBs in a nonliquid state, at any concentration where the concentration at the time of designation for disposal was =50 ppm PCBs. PCB bulk product waste does not include PCBs or PCB items regulated for disposal under 40 CFR Part 761.60(a) through (c), 40 CFR Part 761.61, 40 CFR Part 761.63, or 40 CFR Part 761.64. PCB bulk product waste includes, but is not limited to:

    (1)   Nonliquid bulk wastes or debris from the demolition of buildings and other manmade structures manufactured, coated, or serviced with PCBs. PCB bulk product waste does not include debris from the demolition of buildings or other manmade structures that is contaminated by spills from regulated PCBs which have not been disposed of, decontaminated, or otherwise cleaned up in accordance with Subpart D of this part.

    (2)   PCB-containing wastes from the shredding of automobiles, household appliances, or industrial appliances.

    (3)   Plastics (such as plastic insulation from wire or cable; radio, television and computer casings; vehicle parts; or furniture laminates); preformed or molded rubber parts and components; applied dried paints, varnishes, waxes or other similar coatings or sealants; caulking; adhesives; paper; Galbestos; sound deadening or other types of insulation; and felt or fabric products such as gaskets.

    (4)   Fluorescent light ballasts containing PCBs in the potting material.

APPLICABILITY

The PCB waste regulation applies to:

- Generators of PCB waste;

- Transporters of PCB waste; and

- Treatment, storage, and disposal facilities for PCB waste (typically not applicable to construction sites).

In these situations, the contractor or subcontractor who first discovers the PCB-containing material typically is responsible for notifying the general contractor, developer, and/or owner. Because the PCB-containing material was present on the site prior to construction activities, the developer or owner typically is responsible for ensuring that all PCB wastes are handled and disposed of properly.

In a typical construction project, PCB wastes are generated in one of two ways:

- PCB-contaminated soils and materials are discovered during grading or digging (i.e., remediation wastes); or

- PCB-contaminated buildings or equipment are discovered during demolition.

Items with a concentration of 50 ppm or greater PCBs are regulated by TSCA. Note that states may regulate PCBs differently. Therefore, the state environmental department should be contacted to determine the site PCB waste requirements.

PCB WASTE HANDLING AND DISPOSAL REQUIREMENTS

When handling or disposing of PCB wastes, these requirements must be followed:

- **Identify and Label.** Identify and label all PCB-containing equipment or material that will be disturbed. There are two approved PCB labels that can be found in 40 CFR Part 761.45; "M_L" is the larger, preferred label and "M_S" is the smaller label that should be used only on items that will not accommodate the M_L.

- **Label Location.** Transport and storage areas should be marked on all sides. Any equipment or container containing PCB materials should be marked at a minimum on the side where access is available.

- **Determine the PCB Concentrations.** Determine the concentration of any items that will be removed either for storage or disposal. To do this either:

  — Assume "worst case" (greater than or equal to 50 ppm) and remove the suspect item(s), or

  — Analyze samples of the items for PCB concentration.

• **Get an EPA Identification Number and Notification of PCB Activity Form.**
If the site is storing or disposing of PCB waste, a Notification of PCB Activity
Form must be completed (see http://www.epa.gov/pcb/data.html) and mailed to
the Fibers and Organics Branch of EPA's Office of Pollution Prevention and
Toxic Substances (OPPTS). EPA will assign an ID number to the construction
site for the handling of PCBs. This ID number is for activities involving PCBs
and may not be used for any other waste activities. If the construction site has
already received an ID number for other regulated wastes (e.g., RCRA), EPA will
verify the number and assign the same ID number for the site's PCB activities. It
is not necessary to have a RCRA ID number to receive a PCB ID number.

• **Storage and Disposal.** Materials can be stored for *reuse* for up to five years in an
approved, permanent, PCB storage area. (Note - The storage-for-reuse provisions
at 40 CFR Part 761.35 are meant to capture equipment such as transformers, and
natural gas systems. The equipment must be manufactured for a particular use. It
is not meant for any item or material containing PCBs. See the definition of PCB
Article at 40 CFR Part 761.30.) The site can store materials for *disposal* for up to
30 days in a temporary storage area or for up to one year in a permanent PCB
storage location. In all cases, the items must be marked with the date they were
removed from service and the area must be inspected every 30 days for any spills
or leaks.

A temporary storage area must meet the following requirements:

—   Be marked with a PCB M_L label,
—   Have a roof and walls to protect the materials from rain or snow,
—   Have impermeable floor with six-inch curbing and no drains,
—   Not be located in the 100-year flood plain, and
—   Have a Spill Prevention Control and Countermeasure (SPCC) Plan.

In temporary storage place all leaking equipment in a nonleaking PCB container
with absorbents. Nonleaking equipment may be stored on pallets.

For more specific details on PCB storage, see 40 CFR Part 761.65. For
information specific to fluorescent light ballast disposal, see EPA's summary
guidance table located at http://www.epa.gov/pcb/Ballastchart.pdf.

If the site plans to install or use a permanent PCB waste storage area, a Notification of PCB
Activity Form must be completed and submitted prior to handling any waste. If the site plans
only to temporarily store materials (<30 days) prior to disposal, the form does not need to be
completed. If the storage plans change or the 30-day temporary storage limit is exceeded, the

form must then be completed. The Activity Form requests general information about the site and related activities and is designed to inform EPA of site activities. For more specific details on PCB storage, see 40 CFR Part 761.65.

For PCB waste disposal, an approved PCB waste disposer must be used. (Note - transporters do not need to be approved, but the generator or whoever is offering the waste for shipment must ensure that the transporter has submitted a Notification of PCB Activity Form and received an ID number for their PCB activities. In addition to the waste going to an approved disposer, that disposer must also have notified and received an ID number for their PCB activities.) To transport the waste for either commercial storage or disposal, complete a hazardous waste manifest. If the site is exempt from having an EPA identification number, it can use the generic identification number "40 CFR Part 761" on manifests, records, and reports. A hazardous waste manifest can be obtained from either the hazardous waste transporter or from the state hazardous waste coordinator. A copy of the completed, signed manifest should be kept in the site records. Once the waste has reached its final destination, the hazardous waste storer/disposer will sign the manifest and return a copy to the site.

An annual documentation log must also be kept for certain storage and disposal activities. For details on the specific requirements of the annual documentation log, see 40 CFR Part 761.180.

Disposal Requirements

The PCB waste transporter must dispose of the waste using the following criteria:

- Proper disposal of PCB-containing liquids:

    — PCB liquids at concentrations of $\geq$ 50 ppm must be disposed of in an incinerator, OR

    — Mineral oil and other liquid dielectric fluids with PCB liquid concentrations of between $\geq$ 50 ppm and < 500 ppm can be disposed of in a high efficiency boiler.

- Proper disposal of PCB containers and large PCB capacitors containing PCBs with concentrations of > 500 ppm or transformers:

    — Disposed of in an incinerator, OR

— Disposed of in a chemical waste landfill after being properly treated. Proper treatment usually includes removal of free flowing liquids and treatment with a solvent.

• Nonliquid PCB remediation waste, soil, rags, debris, sludges, and sediment can also be disposed of in this manner. Small PCB capacitors or containers storing PCBs with concentrations of < 500 ppm may be disposed of as municipal solid waste.

• Proper disposal of PCB-contaminated electrical equipment, PCB hydraulic machine, or large PCB capacitors containing PCBs with concentrations of ≥ 50 ppm and < 500:

— Disposed of in an incinerator, OR

— Disposed of in a chemical waste landfill after being properly treated; proper treatment usually includes removing free flowing liquids and treating with a solvent, OR

— Decontaminated in accordance to 40 CFR Part 761.79, OR

— In a scrap metal recovery oven, OR

— A licensed municipal solid waste or nonmunicipal nonhazardous waste management or other approved facility.

• Small PCB capacitors may be disposed of as municipal solid waste.

• If the PCBs are being transported, is the transport vehicle properly marked? A transport vehicle requires marking on all sides with the M_L mark (Appendix A) if it meets the following requirements:

— Loaded with PCB containers that contain more than 45 kilograms (kg) of liquid PCBs at concentrations of ≥ 50 ppm, OR

— Loaded with one or more PCB transformer.

Spills and Remediation Waste

If at any time during site inspection or material handling a spill or leak is discovered, it must be cleaned up within 72 hours of discovery. EPA has provided a detailed spill cleanup policy in 40 CFR Part 761, Subpart G. The requirements of this plan vary depending on the size and concentration of the spill but can include spill testing to determine the concentration of PCBs that were spilled, double wash/rinsing of the contaminated surfaces, soil excavating, and even contacting the National Response Center. If during construction activities any preexisting PCB spills or disposals are discovered, the local EPA Administrator should be contacted to determine the best way to handle these "remediation" wastes.

Self-implementing on-site cleanup and disposal of remediation waste is allowed for moderately sized sites since there should be low residual environmental impact. It is not allowed to clean up the following:

- Surface or ground waters;
- Sediments in marine and freshwater ecosystems;
- Sewers or sewage treatment systems;
- Any private or public drinking water sources or distribution systems;
- Grazing lands; or
- Vegetable gardens.

At least 30 days prior to the date that the cleanup of a site begins, the person in charge of the cleanup or the owner of the property where the PCB remediation waste is located shall notify, in writing, the EPA Regional Administrator, the Director of the state or tribal environmental protection agency, and the Director of the county or local environmental protection agency where the cleanup will be conducted. Within 30 calendar days of receiving the notification, the EPA Regional Administrator will respond in writing to the request. If the EPA Regional Administrator does not respond within 30 calendar days of receiving the notice, the site may assume that it is complete and acceptable and proceed with the cleanup. Once cleanup is underway, the site must notify the EPA Regional Administrator, in writing, within 14 calendar days of any proposed changes.

Remediation Cleanup Requirements

The area must meet specific cleanup levels based on the occupancy levels in the area. A more detailed procedure for remediating the site is provided in 40 CFR Part 761, Subpart 61. The requirements for disposing of the remediated waste are described in 40 CFR Part 761, Subpart 62.

- For high-occupancy areas, the remediation activity must meet the following cleanup levels:

  — Bulk remediation wastes, porous surfaces, or liquids ≤ 1 ppm, OR

  — Bulk remediation wastes, porous surfaces, or liquids > 1 ppm and ≤ 10 ppm and covered with a cap, OR

  — Nonporous surfaces ≤ 10 μg/ 100 cm^2.

- For low-occupancy areas, the remediation activity must meet the following cleanup levels:

  — Bulk remediation wastes, porous surfaces, or liquids ≤ 25 ppm, OR

  — Bulk remediation wastes, porous surfaces, or liquids > 25 ppm and ≤ 50 ppm and the area is secured with a fence and marked with the M_L mark, OR

  — Bulk remediation wastes > 25 ppm and ≤ 100 ppm and covered with a cap, OR

  — Non-porous surfaces ≤ 100 μg/ 100 cm^2.

Attachment A. Potential PCB-Containing Wastes at Construction Sites

- Mineral-oil filled electrical equipment such as motors or pumps manufactured prior to July 2, 1979;

- Capacitors or transformers manufactured prior to July 2, 1979;

- Plastics[2], molded rubber parts, applied dried paints, coatings or sealants, caulking, adhesives, paper, Galbestos, sound-deadening materials, insulation, or felt or fabric products such as gaskets manufactured prior to July 2, 1979;

- Fluorescent light ballasts manufactured prior to July 2, 1979;

- Waste or debris from the demolition of buildings and equipment manufactured, serviced, or coated with PCBs; and

- PCB remediation waste such as materials disposed of prior to May 4, 1987, or waste containing PCBs from spills, such as floors or walls contaminated by a leaking transformer.

Excluded PCB products are materials with PCB concentrations below 50 ppm. The PCB concentration can not be a result of dilution, leaks, or spills of PCBs with concentrations greater than 50 ppm. These products are exempt from TSCA regulations. These materials may include the following:

- Products contaminated with PCB materials;

- Recycled fluids or equipment contaminated during use of PCB-containing products; and

- Used oils.

To identify PCB wastes, contact the state or EPA Region for assistance (EPA's *Notification of Regulated Waste Activities: Instructions and Forms* includes a list of state contacts).

---

[2]Plastics can include a variety of products including insulation from wire or cable; radio, television, and computer casings; vehicle parts; or furniture laminates.

Attachment B. PCB Trade Names and Other Synonyms To Help
Identify PCB-Containing Equipment

Aceclor	Dicolor	Orophene PCB
Adkarel	Diconal	PCB's
ALC	Diphenyl, chlorinated	PCBs
Apirolio	DK	Pheaoclor
Apirorlio	Duconal	Phenochlor
Arochlor	Dykanol	Phenoclor
Arochlors	Educarel	Plastivar
Aroclor	EEC-18	Polychlorinated biphenyl
Aroclors	Elaol	Polychlorinated biphenyls
Arubren	Electrophenyl	Polychlorinated diphenyl
Asbestol	Elemex	Polychlorinated diphenyls
ASK	Elinol	Polychlorobiphenyl
Askael	Eucarel	Polychlorodiphenyl
Askarel	Fenchlor	Prodelec
Auxol	Fenclor	Pydraul
Bakola	Fenocloro	Pyraclor
Biphenyl, chlorinated	Gilotherm	Pyralene
Chlophen	Hydol	Pyranol
Chloretol	Hyrol	Pyroclor
Chlorextol	Hyvol	Pyronol
Chlorinated biphenyl	Inclor	Saf-T-Kuhl
Chlorinated diphenyl	Inerteen	Saf-T-Kohl
Chlorinol	Inertenn	Santosol
Chlorobiphenyl	Kanechlor	Santotherm
Chlorodiphenyl	Kaneclor	Santothern
Chlorphen	Kennechlor	Santovac
Chorextol	Kenneclor	Solvol
Chorinol	Leromoll	Sorol
Clophen	Magvar	Soval
Clophenharz	MCS 1489	Sovol
Cloresil	Montar	Sovtol
Clorinal	Nepolin	Terphenychlore
Clorphen	No-Flamol	Therminal
Decachlorodiphenyl	NoFlamol	Therminol
Delor	Non-Flamol	Turbinol
Delorene Diaclor	Olex-sf-d	

**Attachment C. PCB Concentration Assumptions for Use
(for Equipment Manufactured Prior to July 2, 1979)**

Item	Concentration Assumption
Transformers with <3 lbs of fluid Circuit breakers Reclosers Oil-filled cable Rectifiers with unestablished PCB concentrations	<50 ppm PCB (not regulated by TSCA)
Mineral-oil filled electrical equipment without any established PCB concentration (pole-top and pad-mounted distribution transformers are considered mineral-oil filled)	>= 50 ppm and <500 ppm
Transformers with >3 lbs of fluid other than mineral oil Capacitors	>= 500 ppm

Any person may assume that mineral oil-filled electrical equipment, transformers, or circuit breakers manufactured after July 2, 1979 are non-PCB and contain less than 50 ppm PCB. If a transformer contains more than 3 pounds of fluid and the date of manufacture as well as the type of dielectric fluid for the transformer are unknown, one must assume the concentration of PCB in the transformer is >= 500 ppm. If the date of manufacture for a capacitor is unknown, one must assume the concentration of PCB in the capacitor is >= 500 ppm.

This Page Is Intentionally Left Blank

VII.   ASBESTOS SELF-AUDIT CHECKLIST

This section contains a checklist and associated background information related to asbestos requirements for construction activities. Activities that could result in the release of asbestos from asbestos-containing materials (ACM) are covered by the Asbestos National Emissions Standards for Hazardous Air Pollutants (NESHAP), promulgated under the Clean Air Act.

Before beginning any demolition or renovation activities on existing buildings, the site should evaluate the potential for releasing asbestos. This should include an inspection of the affected facility to determine the presence and quantities of Category I and Category II ACM as well as friable asbestos material. Owners, developers, architects, contractors, and subcontractors can use the checklist to identify who will be responsible for addressing each requirement, and to conduct a self-audit. The checklist can also be used by compliance inspectors to conduct an inspection of a construction site. Check with the state and local authorities to confirm the appropriate Administrator for the site asbestos activities.

More information on asbestos waste requirements can be found in Section X in Part I of this guide and in the Background section following the checklist. Attachment A of this checklist provides a list of common asbestos-containing materials.

CHECKLIST FOR ASBESTOS REQUIREMENTS FOR
CONSTRUCTION PROJECTS

BACKGROUND INFORMATION

Name of Auditor: _____

Date of Audit: _____

Name of Project/Site: _____

A "notes" area is provided at the end of each section of this checklist. For every "No" answer, enter a description of the missing information and the action required to bring the site into compliance in the "notes" area.

ASBESTOS NESHAP

Yes	No	
		Does the Asbestos NESHAP Apply to Site Activity? *The Asbestos NESHAP will apply to the site activity if any of the following questions are answered "Yes." Only the notification requirements apply if the demolition activities contain Regulated Asbestos-Containing Material (RACM) below the following thresholds.*
❑	❑	1. Do the site renovations or demolitions include at least 80 linear meters (260 linear feet) of RACM on pipes?
❑	❑	2. Do the site renovations or demolitions include 15 square meters (160 square feet) of RACM on other facility components?
❑	❑	3. Do the site renovations or demolitions include at least one cubic meter (35 cubic feet) of facility components where the amount of RACM previously removed from pipes and other facility components could not be measured before stripping?
❑	❑	4. Do the site renovations or demolitions occur at residential structures with five or more dwellings (i.e., apartments or single family homes)?
		Will Category I ACM Become RACM and Require Removal? *Category I ACM will become RACM if the answer to any of the following questions is "Yes."*
❑	❑	5. Is Category I material friable or in poor condition?
❑	❑	6. Has the Category I material been or will it be subjected to sanding, cutting, grinding, or abrading?

Yes	No	
❏	❏	7. Has a floor tile removal process, such as using a shot-blaster, resulted in extensive damage to the tiles?
❏	❏	8. Is debris from Category I roofing material created by sawing activities?
❏	❏	9. Will a building containing asbestos-cement products be demolished using cranes, hydraulic excavaters, or implosion/explosion techniques?
❏	❏	10. Will jackhammers or other mechanical devices be used to break up asbestos-containing concrete or other materials coated with Category I non-friable ACM?
❏	❏	11. Will bulldozers, tree chippers, or other equipment be used to reduce the volume of Category I materials?

Will Category II ACM Become RACM and Require Removal?

Category II ACM will become RACM if the answer to any of the following questions is "Yes."

Yes	No	
❏	❏	12. Has Category II material been or will it be subjected to sanding, cutting, grinding, or abrading?
❏	❏	13. Will demolition activities be conducted using heavy equipment such as bulldozers and hydraulic excavaters?
❏	❏	14. Will equipment such as wrecking balls or buckets be used in demolishing asbestos-cement?
❏	❏	15. Will the building be demolished using explosion/implosion?

Notification

The following notification requirements apply if the renovation/demolition activities have RACM below the thresholds listed above.

Yes	No	
❏	❏	16. Did the site provide the Administrator with a complete written notice of intention to demolish or renovate? The notification must be postmarked no later than 10 working days before any stripping/removal activity begins and must contain the following:
❏	❏	Indication if this is the original or a revised notification.
❏	❏	Name, address, and telephone number of both the facility owner and operator and the asbestos removal contractor owner or operator.
❏	❏	Type of operation: demolition or renovation.

Yes	No	
❑	❑	Description of the facility or affected part of the facility including the size (square feet and number of floors), age, and present and prior use of the facility.
❑	❑	The procedure, including analytical methods, used to detect the presence of RACM and Category I and Category II non-friable ACM.
❑	❑	The approximate amount of RACM to be removed from the facility in terms of length of pipe in linear meters (linear feet), surface area in square meters (square feet) on other facility components, or volume in cubic meters (cubic feet) if off the facility components.
❑	❑	Approximate amount of Category I and Category II non-friable ACM in the affected part of the facility that will not be removed before demolition.
❑	❑	Location and street address (including building number or name and floor or room number, if appropriate), city, county, and state, of the facility being demolished or renovated.
❑	❑	Scheduled start and completion dates of asbestos removal work for the demolition or renovation.
❑	❑	Scheduled start and completion dates of demolition or renovation.
❑	❑	Description of work practices and engineering controls to be used to comply with the requirements of this subpart, including asbestos removal and waste-handling emission control procedures.
❑	❑	The name and location of the waste disposal site where the asbestos-containing waste material will be deposited.
❑	❑	Certification that at least one person trained as required by the Asbestos NESHAP will supervise the stripping and removal described by the notification.
❑	❑	If the building is being demolished because it has been declared unsound, the name, title, and authority of the state or local government representative who has ordered the demolition, the date that the order was issued, the date on which the demolition was ordered to begin, and a copy of the order shall be attached to the notification.
❑	❑	For emergency renovations, the date and hour that the emergency occurred; a description of the sudden, unexpected event; and an explanation of how the event caused an unsafe condition, or would cause equipment damage or an unreasonable financial burden.

Yes	No	
❏	❏	Description of procedures to be followed in the event that unexpected RACM is found or Category II non-friable ACM becomes crumbled, pulverized, or reduced to powder.
❏	❏	The name, address, and telephone number of the waste transporter.
❏	❏	17. If the amount of asbestos in the renovation/demolition changed by at least 20 percent, did the site update the notice?
❏	❏	18. If the actual start date is after the start date in the original notification, did the site provide the Administrator with a written notification with the new start date?
❏	❏	19. If the actual start date is before the start date in the original notification, did the site provide the Administrator with a written notification with the new start date and notify by telephone as soon as possible before the original start date?

NOTES / ACTIONS NEEDED TO BRING SITE INTO COMPLIANCE: _____

_____

_____

_____

_____

_____

_____

_____

ASBESTOS EMISSION CONTROL

If the answer is "Yes" to the following applicable questions below, the site is complying with the procedures for asbestos emission control. No visible emissions are allowed under any circumstances.

Yes	No	
❑	❑	20. Has all RACM from the facility being demolished or renovated been removed before any activity begins that would break up, dislodge, or similarly disturb the material or preclude access to the material for subsequent removal? **OR** If the building is being demolished because it has been declared structurally unsound and in danger of imminent collapse or RACM is discovered after demolition, is the portion of the facility containing RACM kept adequately wet?
❑	❑	21. Is at least one on-site representative, such as a foreman or management-level person or other authorized representative, trained in the provisions of the Asbestos NESHAP and the means of complying with them present during the demolition or renovation activities?
❑	❑	22. If the facility is being demolished by intentional burning, has all RACM including all Category I and Category II non-friable ACM been removed?

When a facility component that contains, is covered with, or is coated with RACM is being taken out of the facility as a unit or in sections:

❑	❑	23. Is the RACM that is exposed during cutting or disjoining operations adequately wet?
❑	❑	24. Does the site carefully lower each unit or section to the floor and to ground level to avoid damaging or disturbing the RACM?

When RACM is stripped from a facility component but it remains temporarily in place in the facility:

❑	❑	25. Does the site adequately wet the RACM during the stripping operation? **OR**
		26. If the site does not wet the RACM:
❑	❑	Does the site obtain prior written approval from the Administrator? OR
❑	❑	Does the site use a local exhaust ventilation and collection system to capture the particulate asbestos material produced by the stripping? OR

Yes	No	
❑	❑	Does the site use a glove-bag system or use leak-tight wrapping to contain the particulate asbestos material? OR
❑	❑	Will the site use an alternate control method (besides a local exhaust ventilation and collection or a glove-bag system) and obtain written approval from the Administrator?

After a facility component covered with, coated with, or containing RACM has been taken out of the facility as a unit or in sections, it shall be stripped or contained in leak-tight wrapping.

Yes	No	
❑	❑	27. If the site does not wet the RACM, does it use a local exhaust ventilation and collection system to capture the particulate asbestos material produced by the stripping?

For large facility components such as reactor vessels or large tanks, the RACM is not required to be stripped if the site meets the following requirements:

Yes	No	
❑	❑	28. Is the component removed, transported, stored, disposed of, or reused without disturbing or damaging the RACM?
❑	❑	29. Is the component encased in a leak-tight wrapping and properly labeled?

For all RACM, including material that has been removed or stripped:

Yes	No	
❑	❑	30. Is the material adequately wet and does it remain wet until collected and contained or treated in preparation for disposal?
❑	❑	31. Does the site carefully lower the material to the ground and floor, not dropping, throwing, sliding, or otherwise damaging or disturbing the material?
❑	❑	32. If the material has been removed or stripped more than 50 feet above ground level and was not removed as units or in sections, does the site transport the material to the ground via leak-tight chutes or containers?

When the temperature at the point of wetting is below 0°C (32°F):

Yes	No	
❑	❑	33. Does the site remove facility components containing, coated with, or covered with RACM as units or in sections to the maximum extent possible?
❑	❑	34. During periods when wetting operations are suspended due to freezing temperatures, does the site record the temperature in the area containing the facility components at the beginning, middle, and end of each workday?

NOTES / ACTIONS NEEDED TO BRING SITE INTO COMPLIANCE: _____

_____

_____

_____

_____

_____

_____

ASBESTOS WASTE DISPOSAL

Waste disposal requirements of the asbestos NESHAP do not apply to Category I and Category II non-friable ACM waste that did not become crumbled, pulverized, or reduced to powder. If the answer to the following applicable questions below is "Yes," the site is complying with the procedures for asbestos waste disposal.

Yes	No	
❑	❑	35. Did the site properly mark vehicles used to transport asbestos-containing waste material so that the signs are visible?

To ensure no discharge of visible emissions to the outside air during the collection, processing (including incineration), packaging, or transporting of any asbestos-containing waste material generated by the source, the site must use all applicable emission control and waste treatment methods.

Yes	No	
❑	❑	36. Does the site adequately wet asbestos-containing waste material?
❑	❑	37. Does the site seal all asbestos-containing waste material in leak-tight containers while wet or put materials into leak-tight wrapping?
❑	❑	38. Does the site properly label the containers or wrapped materials?
❑	❑	39. Does the label contain the name of the waste generator and the location at which the waste was generated?
❑	❑	40. Does the site process asbestos-containing waste material into non-friable forms?

<u>**Yes**</u>   <u>**No**</u>

❑	❑	41. If the building is being demolished because it has been declared unsound: Does the site adequately wet asbestos-containing waste material at all times after demolition and keep wet during handling and loading for transport to a disposal site? OR Does the site use an alternative emission control and waste treatment method that has received prior approval by the Administrator?

All asbestos-containing waste material shall be disposed as soon as is practical by the waste generator. This does not apply to Category I and Category II non-friable ACM that is not RACM.

❑	❑	42. Is the material sent to an active waste disposal site authorized to receive asbestos-containing material?
❑	❑	43. Is the material sent to an EPA-approved site that converts asbestos-containing waste material into asbestos-free material?

For all asbestos-containing waste material transported off the facility site:

		44. Does the site maintain waste shipment records using the required format?
❑	❑	Name, address, and telephone number of the waste generator.
❑	❑	Name and address of the local, state, or EPA Regional office responsible for administering the asbestos NESHAP program.
❑	❑	Approximate quantity of waste in cubic meters.
❑	❑	Name and telephone number of the disposal site operator.
❑	❑	Name and physical site location of the disposal site.
❑	❑	Date the shipment was transported.
❑	❑	Name, address, and telephone number of the transporter.
❑	❑	Certification that the contents of this consignment are accurately described by proper shipping name and are in proper condition for transport by highway.

Yes	No	
❏	❏	45. Did the site provide a copy of the waste shipment record to the disposal site owners or operators as the asbestos-containing waste material was delivered to the disposal site?
❏	❏	46. Has the site retained a copy of all waste shipment records for at least two years?
❏	❏	47. If the site did not receive a copy of the waste shipment record signed by the owner or operator of the designated disposal site within 45 days of the date the waste was accepted by the initial transporter, was the transporter and/or the owner or operator of the designated disposal site contacted to determine the status of the waste shipment?
❏	❏	48. If a copy of the waste shipment record, signed by the owner or operator of the designated waste disposal site, was not received within 45 days of the date the waste was accepted by the initial transporter, did the site report this in writing to the office responsible for administering the asbestos NESHAP program for waste generators?

NOTES / ACTIONS NEEDED TO BRING SITE INTO COMPLIANCE: _____

_____

_____

_____

_____

_____

_____

AIR-CLEANING

If the site chooses to use a local exhaust ventilation and collection system to capture particulate asbestos material emissions, it must be designed and operated in accordance with the requirements of 40 CFR Part 61 Subpart 152. The site is complying with this Subpart if the answer to all of the following applicable questions is "Yes."

<u>Yes</u>   <u>No</u>

If the site uses fabric filter devices:		
❑	❑	49. Does the site ensure that the airflow permeability does not exceed 9 $m^3/min/m^2$ (30 $ft^3/min/ft^2$) for woven fabrics or 11 m^2 (35 $ft^3/min/ft^2$) for felted fabrics?
❑	❑	50. Does the site ensure that felted fabric weighs at least 475 grams per square meter (14 ounces per square yard) and is at least 1.6 millimeters (one-sixteenth inch) thick throughout?
❑	❑	51. Does the site avoid the use of synthetic fabrics that contain fill yarn other than that which is spun?
❑	❑	52. Does the site properly install, use, operate, and maintain all air-cleaning equipment?
If the site does not use fabric filter devices:		
❑	❑	53. Does the site utilize wet collectors designed to operate with a unit contacting energy of at least 9.95 kilopascals (40 inches water gage pressure)? OR
❑	❑	Does the site use a HEPA filter that is certified to be at least 99.97 percent efficient for 0.3 micron particles? OR
❑	❑	Is the site authorized to use alternative filtering equipment?

NOTES / ACTIONS NEEDED TO BRING SITE INTO COMPLIANCE: _____

_____

_____

_____

_____

_____

This Page Is Intentionally Left Blank

BACKGROUND ON ASBESTOS REQUIREMENTS FOR CONSTRUCTION ACTIVITIES

DEFINITIONS

- **Adequately Wet.** Sufficiently mixed with liquid to prevent the release of particulates. If visible particles or dust is observed coming from asbestos-containing material, then that material has not been adequately wetted.

- **Asbestos.** The name given to a number of naturally occurring fibrous silicate minerals that have been mined for their useful properties such as thermal insulation, chemical and thermal stability, and high tensile strength. The NESHAP defines asbestos to be the asbestiform varieties of serpentine (chrysotile), riebeckite (crocidolite), cummingtonite-grunerite, anthophyllite, and actinolite-tremolite.

- **Demolition.** The wrecking or taking out of any load-supporting structural member of a facility together with any related handling operations or the intentional burning of any facility.

- **Friable.** Material containing more than 1 percent asbestos that can be reduced to dust by hand pressure.

- **Non-friable.** Material containing more than 1 percent asbestos that is too hard to be reduced to dust by hand. Non-friable asbestos is grouped as Category I or Category II.

    — Category I - Asbestos-containing resilient floor covering, asphalt roofing products, packings, and gaskets. Asbestos-containing mastic is also considered a Category I material (EPA determination - April 9, 1991).

    — Category II - All remaining types of non-friable ACM not included in Category I that, when dry, cannot be crumbled, pulverized, or reduced to powder by hand pressure. Non-friable asbestos-cement products such as transite are an example of Category II material.

- **Owner or Operator of a Demolition or Renovation Activity.** Any person who owns, leases, operates, controls, or supervises the facility being demolished or renovated or any person who owns, leases, operates, controls, or supervises the demolition or renovation operation, or both.

- **Regulated Asbestos-Containing Material (RACM).** This includes:

  — Friable asbestos material;

  — Category I non-friable ACM that has become friable;

  — Category I non-friable ACM that will be or has been subjected to sanding, grinding, cutting, or abrading; and

  — Category II non-friable ACM that has a high probability of becoming or has become crumbled, pulverized, or reduced to powder by the forces expected to act on the material in the course of demolition or renovation operations.

- **Remove.** To take out RACM or facility components that contain or are covered with RACM from any facility.

- **Renovation.** Altering a facility or one or more facility components in any way, including stripping or removing RACM from a facility component. Operations in which load-supporting structural members are wrecked or taken out are considered demolition.

ASBESTOS NESHAP REQUIREMENTS

RACM must be removed before demolition of a building can begin. Attachment A provides a list of materials that are considered RACM. If demolition will be by intentional burning, then all Category I and Category II non-friable materials as well as RACM must be removed from the building. If suspect ACM becomes exposed during demolition activities and there was no prior knowledge of its existence, compliance with the asbestos NESHAP is still required.

In order to avoid NESHAP requirements before and during demolition activities, some groups have had buildings declared unsafe. The condition of a building should be confirmed independently. Even if a building is declared unsafe, it has no effect on requirements for disposal of RACM after demolition activities.

When preparing for any construction project, the site must determine if it is expected to comply with the asbestos NESHAP. The construction project must comply with the asbestos NESHAP if renovations or demolitions meet the following criteria:

- The renovations or demolitions include at least 80 linear meters (260 linear feet) of RACM on pipes;

- The renovations or demolitions include 15 square meters (160 square feet) of RACM on other facility components; or

- The renovations or demolitions include at least one cubic meter (35 cubic feet) of facility components where the amount of RACM previously removed from pipes and other facility components could not be measured before stripping.

The asbestos NESHAP only applies to renovations or demolitions that occur at residential structures with five or more dwellings (i.e. apartments or single family homes).

If a building is being demolished and the RACM being removed is less than the above-stated threshold, then only the notification requirements of the asbestos NESHAP are required.

If the building to be demolished is structurally unsound and in danger of imminent collapse (such as may occur due to a tornado, hurricane or flood damage, cataclysmic event, or extensive deterioration), the RACM are not required to be removed first. However, notification requirements and emission control requirements still apply to the demolition operation (40 CFR Part 61.145 (a)(3)). A review of the structure and the work plan may be required by the Administrator before this approach may be taken.

The following materials are not exempt from the asbestos NESHAP requirements:

- Category I non-friable ACM that has become friable; and

- Category II non-friable ACM that has a high probability of becoming or has become crumbled, pulverized, or reduced to powder by the forces expected to act on the material in the course of demolition or renovation operations.

Attachment A. Asbestos-Containing Materials

- Cement Pipes
- Cement Wallboard
- Cement Siding
- Asphalt Floor
- Vinyl Floor Tile
- Vinyl Sheet Flooring
- Flooring Backing
- Heating and Electrical Ducts
- Acoustical Plaster
- Electrical Cloth
- Electric Wiring Insulation
- Spray-Applied Insulation
- Blown-in Insulation
- Fireproofing Materials
- Taping Compounds (thermal)
- High Temperature Gaskets
- Laboratory Hoods/Table Tops
- Laboratory Gloves
- Fire Blankets
- Fire Curtains
- Elevator Equipment Panels
- Chalkboards
- Construction Mastics (floor tile, carpet, ceiling tile, etc.)
- Packing Materials (for wall/floor penetrations)
- Elevator Brake Shoes
- HVAC Duct Insulation
- Boiler Insulation
- Tile Breaching Insulation
- Ductwork Flexible Fabric Connections
- Cooling Towers
- Pipe Insulation (corrugated air-cell, block, etc.)
- Electrical Panel Partitions
- Decorative Plaster
- Textured Paints/Coatings
- Ceiling Tiles and Lay-in Panels
- Roofing Shingles
- Roofing Felt
- Base Flashing
- Thermal Paper Products
- Caulking/Putties
- Adhesives
- Wallboard
- Joint Compounds
- Vinyl Wall Coverings
- Spackling Compounds
- Fire Doors

U.S. Environmental Protection Agency
Office of Enforcement and Compliance Assurance
1200 Pennsylvania Avenue, NW (MC 2224-A)
Washington, D.C. 20460

EPA/305-B-04-003
April 2005

www.epa.gov/compliance

SAMPLE
Construction
Storm Water Pollution
Prevention Plan

Magerr's Quality Circuits, Inc.

September 15, 2000

The best management practices included in this sample SWPPP are just examples. Your plan may need to include other requirements.

TABLE OF CONTENTS

LIST OF TABLES

LIST OF FIGURES

1.0   INTRODUCTION

1.1   <u>Background</u>

In 1972, Congress passed the Federal Water Pollution Control Act (FWPCA), also known as the Clean Water Act (CWA), to restore and maintain the quality of the nation's waterways. The ultimate goal was to make sure that rivers and streams were fishable, swimmable, and drinkable. In 1987, the Water Quality Act (WQA) added provisions to the CWA that allowed the EPA to govern storm water discharges from construction sites. In 1998, EPA published the final notice for General Permits for Storm Water Discharges from Construction Activities Disturbing 5 Acres or Greater (63 Federal Register 7898, February 14, 1998). The general permit includes provisions for development of a Storm Water Pollution Prevention Plan (SWPPP) to maximize the potential benefits of pollution prevention and sediment and erosion control measures at construction sites.

Development, implementation, and maintenance of the SWPPP will provide Capital Construction Company (general contractor) with the framework for reducing soil erosion and minimizing pollutants in storm water during construction of Magerr's Quality Circuits' manufacturing facility. The SWPPP will:

> Define the characteristics of the site and the type of construction which will be occurring;

> Describe the site plan for the facility to be constructed;

> Describe the practices that will be implemented to control erosion and the release of pollutants in storm water;

> Create an implementation schedule to ensure that the practices described in this SWPPP are in fact implemented and to evaluate the plan's effectiveness in reducing erosion, sediment, and pollutant levels in storm water discharged from the site; and

> Describe the final stabilization/termination design to minimize erosion and prevent storm water impacts after construction is complete.

1.2   **SWPPP Content**

This SWPPP includes the following:

> Identification of the SWPPP coordinator with a description of this person's duties;
>
> Identification of the storm water pollution prevention team that will assist in implementation of the SWPPP during construction.
>
> Description of the existing site conditions including existing land use for the site (i.e., wooded areas, open grassed areas, pavement, buildings, etc.), soil types at the site, as well as the location of surface waters which are located on or next to the site (wetlands, streams, rivers, lakes, ponds, etc.);
>
> Identification of the body of water(s) which will receive runoff from the construction site, including the ultimate body of water that receives the storm water;
>
> Identification of drainage areas and potential storm water contaminants;
>
> Description of storm water management controls and various Best Management Practices (BMPs) necessary to reduce erosion, sediment and pollutants in storm water discharge;
>
> Description of the facility monitoring plan and how controls will be coordinated with construction activities; and a
>
> Description of the implementation schedule and provisions for amendment of the plan.

2.0   SWPPP COORDINATOR AND DUTIES

The construction site SWPPP coordinator for the facility is Mr. Jack Smith (phone number: (301) 555-6434) with Capital Construction, Inc. (general contractor). Mr. Smith's duties include the following:

> Implement the SWPPP plan with the aid of the SWPPP team;
>
> Oversee maintenance practices identified as BMPs in the SWPPP;
>
> Implement and oversee employee training;
>
> • Conduct or provide for inspection and monitoring activities;
>
> Identify other potential pollutant sources and make sure they are added to the plan;
>
> • Identify any deficiencies in the SWPPP and make sure they are corrected; and
>
> Ensure that any changes in construction plans are addressed in the SWPPP.

To aid in the implementation of the SWPPP plan, the members of the SWPPP team are Tom Johnson and Mike Carter. Tom Johnson will ensure that all housekeeping and monitoring procedures are implemented, while Mike Carter will ensure the integrity of the structural BMPs.

3.0   FACILITY DESCRIPTION

3.1   Site Location

The construction site is located at 1200 Towne Ter Road in Suitland District Heights, Maryland. Figure 1 is an area map showing the location of the site. The facility is a 32.1-acre parcel located in Section 30, Township 7N, Range 21 East. The facility is bound to the north by a wooded area, to the west by Old Mill Stream, to the south by Towne Ter Road, and to the east by residential property.

3.2   Construction Type

Capital Construction is planning to build a manufacturing facility for Magerr's Quality Circuits, Inc. The facility will consist of a single building that will house offices and manufacturing operations, a drive and parking area, and a loading/receiving dock. Two storm system inlets will be placed in the front parking area and two storm system inlets will be placed in the loading dock area to collect and convey storm water to a proposed sedimentation basin. Roof drains on the building will convey storm water to the storm system inlets for eventual discharge to the proposed sedimentation basin. Capital Construction and their various subcontractors will be on site from approximately 7 AM until 5 PM, five days per week. Clearing and grading, construction of the building and parking areas, and site landscaping is expected to be complete with 10 months following ground breaking.

3.3   Existing Site Conditions

The 32.1 acre property is currently a mix of heavy wooded areas and grassy, open swales. The property slopes from east to west toward the Old Mill Stream, an intermittent dry stream bed. Top soils range from a silty-sand on the east side of the property to a heavy loam on the west nearest the intermittent dry stream bed. Surface waters which do not infiltrate the soils, migrate to Old Mill Stream which ultimately discharges to Cabin Branch Creek. Cabin Branch Creek discharges into Beaver Dam Creek approximately 2-miles downstream, which in turn, empties

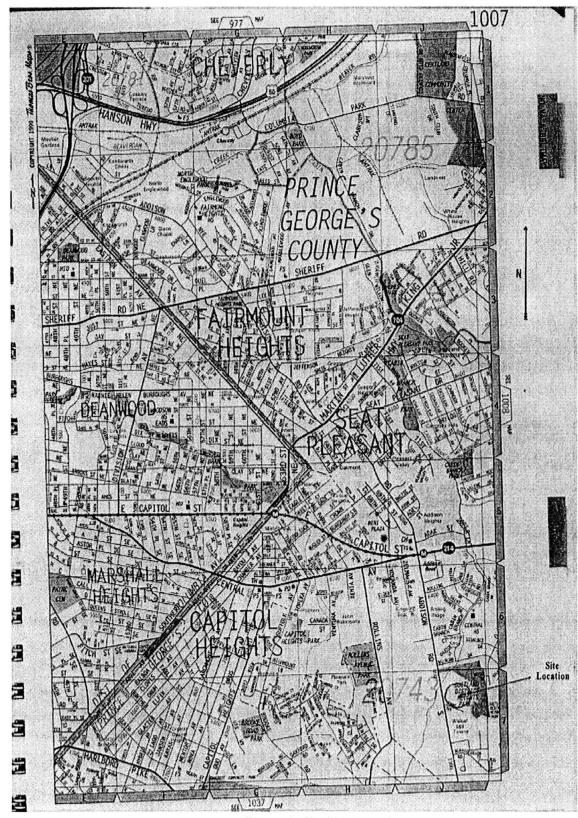

Figure 1. Facility Location

into the Anacostia River approximately 8 miles downstream. The Anacostia River is a major tributary to Chesapeake Bay.

3.4   Site Plan

Figure 2 is a site map showing property boundaries, the proposed location of the building, paved parking and drive areas, storm system inlets, the proposed limits of clearing and grading, and the various drainage areas. A total of 15.8 acres will be cleared and grubbed during construction activities. Approximately 2.3 acres of the heavily wooded area along the eastern portion of the property will be clear-cut and the timber removed for resale. The concrete block building will have an area of 52,500 square feet. The parking area on the south side of the building and the loading dock area on the north side of the building will be 177,500 square feet and 30,000 square feet, respectively. Four storm system inlets will collect storm water from roof drains, parking areas, and the loading dock area and convey it to a 1-acre storm water sedimentation basin. Overflow from the sedimentation basin will discharge into Old Mill Stream and the discharge rate will be controlled to prevent flooding of the receiving stream.

Since the building will be slab-on-grade construction, rough grading and excavation for concrete footings will be the primary soil disturbing activities. All soils excavated for footings will be stockpiled on site prior to finish grading to allow drainage away from the building foundation. All soils excavated from storm systems trenches will be stock piled and then finished graded during construction of the paved drive, parking, and loading dock areas. All exposed soils will be reseeded and new vegetation will be planted as soon as possible.

Figure 2 also shows the locations of the drainage areas and the apparent storm water drainage patterns. Drainage area DA-01 located along the western one-third of the property currently drains toward Old Mill Stream, however, after clearing and grubbing, the majority of storm water will drain to the proposed sedimentation basin. Drainage area DA-02 includes the loading dock area plus the roof drains from the building. Storm water from DA-02 will collect in one of two

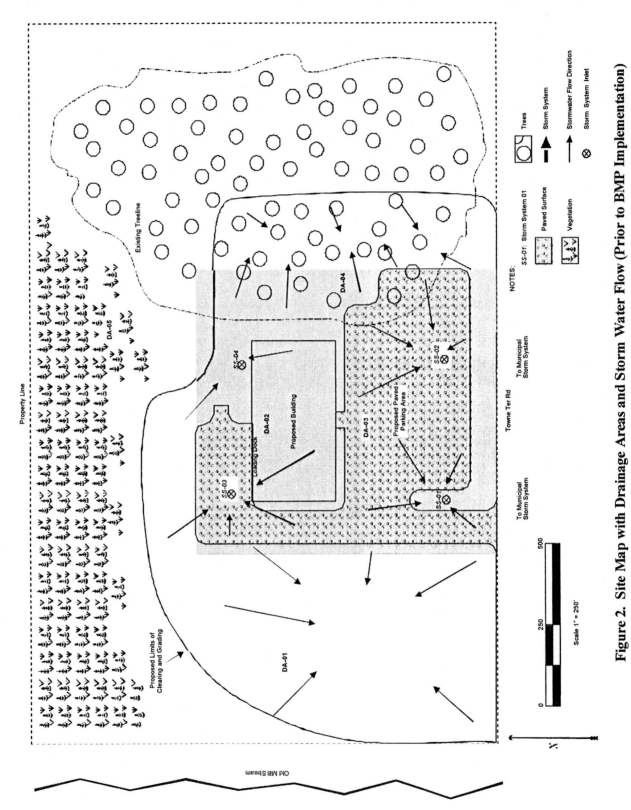

Figure 2. Site Map with Drainage Areas and Storm Water Flow (Prior to BMP Implementation)

storm system inlets before discharging to the sedimentation basin. Drainage area DA-03 includes the proposed parking area south of the building. Storm water from DA-03 will empty into one of two storm system that discharge to the sedimentation basin. Drainage area DA-04 begins along the eastern edge of the parking area and continues east through the area where tree removal will occur. A vegetated swale will be developed in this area following construction and soil stabilization. The vegetated swale will improve storm water infiltration. Drainage area DA-05 located along the northern and eastern one-third of the property is generally covered by vegetation. Because of the high permeability of the soils and the absence of site activities (clearing and grading) in this area, this drainage area is not significant and will not be addressed further in this SWPPP. A description of each drainage area is provided in Table 1.

Table 1

Characteristics of Storm Water Drainage

Drainage Area[1]	Storm Water Flow Description During Construction Activities	Total Size (sq. feet)	Impervious Surface Area During Construction (sq. feet)	Runoff Coefficient[2]	Drainage Discharge Point
DA-01	**Western Portion:** Overland flow across the cleared and graded area to the proposed sedimentation basin.	240,000	0	Low	Old Mill Stream
DA-02	**Proposed Loading Dock Area:** Overland flow across the area to the two new storm inlets SS-03 and SS-04. Roof drains from the building during construction will also discharge to the compacted gravel area before entering either SS-03 or SS-04. This area will be paved following building construction.	82,500	52,500	High	Old Mill Stream
DA-03	**Parking Area and Construction Entrance Area:** Overland flow across the compacted gravel area to storm inlets SS-01 and SS-02. This area will be paved following construction.	177,500	0	Medium	Old Mill Stream
DA-04	**Eastern Portion:** Cleared and graded areas where timber will be removed. Flow from this area will be toward the proposed vegetated swale for infiltration.	100,200	0	Low	Vegetated Swale
DA-05	All vegetation covered areas outside the clearing and grading limits	798,000	0	Low	None

(1) See Figure 2 for drainage areas
(2) Runoff Coefficient:
High: 70-100% impervious (example: asphalt, buildings, paved surfaces)
Medium: 40-70% impervious (example: packed soils)
Low: 0-40% impervious (example: grassy areas)

4.0 IDENTIFICATION OF POTENTIAL STORM WATER CONTAMINANTS

The purpose of this section is to identify pollutants that could impact storm water during construction of the facility.

4.1 Significant Material Inventory

Pollutants that result from clearing, grading, excavation, and building materials and have the potential to be present in storm water runoff are listed in Table 2. This table includes information regarding material type, chemical and physical description, and the specific regulated storm water pollutants associated with each material.

4.2 Potential Areas for Storm Water Contamination

The following potential source areas of storm water contamination were identified and evaluated:

Cleared and graded areas;

Asphalt loading dock construction and building construction;

Construction site entrance and asphalt parking area construction;

- Tree removal area; and

All undisturbed areas.

Table 3 presents site specific information regarding storm water pollution potential from each of these areas.

4.3 A Summary of Available Storm Water Sampling Data

No storm water sampling data is available for the site.

Table 2

Potential Construction Site Storm Water Pollutants

Trade Name Material	Chemical/Physical Description[1]	Storm Water Pollutants[1]
Pesticides (insecticides, fungicides, herbicides, rodenticides)	Various colored to colorless liquid, powder, pellets, or grains	Chlorinated hydrocarbons, organophosphates, carbamates, arsenic
Fertilizer	Liquid or solid grains	Nitrogen, phosphorous
Plaster	White granules or powder	Calcium sulphate, calcium carbonate, sulfuric acid
Cleaning solvents	Colorless, blue, or yellow-green liquid	Perchloroethylene, methylene chloride, trichloroethylene, petroleum distillates
Asphalt	Black solid	Oil, petroleum distillates
Concrete	White solid	Limestone, sand
Glue, adhesives	White or yellow liquid	Polymers, epoxies
Paints	Various colored liquid	Metal oxides, stoddard solvent, talc, calcium carbonate, arsenic
Curing compounds	Creamy white liquid	Naphtha
Wastewater from construction equipment washing	Water	Soil, oil & grease, solids
Wood preservatives	Clear amber or dark brown liquid	Stoddard solvent, petroleum distillates, arsenic, copper, chromium
Hydraulic oil/fluids	Brown oily petroleum hydrocarbon	Mineral oil
Gasoline	Colorless, pale brown or pink petroleum hydrocarbon	Benzene, ethyl benzene, toluene, xylene, MTBE
Diesel Fuel	Clear, blue-green to yellow liquid	Petroleum distillate, oil & grease, naphthalene, xylenes
Kerosene	Pale yellow liquid petroleum hydrocarbon	Coal oil, petroleum distillates
Antifreeze/coolant	Clear green/yellow liquid	Ethylene glycol, propylene glycol, heavy metals (copper, lead, zinc)
Erosion	Solid Particles	Soil, Sediment

(1) Data obtained from MSDSs when available

Table 3

Locations of Potential Sources of Storm Water Contamination

Drainage Area[1]	Potential Storm Water Contamination Point	Potential Pollutants	Potential Problem
DA-01	Cleared and graded areas	Soil erosion, fertilizer, pesticides	Erosion of soils from cleared and graded areas have the potential to discharge into Old Mill Stream.
DA-02	Asphalt loading dock construction and building construction	Plaster, cleaning solvents, asphalt, concrete, paints, hydraulic oil, gasoline, antifreeze, soil erosion, fertilizer, pesticides, glue adhesives, curing compounds, wood preservatives, kerosene	Accidental spills of paints and cleaning solvents, leaking hydraulic oil and antifreeze from construction equipment, gasoline and diesel fuel spills while fueling construction equipment, erosion of exposed and stockpiled soils, and degradation of scrap dry wall can potentially contaminate storm water. Asphalt chemicals can be released to storm water if a rain event occurs before curing is complete.
DA-03	Construction site entrance Asphalt parking area construction	Asphalt, hydraulic oil, gasoline, antifreeze, soil erosion, fertilizer, pesticides	Leaking hydraulic oil and antifreeze from clearing, grading and asphalt application construction equipment. Gasoline and diesel fuel spills while fueling construction equipment, and erosion of exposed and stockpiled soils. Asphalt chemicals can be released to storm water if a rain event occurs before curing is complete. Tracking of soil into the road through the construction site entrance.
DA-04	Tree removal area	Soil erosion, fertilizer, pesticides	Ruts caused by logging equipment can fill with water, preventing complete re-vegetation.
DA-05	All undisturbed areas	None	No storm water related issues with this completely vegetated area

(1) See Figure 2 for drainage areas

4-3

5.0   STORM WATER MANAGEMENT CONTROLS

The purpose of this section is to identify the types of temporary and permanent erosion and sediment controls that will be used during construction activities. The controls will provide soil stabilization for disturbed areas and structural controls to divert runoff and remove sediment. This section will also address control of other potential storm water pollutant sources such as construction materials (paints, concrete dust, solvents, plaster), waste disposal, control of vehicle traffic, and sanitary waste disposal.

5.1   Temporary and Permanent Erosion Control Practices

A list of best management procedures (BMPs) has been developed and the locations of these BMPs are shown in Figure 3. A number of the BMPs included in this plan have been developed to serve as post-construction storm water controls.

Site Wide Control Measures

To prevent soil from washing into Old Mill Stream or the undisturbed areas of the site, the following BMPs will be implemented:

- Silt fencing and straw bale barriers will be placed along the perimeter of the area to be cleared and graded before any clearing or grading takes place. Supersilt fencing will be used on steep slopes at appropriate locations.

- A sedimentation basin will be constructed near the southwest corner of the construction site before any construction begins. The sedimentation basin, with an approximate depth of ten feet and a surface area of 1 acre, will be constructed to a volume of 435,600 cubic feet and is expected to remove 80 percent of suspended solids from the site's storm water runoff. The sedimentation basin has been designed by a professional engineer to keep peak flow rates in Old Mill Stream from the 2- and 10-year/24-hour storms at their pre-site development rates. The sedimentation basin will remain as a permanent storm water detention structure following construction activities. When up slope areas are stabilized, the accumulated sediment will be removed from the sedimentation basin and a geotextile will be placed along the sides for slope stabilization.

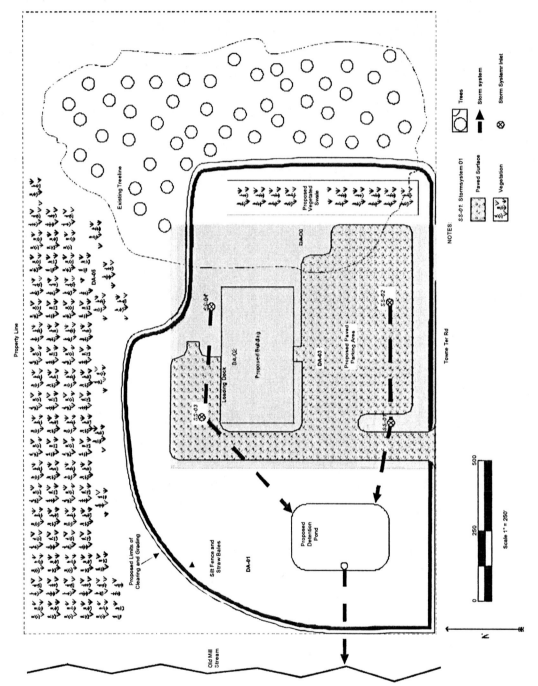

Figure 3. Site Map with Structural BMPs

Influent points to the sedimentation basin will be stabilized with crushed stone to avoid washout. The distance between the influent location and the effluent location in the sedimentation basin will be maximized (e.g., the length to width ratio of the basin will be a minimum of 2:1). The basin will drain through a 12-inch diameter corrugated metal riser and outlet pipe to a rip rap outlet apron leading to Old Mill Stream. Influent to the sedimentation basin will be supplied from two storm water pipes and natural site drainage. The influent pipes will be placed at a depth of approximately 3 feet above the bottom of the basin to facilitate sediment removal.

- All cleared and graded soils will be sloped to the sedimentation basin.

- Within fourteen days after clearing and grading, 4,000 pounds of ground agricultural limestone and 2,000 pounds of 10-10-10 fertilizer will be applied to each acre to be stabilized.

- After fertilizing, all areas which will not be impacted by construction of the building will be seeded. The permanent seed mix shall consist of 80 lbs/acre tall fescue and 40 lbs/acre kobe lespedeza.

- After seeding, each area will be mulched with 4,000 pounds per acre of straw. The straw mulch is to be tacked into place by a disk with blades set nearly straight.

- Top soil stock piles will be stabilized with temporary seed and mulch no later than fourteen days from the last construction activities in that area. The temporary seed shall be Rye (grain) applied at the rate of 120 pounds per acre.

- Areas of the site which are to be paved will be temporarily stabilized by applying geotextile and stone sub-base until asphalt is applied.

- Once construction at the site is nearly complete, a vegetated swale will be constructed in DA-04 where the majority of trees were removed. Soils along the east side of the parking area and the building will be sloped toward the swale, creating a natural depression to retain storm water and promote reinfiltration. The vegetated swale will remain as a permanent storm water control measure.

5.2   <u>**Construction Practices to Minimize Storm Water Contamination**</u>

All waste materials will be collected and stored in a securely lidded metal dumpster rented from BFI Waste Inc, which is a licensed solid waste management company located in Capital Heights, Maryland. All trash and construction debris from the site will be deposited in the dumpster. The dumpster will be emptied a minimum of twice per week and the trash will be hauled to Doe Run landfill. No construction materials will be buried on-site. All personnel will be instructed regarding the correct procedure for waste disposal. All sanitary waste will be collected from the portable units a minimum of three times per week by Johnson Waste Hauling, a licensed sanitary waste management contractor. Good housekeeping and spill control practices will be followed during construction to minimize storm water contamination from petroleum products, fertilizers, paints, and concrete. Good housekeeping practices for each drainage area are list below.

DA-01

To prevent storm water contamination from DA-01, the following BMPs will be implemented:

- Fertilizers will be applied only in the minimum amounts recommenced by the manufacturer.

- Fertilizers will be worked into the soil to limit exposure to storm water.

- Fertilizers will be stored in a covered shed and partially used bags will be transferred to a sealable bin to avoid spills.

DA-02

To prevent storm water contamination from DA-02, the following BMPs will be implemented:

- All vehicles on site will be monitored for leaks and receive regular preventive maintenance to reduce the chance of leakage.

- Petroleum products will be stored in tightly sealed containers which are clearly labeled.

- Spill kits will be included with all fueling sources and maintenance activities.

- Any asphalt substances used onsite will be applied according to the manufacturer's recommendation.

- Sanitary waste will be collected from portable units a minimum of two times a week to avoid overfilling.

- A covered dumpster will be used for all waste materials.

- All paint containers and curing compounds will be tightly sealed and stored when not required for use. Excess paint will not be discharged to the storm system, but will be properly disposed according to the manufacturer's instructions.

- Materials and equipment necessary for spill cleanup will be kept in the temporary material storage trailer onsite. Equipment will include, but not be limited to, brooms, dust pans, mops, rags, gloves, goggles, kitty litter, sand, saw dust, and plastic and metal trash containers.

- Spray guns will be cleaned on a removable tarp.

- All spills will be cleaned up immediately upon discovery. Spills large enough to reach the storm system will be reported to the National Response Center at 1-800-424-8802.

- Concrete trucks will not be allowed to wash out or discharge surplus concrete or drum wash water on the site.

- Two storm system will be installed to collect and deliver storm water to the sedimentation basin.

- Form release oil used for decorative stone work will be applied over a pallet covered with an adsorbent material to collect excess fluid. The absorbent material will be replaced and disposed of properly when saturated.

- When testing/cleaning of water supply lines, the discharge from the tested pipe will be collected and conveyed to a completed storm water pipe system for ultimate discharge into the sedimentation basin.

DA-03

To prevent storm water contamination from DA-03, the following BMPs will be implemented:

- A stabilized construction entrance will be constructed to reduce vehicle tracking of sediments.

- The paved street adjacent to the site entrance will be swept daily to remove excess mud, dirt, or rock tracked from the site.

- Dump trucks hauling material from the construction site will be covered with a tarpaulin.
  Two storm system will be installed to collect and deliver storm water to the sedimentation basin.

DA-04

To prevent storm water contamination from DA-04, the following BMPs will be implemented:

All ruts caused by equipment used for cutting and removing of trees will be graded.

5.3   Coordination of BMPs with Construction Activities

Structural BMPs will be coordinated with construction activities so the BMP is in place before construction begins. The following BMPs will be coordinated with construction activities:

The temporary perimeter controls (silt fences and straw bails) will be installed before any clearing and grading begins.

Clearing and grading will not occur in an area until it is necessary for construction to proceed.

The stabilized construction site entrance and sedimentation basin will be constructed before clearing and grading begins.

Once construction activity ceases permanently in an area, that area will be stabilized with permanent seed and mulch.

After the entire site is stabilized, the accumulated sediment will be removed from the basin and the permanent geotextile membrane will be placed along the sides.

The vegetated swale will not be constructed until the entire site is stabilized.

The temporary perimeter controls (silt fencing and straw bails) will not be removed until all construction activities at the site are complete and soils have been stabilized.

5.4 Certification of Compliance with Federal, State, and Local Regulations

This SWPPP reflects Suitland District Heights requirements for storm water management and erosion and sediment control, as established in Suitland District Heights Ordinance 5-188. To ensure compliance, this plan was prepared in accordance with the Suitland District Heights Storm Water Management, Erosion and Sediment Control Handbook, published by the Suitland District Heights Department of Planning, Storm Water Management Section. There are no other applicable State or Federal requirements for sediment and erosion site plans (or permits), or storm water management site plans (or permits).

6.0   MAINTENANCE/INSPECTION PROCEDURES

6.1   Inspections

Visual inspections of all cleared and graded areas of the construction site will be performed daily and within 12 hours of the end of a storm with rainfall amounts greater than 0.5 inches. The inspection will be conducted by the SWPPP coordinator or his designated storm water team members. The inspection will verify that the structural BMPs described in Section 5 of this SWPPP are in good condition and are minimizing erosion. The inspection will also verify that the procedures used to prevent storm water contamination from construction materials and petroleum products are effective. The following inspection and maintenance practices will be used to maintain erosion and sediment controls:

Built up sediment will be removed from silt fencing when it has reached one-third the height of the fence.

Silt fences will be inspected for depth of sediment, for tears, to see if the fabric is securely attached to the fence posts, and to see that the fence posts are firmly in the ground.

The sediment basin will be inspected for depth of sediment and built up sediment will be removed when it reaches 1 foot in depth.

Temporary and permanent seeding will be inspected for bare spots, washouts, and healthy growth.

- The stabilized construction entrance will be inspected for sediment tracked on the road, for clean gravel, and to make sure that the culvert beneath the entrance is working and that all traffic use the stabilized entrance when leaving the site.

The maintenance inspection report will be made after each inspection. A copy of the report form to be completed by the SWPPP coordinator is provided in Appendix A of this SWPPP. Completed forms will be maintained on-site during the entire construction project. Following construction, the completed forms will be retained at the general contractors office, Capital Construction, for a minimum of 1 year.

If construction activities or design modifications are made to the site plan which could impact storm water, this SWPPP will be amended appropriately. The amended SWPPP will have a description of the new activities that contribute to the increased pollutant loading and the planned source control activities.

6.2   Employee Training

An employee training program will be developed and implemented to educate employees about the requirements of the SWPPP. This education program will include background on the components and goals of the SWPPP and hands-on training in erosion controls, spill prevention and response, good housekeeping, proper material handling, disposal and control of waste, equipment fueling, and proper storage, washing, and inspection procedures. All employees will be trained prior to their first day on the site.

6.3   **Certification**

Corporate Certification (Magerr's Quality Circuits - Owner)

I certify under penalty of law that this document and all attachments were prepared under my direction or supervision in accordance with a system designed to assure that qualified personnel properly gathered and evaluated the information submitted. Based on my inquiry of the person or persons who manages the system, or those persons directly responsible for gathering the information, the information submitted is, to the best of my knowledge and belief, true, accurate, and complete. I am aware that there are significant penalties for submitting false information, including the possibility of fine and imprisonment for knowing violations.

                                             _____
                                             Name

                                             _____
                                             Title

                                             _____
                                             Date

Contractor Certification (Capital Construction - General Contractor)

I certify under penalty of law that I understand the terms and conditions of the general National Pollutant Discharge Elimination System (NPDES) permit that authorizes the storm water discharges associated with industrial activity from the construction site identified as part of this certification.

_____
Name

_____
Title

_____
Date

Contractor Certification (Dirt Movers, Inc. - Excavations and Grading Subcontractor)

I certify under penalty of law that I understand the terms and conditions of the general National Pollutant Discharge Elimination System (NPDES) permit that authorizes the storm water discharges associated with industrial activity from the construction site identified as part of this certification.

_____
Name

_____
Title

_____
Date

Contractor Certification (Marvin Gardens, Inc. - Landscaping Subcontractor)

I certify under penalty of law that I understand the terms and conditions of the general National Pollutant Discharge Elimination System (NPDES) permit that authorizes the storm water discharges associated with industrial activity from the construction site identified as part of this certification.

_____
Name

_____
Title

_____
Date

Appendix A

Inspection Logs

Magerr's Quality Circuits

Storm Water Pollution Prevention Plan

Inspection and Maintenance Report Form

To be completed every 7 days and within 24 hours of a rainfall event of 0.5 inches or more

Inspector: _____   Date: _____

Inspector's Qualifications:

Days since last rainfall: _____   Amount of last rainfall: _ inches

Stabilization Measures

Drainage Area	Date Since Last Disturbance	Date of Next Disturbance	Stabilized (Yes/No)	Stabilized With	Condition
DA-01					
DA-02					
DA-03					
DA-04					

Stabilization required:

.

.

.

To be performed by: _____   On or before: _____

Magerr's Quality Circuits

Storm Water Pollution Prevention Plan

Inspection and Maintenance Report Form

Sediment Basin:

Depth of Sediment Basin	Condition of Basin Side Slopes	Any Evidence of Overtopping of the Embankment	Condition of Outfall from Sediment Basin

Maintenance required for sediment basin:

To be performed by: _____   On or before: _____

Other Controls

Stabilized Construction Entrance:

Does Much Sediment Get Tracked on to Road?	Is the Gravel Clean or is it Filled with Sediment?	Does all Traffic use the Stabilized Entrance to Leave the Site?	Is the Culvert Beneath the Entrance Working?

Maintenance required for stabilized construction entrance:

_____

To be performed by: _____   On or before: _____

Magerr's Quality Circuits

Storm Water Pollution Prevention Plan

Inspection and Maintenance Report Form

Perimeter Structural Controls:

Date: _____

Silt Fence and Straw Bails

Drainage Area Perimeter	Has Silt Reached 1/3 of Fence Height?	Is Fence Properly Secured?	Is There Evidence of Washout or Over-topping?
DA-01			
DA-02			
DA-03			
DA-4			

Maintenance required for silt fence and straw bails:

To be performed by: _____   On or before: _____

Magerr's Quality Circuits

Storm Water Pollution Prevention Plan

Inspection and Maintenance Report Form

Changes required to the pollution prevention plan:

Reasons for changes:

I certify under penalty of law that this document and all attachments were prepared under my direction or supervision in accordance with a system designed to assure that qualified personnel properly gathered and evaluated the information submitted. Based on my inquiry of the person or persons who manage the system, or those persons directly responsible for gathering the information, the information submitted is, to the best of my knowledge and belief, true, accurate, and complete. I am aware that there are signification penalties for submitting false information, including the possibility of fine and imprisonment for knowing violations.

Signature: _____   Date: _____